NIGHT JOYCE OF A THOUSAND TIERS
Petr Škrabánek: Studies in Finnegans Wake

edited by Louis Armand & Ondřej Pilný

þ

Litteraria Pragensia
Prague 2002

Published 2002 by Litteraria Pragensia
Faculty of Philosophy, Charles University
Náměstí Jana Palacha 2, 116 38 Prague 1
Czech Republic
lazarus@ff.cuni.cz

Typeset & design by Lazarus
Printed in the Czech Republic by PB Tisk

This publication has been assisted by a grant from the Cultural Relations Committee of Ireland / Comhar Cultúra Éireann of the Ministry of Foreign Affairs, Ireland.

ISBN: 80-238-8853-6

This book is dedicated to Věra, Lucy and Nora.

CONTENTS

ABBREVIATIONS

Finnegans Wake has been cited following the standard form used by Joyce scholars, either by page number and line—viz. (278.13)—or, with reference to the accepted division of the text into four books with chapters, by Roman numeral (book) and Arabic numeral (chapter)—viz. (III.2). The following abbreviations are used throughout the text:

D	*Dubliners*, ed. Robert Scholes with Richard Ellmann. New York: Viking Press, 1967.
P	*A Portrait of the Artist as a Young Man*. The definitive text corrected from the Dublin Holograph by Chester G. Anderson and edited by Richard Ellmann. New York: Viking Press, 1966.
U	*Ulysses*. New York: Random House, 1934, reset and corrected 1961.
FW	*Finnegans Wake*. London: Faber and Faber, 1939.
CW	*The Critical Writings of James Joyce*. Eds. Ellsworth Mason and Richard Ellmann. New York: Viking Press, 1959.
L	*Letters of James Joyce*. Vol. I, ed. Stuart Gilbert. New York: Viking Press, 1957; re-issued with corrections 1966. Vols. II and III, ed. Richard Ellmann. New York: Viking Press, 1966.
SL	*Selected Letters*, ed. Richard Ellmann. New York: Viking Press, 1975.
Census	Adaline Glasheen, *A Census of Finnegans Wake*, III vols. Evanston: Northwestern University Press, 1952; 1963; 1977.
JJI	Ellmann, Richard. *James Joyce*. London: Oxford University Press, 1959.
JJII	Ellmann, Richard. *James Joyce*. Revised edition. London: Oxford University Press, 1982.
AWD	*A Wake Digest*, eds. Clive Hart and Fritz Senn. Sydney: Sydney University Press, 1968.
AWN	*A Wake Newslitter*
FWC	*A Finnegans Wake Circular*
JJLS	*James Joyce Literary Supplement*
JJQ	*James Joyce Quarterly*
JJR	*James Joyce Review*
BM	*British Museum* + catalogue number (documents belonging to Joyce, including *Finnegans Wake* drafts, lodged with the British Museum by Harriet Shaw Weaver. Cf. *JJA*).
JJA	*The James Joyce Archive*, ed. Michael Groden, *et al.* New York and

London: Garland Publishing, 1977-79. N.B. The correlation of the *Finnegans Wake* notebooks and drafts within *The James Joyce Archive* are as follows:

JJA 28	*Finnegans Wake*: Buffalo Notebooks VI.A
JJA 29	*Finnegans Wake*: Buffalo Notebooks VI.B.1-4
JJA 30	*Finnegans Wake*: Buffalo Notebooks VI.B.5-8
JJA 31	*Finnegans Wake*: Buffalo Notebooks VI.B.9-12
JJA 32	*Finnegans Wake*: Buffalo Notebooks VI.B.13-16
JJA 33	*Finnegans Wake*: Buffalo Notebooks VI.B.17-20
JJA 34	*Finnegans Wake*: Buffalo Notebooks VI.B.21-24
JJA 35	*Finnegans Wake*: Buffalo Notebooks VI.B.25-28
JJA 36	*Finnegans Wake*: Buffalo Notebooks VI.B.29-32
JJA 37	*Finnegans Wake*: Buffalo Notebooks VI.B.33-36
JJA 38	*Finnegans Wake*: Buffalo Notebooks VI.B.37-40
JJA 39	*Finnegans Wake*: Buffalo Notebooks VI.B.41-44
JJA 40	*Finnegans Wake*: Buffalo Notebooks VI.B.45-50
JJA 41	*Finnegans Wake*: Buffalo Notebooks VI.C.1,2,3,4,5,7
JJA 42	*Finnegans Wake*: Buffalo Notebooks VI.C.6,8,9,10,16,15
JJA 43	*Finnegans Wake*: Buffalo Notebooks VI.C.12,13,14,17,11,18
JJA 44	*Finnegans Wake*: Bk. I.1, Drafts, TSS and Proofs
JJA 45	*Finnegans Wake*: Bk. I.2-3, Drafts, TSS and Proofs
JJA 46	*Finnegans Wake*: Bk. I.4-5, Drafts, TSS and Proofs
JJA 47	*Finnegans Wake*: Bk. I.6-7, Drafts, TSS and Proofs
JJA 48	*Finnegans Wake*: Bk. I.8, Drafts, TSS and Proofs
JJA 49	*Finnegans Wake*: Bk. I, Galley Proofs, Vol.1
JJA 50	*Finnegans Wake*: Bk. I, Galley Proofs, Vol.2
JJA 51	*Finnegans Wake*: Bk. II.1, Drafts, TSS and Proofs
JJA 52	*Finnegans Wake*: Bk. II.2, Drafts, TSS and Proofs, Vol.1
JJA 53	*Finnegans Wake*: Bk. II.2, Drafts, TSS and Proofs, Vol.2
JJA 54	*Finnegans Wake*: Bk. II.3, Drafts, TSS and Proofs, Vol.1
JJA 55	*Finnegans Wake*: Bk. II.3, Drafts, TSS and Proofs, Vol.2
JJA 56	*Finnegans Wake*: Bk. II.4, Drafts, TSS and Proofs
JJA 57	*Finnegans Wake*: Bk. III.1-2, Drafts, TSS and Proofs
JJA 58	*Finnegans Wake*: Bk. III.3, Drafts, TSS and Proofs, Vol.1
JJA 59	*Finnegans Wake*: Bk. III.3, Drafts, TSS and Proofs, Vol.2
JJA 60	*Finnegans Wake*: Bk. III.4, Drafts, TSS and Proofs
JJA 61	*Finnegans Wake*: Bk. III, *transition* Pages
JJA 62	*Finnegans Wake*: Bk. III, Galley Proofs
JJA 63	*Finnegans Wake*: Bk. IV, Drafts, TSS and Proofs

EDITORIAL STATEMENT

This edition collects the extant writings by Petr Škrabánek on the work of James Joyce, almost all of which deal exclusively with *Finnegans Wake*. In preparing this edition we have chosen to present the work as it originally appeared in print, in chronological order, with a number of exceptions.

In order to frame the edition and give it some form of overall coherence, the title piece, *"Finnegans Wake*—Night Joyce of a Thousand Tiers," has been placed at the beginning of the book. This was in fact the last work published by Petr Škrabánek on Joyce (1990), and in many respects it ties together the broad-ranging concerns which directed his investigations into *Finnegans Wake* during the preceding twenty years. The final piece in the main body of this edition, "Joyce in Exile," was originally conceived as the Thomas Davis Lecture, broadcast by Radio Éireann on April 18, 1982, but left unpublished. In many ways it is a companion piece to "Night Joyce of a Thousand Tiers," and so the two pieces may be read as framing the rest of the work. Petr Škrabánek wrote only a handful of reviews of critical works on Joyce. These are reproduced here as appendices, along with a letter from Škrabánek to the editor of the *Times Literary Supplement* regarding the Parisian literary journal *transitions*, along with a reply from Maria Jolas, author of *A James Joyce Yearbook* (Paris: Transition Press, 1949) and daughter of Eugene Jolas.

While preparing the original texts for publication we have also chosen to incorporate, wherever possible, the author's corrections. Most of these took the form of marginal annotations, many of which required patient decipherment with the assistance of Petr Škrabánek's widow, Věra Čapková. In one important instance, where the author published addenda to the "Slavonic Dictionary" (cf. "Addenda to Slavonic List in *AWN* 10.4," *AWN* 11.2 (1974): 32-33), the additional text has been incorporated into the original. Subsequent corrections by the author, not published in the "Addenda," have been indicated in the text by an asterix. The very few entries in the original list which were deleted by the author in the typescript have been retained in the text and indicated by a "strikethrough" line.

Throughout this edition obvious typographical errors in the originals and in the typescripts have been corrected. Wherever possible the referencing style has been standardised and, when incomplete, missing details have been supplied. In a number of instances we have chosen to elaborate upon points glossed over in the original, for example where etymological variations are left unstated, or prior specialised knowledge has been assumed. A number of historical details have been added in order to make entries in the "Slavonic Dictionary" internally consistent. When a reference needed clarification, we have supplied it and cited the appropriate texts. In almost all cases, however, editorial intervention has taken the form of a footnote, distinguished from the author's notes by (Ed.) in parentheses.

All abbreviations used in this edition correspond to the standard abbreviations used in Joyce scholarship. These are listed along with the parallel references for the *James Joyce Archive* and the *Finnegans Wake* notebooks, at SUNY Buffalo, and the typescripts lodged in the British Museum. Throughout the text the author makes use of the original catalogue number, preceded either by VI, BM or MS. Only on rare occasions are these directly correlated in the text to the volume and page number of the *Archive*. Throughout this edition *Finnegans Wake* is usually cited without the abbreviation *FW*, employing simply the page and line number according to the established convention. Wherever the context does not indicate otherwise, references unaccompanied by an abbreviation should be taken as referring to the *Wake*.

Original publication details for each of the pieces reproduced in this edition are as follows: "Cheka and OGPU," *AWN* 8.1 (1971): 13-14. "355.11 Slavansky Slavar, R. Slavanskii Slovar (Slavonic Dictionary)," *AWN* 9.4 (1972): 5-68; "Imaginable Itinerary through the Particular Universal," *AWN* 10.2 (1973): 22-23; "Wassaily Booslaeugh of Riesenborg," *AWN* 10.3 (1973): 42-43; "Havvah-ban-Annah (38.30)," *AWN* 10.4 (1973): 65; "O Quanta Virtus est in Intersecationibus Circulorum," *AWN* 10.6 (1973): 86-87; "More Hebrew," *AWN* 10.6 (1973): 88-91; "Addenda to Slavonic List in *AWN* 10.4," *AWN* 11.2 (1974): 32-33; "A and aa ab ad abu abiad (254.16)," *AWN* 11.2 (1974): 33; "Structure and Motif in Thunderwords—A Proposal," *AWN* 12.6 (1975): 108-111; "A Note on 'Polish in *Finnegans Wake*,'" *AWN* 12.6 (1975): 111; "294.F4," *AWN* 12.6 (1975): 112; "Infinite Variety," *AWN* 13.3 (1976): 51-52; "Anglo-Irish in *Finnegans Wake*," *AWN* 13.5 (1976):

79-85; "The Peter the Painter (85.05),"' *AWN* 13.5 (1976): 99; "The key No. one to No-one," *AWN* 14.1 (1977): 16; "Signs on it!" *AWN* 14.6 (1977): 96; "Semisigns of His Zooteach (III)," *AWN* 14.6 (1977): 98; "Nash of Girahash (75.20)," *AWN* 14.6 (1977): 100; "The Whole Gammat (492.04)," *AWN* 14.6 (1977): 100-101; "The Chess Elephant in the Belly," *AWN* 15.4 (1978): 61; "Basque Beginning," *AWN* 15.4 (1978): 61; "Epscene License," *AWN* 15.5 (1978): 74-75; "A Born Gentleman is (?) (116.25)," *AWN* 15.6 (1978): 90; "The Turning of the Ш," *AWN* 15.6 (1978): 94; "Slavonicisms in *Finnegans Wake*," *Irish-Slavonic Studies* 2 (1981): 3-8; rpr. *Litteraria Pragensia* 4.8 (1994): 92-99; "Gambariste della porca!" *AWN: Occasional Paper No. 1* (1982): 8; "Letter on *transition*," *Times Literary Supplement* 5 March, 1982; "*Finnegans Wake*—The Condom Conundrum of a French letter," *Third Degree: James Joyce Centenary Issue* 6 (1983): 11-14; "St. Patrick's Nightmare Confession," *FWC* 1.1 (1985): 5-20; "29 Pacifettes," *FWC* 1.2 (1985): 33-37; "Notes on 29 Death Words," *FWC* 1.2 (1985): 38-40; "Notes on Armenian in *Finnegans Wake*," *FWC* 1.3 (1986): 45-58; "Notes on Ruthenian in II.3," *FWC* 2.2 (1986): 23-28; "Review of *James Joyce and Heraldry*," *FWC* 2.2 (1986): 33-40; "Cushitic Cant: Kant in Afar," *FWC* 2.4 (1987): 72-75; "Anna's Ainu," *FWC* 3.1 (1987): 7-10; "Review of *An Anglo-Irish Glossary for Joyce's Works*," *FWC* 3.1 (1987): 16-18; "Cunniform Letters," *FWC* 3.4 (1988): 75-76; "Review of *James Joyce 1. Scribble 1. Genèse des textes*," *FWC* 4.1 (1988): 19-20; "*Finnegans Wake*— Night Joyce of a Thousand Tiers," *The Artist and the Labyrinth*, ed. Augustine Martin (London: Ryan Publishing, 1990) 229-240; "Joyce in Exile," *Thomas Davis Lecture*, Radio Éireann, 18 April, 1982.

By way of acknowledgement, the editors wish to express their thanks to Věra Čapková for her permission to publish the work of her late husband and for her assistance in editing the manuscripts. Her generosity and kindness has been unstinting in all aspects of this book's conception and publication. The editors also wish to express their thanks to Lucie Koutková for retyping the entire text; to Clare Wallace for her painstaking efforts in proof-reading each of the drafts and for her invaluable help in locating references; to the Irish Embassy in the Czech Republic for their ongoing assistance of the Irish Studies Centre at Charles University; to Fritz Senn for his long-standing support and suggestions in all things Joycean; to Sam Slote and Michael Powers for their help with *Finnegans Wake* sigla; to Dirk Van Hulle, Daniel Ferrer and Geert Lernout for their general encouragement; and to David Sehnal, Bohumil Palek and Michal Bareš for their assistance with computer typography. We would also like to acknowledge the support of the Cultural Relations Committee of the Ministry of Foreign Affairs, Ireland, who have provided the major part of the funding necessary for this publication.

PREFACE: PETR ŠKRABÁNEK

I am trying to remember when I first came across a new philological contributor to Joyce exegesis by the name of Petr Škrabánek; it must have been in the early seventies. He had set up a detailed list of Slavonic words in *Finnegans Wake* and was able even to distinguish between Russian, Polish, Czech, etc. all the way to "Panslavonic." So there was someone who had a command of many of those languages that Joyce may have tucked into the Wakean texture and were entirely out of our own reach when most of us felt already competent with a bit of French and a smattering of what was spoken in Central Europe.

Then, during one of my trips in Ireland, we did meet, I think it was a Sunday and some of us took a long walk. I learned that, during the Prague Spring of 1968 when Petr Škrabánek and his wife were vacationing in Ireland, they had decided to stay in the country, and so they settled in Dublin. Such is my recollection. The immigrants must have taken roots fairly soon, no wonder considering their gifts. An appointment at Trinity College soon to follow, where Petr Škrabánek taught Medicine. Věra, his wife, an extremely versatile and knowledgeable linguist, was employed at UCD—this at any rate was the situation when, years later, I visited the family in their suburban home on the first Dublin Pilgrimage undertaken by the Zürich Foundation. Both Petr and Věra were great to listen and talk to, perceptive and witty with, it seemed, the best of the old European humanist tradition effortlessly (and unostentatiously) at their fingertips. There were also two lovely daughters. All in all a cherished memory.

In the wake of this visit and fruitful contact, the same year Petr took part in the Zürich James Joyce Foundation's August workshop on a particular theme: it was devoted to "Synaesthesia." My impression is that he could have easily fitted into almost any topic and come up with something pertinent as he was always inspiring and often agreeably provocative.

We were pleased to have Petr Škrabánek again in Zürich for one of the occasional, informal talks (solemnly but erroneously termed "Strauhof Lectures"): in November 1989 he informed and entertained us in his usual lively and spirited manner and talked about "Night Joyce of a Thousand Tiers" to an intimate, attentive and exhilarated audience.

Petr Škrabánek was a Joycean amateur in the best sense. He had an excellent grasp of the texts and a great sense for, and disgust of, pomposities. His main subject however was medicine; there again his views were entirely autonomous and unorthodox. He played more than just *advocatus diaboli* when in conversation, lectures and publications he maintained that medical doctors are generally not of much use and patients might be better off without them altogether, allowing Nature to take care of their illnesses. This did not universally amuse his medical colleagues.

It would have been wonderful to keep in constant touch and it was a great shock when we heard that Petr Škrabánek was suffering from cancer. He died quite unexpected, much regretted, a man of multiple talents and inspiration and of uncommon charisma.

Fritz Senn
Zürich James Joyce Foundation

FOREWORD: PETR ŠKRABÁNEK 1940-1994

Petr Škrabánek was born in Náchod, a small town in north-eastern Bohemia. After he left the local secondary school, he went to study at the Faculty of Natural Sciences at Charles University in Prague. While still a student, he started doing research in toxicology. He also frequently contributed short articles to the Czechoslovakian science journal *Vesmír* (Cosmos). At the early age of twenty-two, he was appointed head of the Toxicology Department at the Institute of Forensic Medicine at Purkyně University in Brno. In 1963, Petr enrolled as a medical student at the same university, while still working in toxicology and also writing résumés from journals published in Slavonic languages for *Chemical Abstracts*.

As an outstanding student, he was granted a short-term research scholarship in 1967 which allowed him to travel abroad. Petr chose Galway Regional Hospital in Ireland and spent a month there, taking besides the opportunity to travel in Ireland. Due to the mild thaw of the Czechoslovak communist regime in 1968, he was able to go to Ireland as a researcher again, this time opting for the Richmond Hospital in Dublin. In August, he was joined in Ireland by his wife, Věra Čapková (who is now a lecturer in linguistics at University College Dublin). Together they met scholars working in Celtic studies and travelled to the West of Ireland. It was while they were visiting Yeats's grave in Sligo that they heard the news of the Soviet invasion of Czechoslovakia. Deeply shocked, they decided not to return and remained in Ireland. Their total assets at that time were two backpacks and a tent.

Due to the generous help and understanding of many Irish friends, Petr and Věra were soon able to settle in Dublin, Petr was offered a job at the Medical Council Laboratories and was allowed to finish the last year of his medical studies at the Royal College of Surgeons. He qualified in 1970, and after a series of house jobs became Senior Research Fellow in the Endocrine Oncology Unit in the Mater Misericordiae Hospital (1975). Entering this position reflected his gradual move away from clinical medicine towards research in neuroendocrinology: Petr became a leading specialist on the neurotransmitter Substance P, publishing widely in a number of professional journals. At the same time he completed his doctoral thesis "Inappropriate Production of Hormonal Peptides in Neoplasia."

It was also during the mid-1970s that he became interested in wider issues of medicine. Occasional articles concerned with the philosophical issues of the discipline, together with frequent letters to editors, attracted the attention of the editors of the eminent British medical journal, *The Lancet.* This resulted in an extensive co-operation—one that Petr valued perhaps the most of his professional achievements—and over the years he became a well known editorialist of the journal. Through *The Lancet,* Petr met his future colleague and collaborator James McCormick, who offered him a position at the Department of Community Health of Trinity College, Dublin (1984). Petr became tenured in 1986, was made a fellow of the College, and also a fellow of the Royal College of Physicians of Ireland. Shortly before his untimely death he was appointed Associate Professor at Trinity College. From his post at Trinity, he maintained his reputation as a stringent and scathing critic of dogmas, sham and wishful thinking pertaining to the areas of preventive medicine and alternative medicine. Apart from hundreds of articles and letters, his views found an expression in *Follies and Fallacies in Medicine* (1989; Glasgow: Tarragon Press, 1992), co-authored with McCormick and promptly translated into Danish, German, Spanish, Italian, French, Dutch and Czech, and ultimately in *The Death of Humane Medicine and the Rise of Coercive Healthism* (London: Social Affairs Unit, 1994), a book which he finished during the last stages of his final illness and which was published posthumously.

Petr Škrabánek died of cancer at his Dublin home on 21 June 1994.

Shortly after his death, friends and associates decided to honour his achievements by establishing the Skrabanek Foundation. The foundation aims to provide a forum for the continuation of the debate concerning general issues of medicine and ethics along the lines of sceptical inquiry so much endorsed by Petr. The first interdisciplinary symposium organised by the Foundation was held in May 1995 in Dublin. The Foundation members have also initiated the publication of a volume of Petr's writings on the broader issues and philosophical aspects of medicine, entitled *False Premises False Promises: Selected Writings of Petr Skrabanek* (Whithorn: Tarragon Press, 2000).

Throughout his life, Petr was deeply interested in languages. Apart from learning several major European tongues during his years as a student, he became a private pupil of the chief rabbi Richard Feder in Brno and learnt to read and write Hebrew. As soon as he arrived in Ireland, he became interested in the Irish language, and his enthusiasm for Irish literature was accompanied by an interest in Hiberno-English (Anglo-Irish). Over the years, he also tackled a number of non-Indo-European languages, chiefly with the help of his foreign friends. In this manner, he acquired for instance a knowledge of Japanese in the early 1980s.

His literary affections were numerous: he loved reading Montaigne's essays and cherished Rabelais. Together with the phonetician Richard Walshe and the composer Gerard Victory he embarked on a translation of Lautréamont's *Les Chants de Maldoror* (publication forthcoming), meeting every Saturday morning to work on a few passages before lunch. Moreover, he nearly accomplished a translation into English of one of the small masterpieces of modern Czech writing, the poetic, experimental novella *Rozmarné léto* (The Capricious Summer, 1926) by Vladislav Vančura, which still remains in manuscript.

However, Petr's greatest literary passion was Joyce. Already in Czechoslovakia he became acquainted with the early Czech translations of *Dubliners* (1933), *A Portrait of the Artist as a Young Man* (1930) and *Ulysses* (1930). After their decision not to return to their native country which was being crushed by a new wave of communist dictatorship, Petr and Věra found an unusual means of improving their basic knowledge of English: they decided to learn the language by reading *Ulysses* to themselves in the evenings, a couple of pages a day...

Petr's first encounter with *Finnegans Wake* was through an excerpt of the "Anna Livia Plurabella" section translated into Czech by Zdeněk Urbánek and published in the literary review *Světová literatura* (World Literature) in 1966 (1: 199-202). His systematic involvement with Joyce's extended riddle began when he was presented a copy of the book by his wife for Christmas in 1969. In 1971 Petr published his first article on Joyce in *A Wake Newslitter*, and at the same time started working on a dictionary of Slavonic expressions in the *Wake* (published in 1972; addenda in 1974). Through his articles he established contacts with a number of Joycean scholars during the 1970s and became respected as an authority on *Finnegans Wake*. Although his scholarly achievement has been widely acknowledged, he tended to express his attitude towards his involvement with Joyce's opus in a manner quite typical of him: he used to say, "other doctors have golf, I have the *Wake*."

In the mid-1980s, Petr was invited by professor Augustine Martin to teach an intensive seminar on the *Wake* to PhD students of Anglo-Irish literature at University College Dublin, a course which he then successfully maintained for a number of years. For the purpose of this seminar, he developed a method of annotating every single word in the passages debated with the students, and preserved his annotations meticulously on separate cards filed in a large cabinet. This methodical way of annotating the *Wake* represented an extension of the earlier notes made in his copy of the book, and also in the issues of *The Wake Newslitter*. The majority of notes reflect the fondness of their author for languages of all kinds, his keenness on dictionaries and grammar-books, but above all his curiosity, learning and sense of humour.

Apart from his professional and literary interests, Petr was also a great lover of jazz and classical music, an accomplished pianist who delighted in playing for his friends at parties and other gatherings. He was a life-long admirer of surrealism in literature and the visual arts, with a special fondness for the work of the Czech avant-garde painters, writers and theoreticians Jindřich Štyrský and Toyen; he himself created plentiful irreverent collages and surrealist paintings.

The early death of Petr Škrabánek meant the demise of a multifaceted, cosmopolitan intellectual, a sharp ironist and a great lover of life, an acerbic critic but also a wonderful companion. We are delighted to honour Petr's memory by the first publication of his complete writings on *Finnegans Wake*.

Ondřej Pilný
Prague, May 2002

Petr Škrabánek in Zürich, 3 December, 1989. Photograph courtesy of Fritz Senn.

Petr Škrabánek at Trinity College, Dublin. Photograph courtesy of Věra Čapková.

INTRODUCTION: "PROBAPOSSIBLE PROLEGOMENA"

In March 1977, in a note meant to accompany an edition of letters from Thornton Wilder written to her between 1950 and 1975, Adaline Glasheen described the early project of *Finnegans Wake* exegesis as one of "amateur" unriddling:

> It was a time when *Finnegans Wake* was yet outside literature, criticism, scholarship, when it had no price on the literary exchange, when it seemed capable of solution or dissolution at any moment.[1]

From the 1940s, Glasheen, along with Wilder, Joseph Campbell, Henry Morton Robinson, Richard Ellmann, James S. Atherton, Hugh Kenner, William York Tindall, Matthew Hodgart, Jack Dalton, and others, pursued the project of amateur unriddling with prodigious energy. Their pioneering attempts made possible, and were to some degree brought to a close by, the major works of *Finnegans Wake* scholarship which emerged in the 1960s and 1970s, in particular those of Clive Hart and Roland McHugh.[2] In these works the project of cataloguing, codifying, and schematising Joyce's text achieved a formalistic nature which separates it as much in spirit as in intent from the earlier attempts at "unriddling." As Glasheen noted:

> The amateur age was over when Mr Hart published his *Concordance to Finnegans Wake* in 1963, and when Mr Hart and Mr Senn founded *A Wake Newslitter* which has been published since 1964.[3] The *Concordance*

1 Adaline Glasheen, Introduction to *A Tour of the Darkling Plain: The Finnegans Wake Letters of Thornton Wilder and Adaline Glasheen*, ed. Edward M. Burns with Joshua A. Gaylord (Dublin: University College Dublin Press, 2001) xiii.
2 Clive Hart, *A Concordance to Finnegans Wake*, corrected ed. (New York: Paul Appel, 1974); and, *Structure and Motif in Finnegans Wake* (London: Faber and Faber, 1962). Roland McHugh, *The Sigla of Finnegans Wake* (London: Edward Arnold, 1976); and, *Annotations to Finnegans Wake* (Baltimore: Jones Hopkins University Press, 1980).
3 Cf. *A Tour of the Darkling Plain*, xix, n3. The first issue of *A Wake Newslitter* appeared in March 1962. Eighteen numbers were published irregularly in mimeograph format, until December 1963. The new series began publication in February 1964 and continued until December 1980. Under the title *A Wake Newslitter: Occasional Paper* four issues were published between August 1982 and September 1984.

makes possible production of useful scholarly work—e.g., studies of verbal motifs, foreign word lists—by those who have not read *Finnegans Wake*. Scholar's time will be cut even shorter when, as is highly desirable, we get the sixty-three thousand [unique] words of *Finnegans Wake* onto computer cards. Amateur unriddlers still flourish, mostly underground. No amateur unriddler of Thornton Wilder's quality and endurance has surfaced of late, but there is sure to be one."[4]

It may be that Petr Škrabánek, who began publishing his readings of *Finnegans Wake* in *A Wake Newslitter* in 1971, was one of those who suggested to Adaline Glasheen the surety that an amateur unriddler of quality and endurance would yet emerge from an activity which, already at that time, had been largely marginalised and virtually driven "underground" by an incipient Joyce Industry.

Glasheen was not to know, however, that apart from devoting a great deal of energy to elaborating "foreign word lists," Škrabánek did indeed read *Finnegans Wake*, and did so compulsively. Like Clive Hart, Škrabánek transcribed and collated thousands of catalogue cards on which he recorded possible variant readings of Joyce's text. Much of this work was linguistic in nature, and while almost all of Škrabánek's published writings on the *Wake* comprise glossaries of Anglo-Irish, Slavonic and Eastern languages, his project taken as a whole vastly extends the interpretative field of *Finnegans Wake* scholarship.

Petr Škrabánek's work on *Finnegans Wake* has remained "underground" in other respects. Škrabánek was indeed an amateur Joycean, devoting his professional life to medicine. From 1968 until his death in 1994 he worked in Dublin at various medical laboratories and hospitals, including the Mater Misericordiae, and at Trinity College, and went on to become a fellow of the Royal College of Physicians of Ireland. Over three hundred medical publications attest to his "quality and endurance" in that field. But while his writings on Joyce appeared consistently enough in mimeograph publications like *AWN*, and while his name often appears among the acknowledgements in the works of better-known critics (McHugh, *et al.*), Škrabánek's own "unriddling" of *Finnegans Wake* has suffered to a certain degree due to the fact that, almost uniquely among the generation of Fritz Senn and Clive Hart, he published nothing on Joyce in book form.

---

[4] Glasheen, *A Tour of the Darkling Plain*, xiv.

The relative neglect of Škrabánek's work in the mainstream of the Joyce Industry may also have to do with the increasing bias of critics towards resurrecting an "Irish" Joyce (Škrabánek cites Patrick Kavanagh, "Who Killed James Joyce," as accusing foreigners of the original "murder").[5] Much of Škrabánek's work draws upon Joyce's well-attested fascination with Slavonic languages, including Czech, Russian, Polish, Slovenian, Serbo-Croat, Ruthenian, Rumanian, and non-Latin writing systems such as Armenian, Hebrew, Cuneiform and Sino-Japanese.

Joyce never schematised his interest in these languages in such a way as, for example, Ezra Pound schematised his interest in Chinese ideograms via the work of Fenollosa. The little enough which is known of Joyce's Czech brother-in-law, František Schaurek, has generally been presumed to have been said, and despite the fact that Joyce lived in Trieste from 1904 to 1915 and spoke Triestino with his family, his one work not to be "set" in Dublin, *Giacomo Joyce*, has been largely overlooked by professional Joyce scholars.[6]

Without question the Cold War, which overshadowed most of Petr Škrabánek's life as a Czech émigré, has much to answer for in this respect too. The same historical events which led to the dispersal of Joyce's papers and to the academic and cultural "centrism" of the United States, may well be one of the prime reasons for the scholarly neglect of the Central-Eastern European Joyce, in tandem with the more recent celebration of the bogey Irish nationalist Joyce.

Doubtless in time these tendencies will be balanced out by the growing amount of work coming to light in Trieste, Prague and other "peripheral" European cities, even as the idea of Europe itself is undergoing modifications, and to a greater or lesser degree coming more to resemble the Europe Joyce himself was most intimate with. The drawing and re-drawing of boundaries is a Wakean theme if ever there was one, and it ought to be pointed out that Joyce's erstwhile preoccupation with a number of the Slavonic languages, for example, corresponds historically to a period of energetic revivalism in the face of imperialistic disenfranchisement. Joyce's sympathy (shared with his brother Stanislaus) for the Irredentist movement in Trieste prior to

---

5   Petr Škrabánek, "Joyce in Exile," *Thomas Davis Lecture*, Radio Éireann, 18 April, 1982.
6   Cf. *Giacomo Joyce: Envoys of the Other*, eds. Louis Armand and Clare Wallace (Bethesda: Academica, 2002).

WWI, may be generalised in terms of like movements throughout the Austro-Hungarian and Russian Empires, just as with the British Empire and the question of Irish Home Rule.

But Joyce himself was never a nationalist in any straightforward sense and could on occasion be scathing of the national revivalism of Lady Gregory and W.B. Yeats. It might be said that his interest was drawn more to the "resistances" of language, and the plurality of languages, as against the Babelian cult of the One. For Joyce, all language is "foreign," above all when we imagine that we can erect claims of sovereignty upon it, or over it.

▲▲▲▲▲

In the early 1970s, when Petr Škrabánek first began publishing on *Finnegans Wake*, Joyce scholarship had already begun to take on the specialised complexion which has led it to be regarded by many as the "Joyce Industry." Škrabánek's detailed exegeses of Joyce's text, however, are of an entirely other order of specialisation to this. His linguistic studies possess a level of detail which nevertheless avails itself of more general application in the theoretical elaboration of the *Wake*'s structure.

Indeed, Škrabánek himself rarely laid claim to any particular theoretical position and was more than usually sceptical of intellectual fashions. His work maintains a high degree of empirical "objectivity," and in many respects this work defines a continuity between the early attempts of Glasheen and Wilder and the more systematic exploration of the Joycean *avant-texte* which has characterised "textual genetics" during the last two decades.

Reviewing *"Scribble" 1. Genèse des textes*, edited by Claude Jacquet (Paris: Lettres Modernes, 1988), Škrabánek indicated at least a nodding acquaintance with the early genetic criticism of, among others, Daniel Ferrer, Jean-Michel Rabaté and Laurent Milesi. The review itself is too brief to draw many conclusions (it at least indicates that the Anglo-European divide had already established itself sufficiently in Joyce studies for the work of *Le Centre de Recherches sur James Joyce de l'Université de la Sorbonne Nouvelle* and *Le Programme Joyce de l'Institut des Textes et Manuscrits Modernes du Centre National de la Recherche Scientifique* to have seemed a novelty at the time). But however Škrabánek consciously measured his relation to such things as textual genetics, it is clear that his own critical methodology significantly predicates that of later critics and genetic theoreticians, particularly in the elaboration of Joyce's notebook and manuscripts.

It is arguable that Petr Škrabánek is the major unacknowledged figure in *Finnegans Wake* scholarship of the late 1970s. His work stands at a critical juncture between the publication of the *Concordance*, the *Annotations* and the *Archive*, and the recently commenced serial publication of *The Finnegans Wake Notebooks at Buffalo*, under the editorship of Vincent Deane, Daniel Ferrer and Geert Lernout.[7]

What most distinguishes Škrabánek's work from that of other exegetes and connects him with figures like Clive Hart (*Structure and Motif in Finnegans Wake*) and Roland McHugh (*The Sigla of Finnegans Wake*) is his abiding concern with the structural significance of the Joycean *avant-texte* and of Joyce's radical use of paronomasia. While it may be argued that Škrabánek's project is not one which attempts to comprehend the theoretical implications of its own activities, it nevertheless is engaged in an exploration into the premises of those activities. That is to say, into the structurality of Joyce's text which in the first place allows, indeed seems to demand, a broadly linguistic approach. Škrabánek's empiricism in this sense can thus be seen as foundational to more theoretically "structuralist" approaches.

In his introduction to *The Sigla of Finnegans Wake*, Roland McHugh states that "*Finnegans Wake* [...] is immensely difficult to read: I should in fact say that it is not a reasonable thing to expect an unaided person to attempt *Finnegans Wake*. There is in consequence a pressing need for exegetical studies which actually work, as opposed to producing a mere tranquillising effect."[8] Indifference to context and continuity are the two principle flaws McHugh identifies in the bulk of exegetical material which came to surround the *Wake* in the 1960s and 70s. Like Clive Hart, McHugh sought to overcome this problem by addressing the relation between linguistic structure and a general schematics. Such an approach is implicit also in Petr Škrabánek's linguistic analysis of foreign language forms in Joyce's text, and in this respect much of his work can be taken as a companion to the structural analyses of Hart and McHugh, and is perhaps best appreciated in this context.

---

[7] *The Finnegans Wake Notebooks at Buffalo*, eds. Vincent Deane, Daniel Ferrer and Geert Lernout (Turnout, Belguim: Brepols, 2002).

[8] McHugh, *The Sigla of Finnegans Wake*, 1.

The structural, "schematic" orientation of Škrabánek's ethno-linguistic tropisms is clearly indicated in a number of short discussion papers and hypotheses, such as the typo-topology of "Imaginable Itinerary through the Particular Universal" and "The Condom Conundrum of a French Letter," with its echo in Hart's Viconian analysis of the *Wake*'s "mandalic" ⊕ structure; likewise in "Structure and Motif in Thunderwords—A Proposal," where Škrabánek argues against syllabification and in favour of a contextual approach. What becomes most evident when taken as a whole, is that, no less than in the writings of Hart and McHugh, Škrabánek's analysis hinges upon the overall structural significance of Joyce's language.

In reading Škrabánek, however, it is important not to allow the work to appear to be overshadowed by that of his more widely known contemporaries. Keeping in mind that Škrabánek never formalised a system for approaching *Finnegans Wake*, we may view the work as tentative, but also as an apparatus of potentialities which, in not been over-burdened by the rigidities of a system, has retained a deal of critical versatility. This should not diminish our appreciation of the seriousness and the profound implications of Škrabánek's work. On the contrary, it is the very tentative nature of these writings which gives them a pertinence today often lacking in the more canonical texts, many of which have become obsolete, succumbing to the redundancies of prematurely formulated theory (the outcome of an excessive dependence upon the timeliness of empirical methodology and the technical means that underwrite it).

Another distinguishing feature of Škrabánek's work is, beyond the dictates of indexical form, a certain minimalism, as opposed to the monumentality of those bodies of work, like Ellmann's and Hart's, which sought to establish certain definitive claims over Joyce's text. Škrabánek's minimalism provides a strategic means of coming to the *Wake* from many directions, through a series of feints and counter-feints which affect a critical "deterritorialisation," transforming, through a type of Joycean parthenogenesis, the assumed boundaries of the interpretative terrain.

While Škrabánek points to the structural significance of Joyce's puns, for example, structurality is never rigidified into a schematic orthodoxy, as it is particularly in the work of Campbell, Robinson and Tindall. There is no attempt to provide any "skeleton key" with which to unlock *Finnegans Wake* (a pretension which is mocked in an originally "anonymous" piece, "The Key No. One to No-One").[9]

▲▲▲▲▲

Arguably Clive Hart's 1962 study *Structure and Motif in Finnegans Wake* represented the first major attempt at investigating Joyce's work in terms of structural principles. Earlier works, like Campbell and Robinson's *A Skeleton Key to Finnegans Wake* (1947) had made what Hart called a "very brave attempt [...] to reveal the general architectural design" of the *Wake*, but Hart's book was amongst the earliest to deal with Joyce's work by analysing it in terms that could be called structuralist.[10] While the importance of paronomasia in the *Wake* was generally acknowledged well before Hart's study, it was Hart who first recognised the "structural" importance of Joyce's puns:

> A pun is effective only when its first term is vividly prepared by the context. By using a vocabulary and style packed with well-worn units Joyce is able to play on what the psychologists call the reader's "readiness" [...]. If Joyce builds [the motifs] up from familiar phrases [...] he is immediately able to make the widest punning excursions while remaining sure of his reader's powers of recognition [...].
>
> The essential value of the pun [...] in *Finnegans Wake* lies not in its elusive and suggestive qualities but in its ability to compress much meaning into little space.[11]

As Hart suggests, the pun is also at work at the schematic or cosmological level of text (the "chaosmos of Alle" [118.21]), in what we might call its structural convergence. For Škrabánek, like Hart, this structural convergence is tropical, orientated by a turning or series of turns, based upon a certain "perversion" of resemblance underwriting the pun's semantic value. This manifests itself most evidently at the structural level of the book itself, for which Škrabánek supplies the tropic mechanism absent from Hart's schematic approach, linking the first and last words of *Finnegans Wake*, "the" and "riverrun," through a pun on the name of the mythological river Lethe:

9   Petr Škrabánek, "The Key No. One to No-One," *AWN* 14.1 (1977): 16.
10 Hart, *Structure and Motif in Finnegans Wake*, 19-20.
11 Hart, *Structure and Motif in Finnegans Wake*, 32.

The book ends (and starts) in the middle of a sentence. "The letter that never begins to find the latter that ever comes to end" (337.10). We are hoping "for the latter to turn up with a cupital tea before her ephumeral comes off" (369.32) but it "comes to nullum in the endth" (298.21)—the end "the."

The last "the" is the dead end, oblivion, the waters of the Lethe (French *Le thé*, the tea. The "obliffious" (317.32) river of Death, the Lethe, meets the water of Life, *uisce beatha*, the Liffey, in the gap between the last "the" and the opening "riverrun." "What a neanderthalltale to unfurl and with what an end" (12.25).[12]

The pun becomes a "lethemuse" (272.F3), forgetting itself and beginning over again in the possibility of other readings, other embodiments. For Škrabánek, the pun itself is a schematic agent, operating across the "whole gammat" of rhetorical categories.

▲▲▲▲▲

In *Structure and Motif*, Hart, working "contrawatchwise" (119.17), commences with the schematic and deduces from it a tropological ground, identifying by this means two major patterns of organisation in the structure of *Finnegans Wake*. The first of these is a three-plus-one pattern which Joyce ostensibly borrowed from Vico's *Principi di Scienza Nuova*, of a cyclical model of history comprising three evolutionary stages and a *ricorso*. The second pattern consists of "Lesser Cycles" which "make up a four-plus-one quasi-Indian" pattern.[13]

According to Hart, these models sustain the *Wake*'s overall double, cyclic structure: the "Major Viconian Cycle" describing the four Books of the *Wake*, while within each of the "three Viconian Ages of Books I, II, and III, Joyce allows four four-chapter cycles to develop," and each of these lesser cycles also sustains an "implicit identification" with one of the four Western "classical elements" of earth, water, fire, and air:

---

[12] Petr Škrabánek, "The Condom Conundrum of a French Letter," *Third Degree: James Joyce Centenary Issue* 6 (1983): 12.

[13] Hart, *Structure and Motif in Finnegans Wake*, 62.

Major Viconian Cycle	*Lesser Cycle*
Book I (Birth)	1. I.1-4: Male H.C.E 2. I.5-8: Female A.L.P.
Book II (Marriage)	3. II—Male and Female battles; fire
Book III (Death)	4. III—Male cycle; Shaun as Earwicker's spirit; air

Hart's work touches closest on contemporary genetic approaches to Joyce's text in his idea of schemata functioning as prototypical models of different levels of textual production, although where Hart focuses on how these emerge within Joyce's text along more traditional lines of character and narrative, genetics tends to focus on how these schemata emerge from different points in the history of the text's composition.[14]

In this way, also, it is possible to see Škrabánek's analysis as working a seam between the two, proceeding from the structural agency of the pun where Hart proceeds from the thematic, and underwriting this through a discursive exploration of etymological geneses (actual or projective) whose elaboration can be regarded as broadly "genetic." Again, here the "evolutionary" approach of Hart proceeds from the

---

[14] Hart's insight into the importance of context and the preparation of the reader in the operation of the pun recalls the structural importance Freud attributed to puns in *Wit and its Relation to the Unconscious* (1916) and anticipates, in many respects, Umberto Eco's later analysis of the *Wake*'s paronomasia in *The Role of the Reader: Explorations in the Semiotics of Texts* (Bloomington: Indiana University Press, 1979). Hart's thinking in this regard also incorporates many of the ideas of the Prague Structuralist and Russian Formalist critics, and anticipates much of later "reader response" or "reception" theory. His historical-schematic rendering of the *Wake* and the *Wake*'s language brings to mind Roman Ingarden and Wolfgang Iser's contention that language offers different "schematised views" through which the subject matter of the work can come to light, although the actual bringing to light is an action of *Konkretisation*. Those schemata that are actualised in this way would also signify and hence constitute a textuality of their own. This is perhaps the most radical point that Hart makes—that the textual schemata not only consist of a semantic content, but comprise that content themselves. Although Hart does not follow this idea through to its possible implications, and while he remains closer to the phenomenological views of Ingarden and Iser, he does pave the way for thinking the "schematic views" of *Finnegans Wake* as *genetic* and *generative* of the *Wake*'s overall signifying structures.

thematic or analogical (Vico) to the particular, although it is arguable as to whether or not this ever engages with the idea of the pun and paronomasia on their own terms. By contrast, the "minimalism" of Škrabánek implicitly requires any generalised poetics to account, in the first place, for those tropological mechanisms which characterise even the least remarkable and diminutive features of Joyce's text.

An example of this can be seen in Hart's analysis of III.1, in which Hart sees Joyce as putting "cyclic ideas to work" in organising individual chapters:

Cycle I

Age i (403.18-405.03):	Description of Shaun as a "picture primitive"; he does not speak (first Viconian Age).
Age ii (405.04-407.09):	Shaun has become a hero ("Bel of Beaus Walk"); there is an illusion to the heroic slaying of the Jabberwock and an entertaining Rabelaisian description of Shaun's heroic eating habits.
Age iii (407.10-414.14):	Introduced by "Overture and beginners'" this is the beginning of the Human Age, in which the gods can appear only in dramatic representation on stage; Shaun has become a popular representative ("vote of the Irish"); the word "Amen" brings to an end the group of three Ages forming the main part of this first Viconian cycle.
Age iv (414.14-414.18):	A short *ricorso* brings us back to the theocratic Age with the introduction to the Fable— Thunder (*FW* 414.19).[15]

Hart suggests that the overall structure of the *Wake*—by the three-plus-one pattern and its four-plus-one schematic compliment—can also be understood in terms of the ⊕ symbol. This "cross of the quaternity"

---

[15] Hart, *Structure and Motif in Finnegans Wake*, 58. Hart then analyses the following sections of the book along the same lines and demonstrates that Cycle IV brings III.1 "to a conclusion with a prayer [...] to Shaun the god-figure, who is to be resurrected in the next chapter" (ibid., 60).

corresponds to the siglum in the *Finnegans Wake* notebooks used to designate what Hart refers to as the "highly important ninth question in I.6.9":

> if a human being duly fatigued [...] having plenxty off time on his gouty hands [...] were [...] accorded [...] with an earsighted view of old hopinhaven [...] then *what* would that fargazer seem to seemself to seem seeming of, dimm it all?" (143.4-27)

The *Wake*'s answer, "A collideorscope" (143.28), can be seen as one of the many terms with which Joyce's text describes itself, and Hart contends that Joyce's use of the ⊕ symbol to designate a passage dealing with the structure of *Finnegans Wake* "suggests that in one structural sense, the whole book forms a *mandala*," which the ⊕ symbol represents ("a quadripartite with diametrically inverted ornaments")[16]:

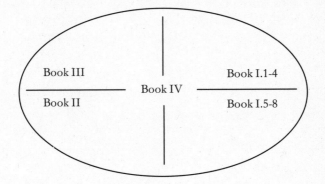

According to Hart, the four quadrants of the circle constitute "the Wheel of Fortune, while Book IV lies at the 'hub.'"[17]

---

16 Cf. McHugh, *The Sigla of Finnegans Wake*, 118. For McHugh the ⊕ symbol "denotes the mental sensation of contemplating the mandala of *Finnegans Wake*, a tranquil equipoise at the hub of time" (ibid., 121). There has been considerable speculation on the relationship between *Finnegans Wake*'s schematic structures and Jung's conception of archetypes and a collective unconscious (in which Jung employed the mandala symbol). Although Joyce was acquainted with Jung (who treated his daughter, Lucia, for part of her illness), and made several references to Jung in the *Wake* ("Jungfraud's" [460.20]), he was more clearly drawn to the ideas of Vico and, to a less certain extent, Freud and the British anthropologist Sir J.G. Frazer.

17 Hart, *Structure and Motif in Finnegans Wake*, 77.

In "Imaginable Itinerary through the Particular Universal" and "The Condom Conundrum of a French Letter," Škrabánek similarly explores the comedic cyclicality of the *Wake*'s structural organisation. However, unlike Hart's directly schematic reading, Škrabánek suggests a tropological way of reading the Wakean mandala ⊕ as a literal turning (between the *Wake*'s terminal "the" and its "initial" term, "riverrun). Punning on the French word for "tea," *thé* (which is pronounced like the letter "T"), Škrabánek suggests that we may read the *Wake*'s terminal signifier of definite articulation *the* as "a cupital tea," T (which might also be read substituting for the letter C [sea?] in an erstwhile acrostic on H.C.E.). Škrabánek proposes that *the* operates a series of substitutions on the theme of recirculation (tea, whiskey, *uisce beatha*, the water of life, the Liffey, urine, Lethe, the waters of death, forgetfulness, etc., oblivion, the sea, and hence, by a commodius vicus of recirculation, "the ... riverrun"). However, by interpolating a little into an otherwise unrelated discussion of sigla in *Finnegans Wake*, "The Turning of the Ш," we might also extend Škrabánek's tropism to Hart's Viconian 3+1 structure as a literal "turning of the T." In this case, the "turning" described by the three notebook sigla representing Isolde as an inverted T and a T tipped over on its left and right sides, ⊢⊥⊣, combined with the siglum for Tristan, T, would thus come to form an approximately squared circle or mandalic T-totem, ⊕ (another symbol, perhaps, for St. Patrick's shamrock, the trinity cum quaternity of the *Wake*'s "tristurned initials" 100.28).

▲▲▲▲▲

Following from Hart's project, Roland McHugh, in 1980, published *Annotations to Finnegans Wake* which thereafter formed the basis for a large body of scholarship devoted to annotating Joyce's texts. McHugh's other important work, *The Sigla of Finnegans Wake* (1976), furnished the first systematic inquiry into Joyce's use of sigla in his writing (e.g. 299.F4):

The Doodles Family, ⋔, △, ⊣, ✕, □, ∧, ⊏. Hoodle doodle, fam.?

McHugh's study, which acknowledges a debt to Škrabánek, is significant to the conceptualisation of Joyce's language because it addresses the way in which textual elements in *Finnegans Wake* signify otherwise than linguistically. These sigla variously appear in the published version of *Finnegans Wake*, in several of Joyce's letters, and in the notebooks, particularly VI.B.8. McHugh records, for example, the appearance of the ⊥ siglum on page 147 of the notebook along with its page and line reference in the *Wake* ("*Miss Horizon, justso all our fannacies dainted her, on the curve of the camber, unsheathing a showlaced limbaloft to the great consternations*"):

VI.B.8.147:	⊥ girl lying on	(340.28-30)
	causeway ~~lacin~~	
	with one leg	
	heavenward, lacing	
	her shoe[18]	

In a letter to Harriet Shaw Weaver (24 March 1924), Joyce wrote: "In making notes I used signs for the chief characters," on the reverse of which the ⊥ siglum appears among a list of other sigla, this time standing for the figure of Isolde, the *inverse* of Tristan (⊤) (*L* I.213). Elsewhere, at VI.B.11.105, ⊥ is given as "mirror of mirror."[19] But as McHugh himself has pointed out, any nominal approach to the sigla is liable to ambiguity, despite Joyce's advertisements.[20]

As with the notational acrostics H.C.E. and A.L.P., the sigla appear to stand in place of different "characters" or characteristics at different times. The ∧ siglum, for example, is taken to stand for Shaun in Joyce's letter to Weaver, while in VI.B.15.153 it stands for "taste," and later for Justius and Kevin (where an apparent relatedness lies in the binary organisation of the fraternal couples Shaun and Shem, Justius and Mercius, Kevin and Jerry, and so on).

Similarly, studies into the *Wake*'s paronomasia have long seen Joyce's phonic and graphic puns and portmanteau words as examples of lexemes or other sublexical units bearing "autonomous" significations beyond simply designating linguistic difference.[21] For

---

18 McHugh, *The Sigla of Finnegans Wake*, 133.
19 McHugh, *The Sigla of Finnegans Wake*, 7.
20 McHugh, *The Sigla of Finnegans Wake*, 135.
21 This effect of verbal atomism has been compared to the "optical mixing" of post-Impressionist artists like Georges Seurat. According to early Joyce biographer and critic Stuart Gilbert, *Finnegans Wake* is "*pointilliste* throughout," and Hart has suggested that

example, how the "E" of H.C.E. is seemingly tipped over to signify "a village inn" (119.27; VI.B.8.145), or when the △ siglum of A.L.P. is suggested to signify "an upside down bridge" (119.28; VI.B.146), the Liffey "delta," and the equilateral triangle of transcendental mystery[22]:

> all tiberiously ambiembellishing the initials majuscule of Earwicker: the meant to be baffling chrismon trilithon sign ⊓, finally called after some hecitency Hec, moved contrawatchwise, represents his title in sigla as the smaller △, fontly called following a certain change of state of grace of nature alp or delta, when single, stands for or tautologically stands beside the consort. (119.16-22)

At the same time, as Škrabánek demonstrates in "The Turning of the Ш," the translational process which seems to assign a material, non-linguistic function to the *Wake*'s sigla, can also give rise to other translational processes of ideographic summation or "literalisation" through their material resemblance to other signifying "scriptsigns."

Škrabánek locates one such instance in the resemblance of the E (from H.C.E.) turned "contrawatchwise" to both the Persian Cuneiform ⊨⫶⫶ and the Cyrillic ШƎⳘ (i.e. "Sheem" 188.05; 580.18). Another instance ("St. Kevin's Nightmare Confession") involves the siglum that Joyce used to designate the figure of Shaun ∧ (*L* I.213), which can be read not only as the Greek lambda Λ, but also as the Sino-Japanese character for "man" 人 (i.e. the counterpart to Shem's noman: "When is a man not a man? [...] When he is [...] Sham" 170.24).

Like McHugh, Škrabánek's elucidations of the *Wake* sigla draw directly upon original source materials. This is similarly the practice with regard to the various "foreign word lists" which are as much elaborations of Joyce's own transcriptions as they are upon the contexts in which they appear in the published text. By tracing Joyce's transcriptions of Armenian terms in the notebooks, for example,

---

the *Wake* describes "The development of a style which involved the manipulation of ever smaller and more autonomous units." Stuart Gilbert, *James Joyce's Ulysses: A Study* (New York: Vintage, 1952) 96; Clive Hart, "Quinet." *James Joyce: A Collection of Critical Essays*, ed. William M. Chance (New Jersey: Prentice Hall, 1974) 130.

[22] McHugh, *The Sigla of Finnegans Wake*, 66-67. Cf. Alan Roughley, "A.L.P.'s 'Sein' and 'Zeit': Questions of *Finnegans Wake*'s Being of Language in a Philosophical Context." *European Joyce Studies. Finnegans Wake: Fifty Years*, ed. Geert Lernout (Amsterdam: Rodopi, 1990) 129.

Škrabánek is able to trace Joyce's likely use of French transliteration tables for Western Armenian (e.g. VI.B.45.128).[23] The significance of this is not merely academic. The phonemic shifts between Eastern and Western Armenian noted by Škrabánek echo similar shifts in systems of transliteration, orthography and pronunciation within English itself and its constituent dialects and etymologies. This in turn bears upon the mechanism of phonemic metamorphosis articulated in *Finnegans Wake*, as a matrix of linguistic genesis.

In this sense Joyce's linguistic experiment can be seen as developing ideas expressed in Ferdinand de Saussure *Cours de Linguistique Général* (1913), in which the structural relation between orthography and semantics is shown to be not only arbitrary but also generative of signifying difference of its own. Phonemic substitution operates as both an agent of ambiguity and as a mark of idiomatic specificity. Above all, it operates a tropic mechanism which underwrites a form of linguistic discursus, investing the entire field of signifying possibility (between and across language/s), "wordloosed over seven seas" (219.16).

While this approach may be viewed as fundamentally materialist, it is so in a way that is never divorced from semantic contingency. Trope and schema are mutually determinate, describing a broadly transverse relation of the "particular universal," in a manner which is not a theoretical construct but, for Škrabánek, necessarily demonstrable. As Joyce's own materialist poetics comes increasingly to the fore in discussions of *Finnegans Wake*, the re-publication of Petr Škrabánek's work takes on an additional relevance. It would not be an idle speculation to suggest that Škrabánek's legacy may yet come to exercise a notable influence over the future of Wakean analysis.

Louis Armand
Prague, May 2002

---

[23] Petr Škrabánek, "Notes on Armenian in *Finnegans Wake*," *FWC* 1.3 (1986): 45-58.

NIGHT JOYCE OF A THOUSAND TIERS

"There is no work more intellectual, more disengaged from worry about contemporary matters, more estranged from time and space, more foreign to politics, war, the torment of wretched Europe, none more preoccupied with the great interests of life, love, desire, death, childhood, fatherhood, the mystery of eternal return." This is how the French Academician, Louis Gillet, described *Finnegans Wake*.

James Stephens said: "it is unreadable ... it is wonderful."

On the other hand, St. John Gogarty, in a fit of blinding envy suggested that *Finnegans Wake* was a gigantic hoax written by an idiot on the backside of beauty. Or, to quote from the *Wake* itself, "the recital of the rigmarole" (174.04), "a stinksome inkestink" (183.06), "a ... riot of blots and blurs and bars and balls and hoops and wriggles and juxtaposed jottings linked by spurts of speed" (118.29).

After "his usylessly unreadable Blue Book of Eccles" (179.26), Joyce wrote the "bluest book in baile's annals" (13.21). As a young artist Joyce started with Ibsen, and ended obscene. *Finnegans Wake* with its "sexophonologistic Schizophrenesis" (123.18) however, in distinction to *Ulysses*, was never banned, despite its "seedy ejaculations" (183.23) and the "fluefoul smut" (183.15), as all the four-letter words have been "variously inflected, differently pronounced, otherwise spelled" (118.26). The scatological eschatology also seems to have escaped the attention of vigilant censors.

The verbal diarrhoea, the riverrun, of the *floozie in the jacuzzi*, is punctuated by ten thunderous farts, totalling 1001 letters. Thousand and One Nights of tails within tales, of tumescence and detumescence, of drinking and pissing, of eating and defecation, "turning breakfarts into lost soupirs" (453.11). In the upside down universe of the *Wake*, God's creative breath becomes Devil's fart, and *paternoster*, "farternoiser" (530.36). The sound of *Finnegans Wake* is that of chamberpot music.

If *Ulysses* was a day book, a stream of consciousness of one man, Everyman Bloom, *Finnegans Wake* is a night book, a nightmare stream from the unconscious of all men, of Nomen. Bloom's day is followed by Noman's night. The action takes place "nowhere," now and here, in Noman's land. "This nonday diary, this allnights newseryreel" (489.35).

The time is "nowtime" (290.17), "noughttime" (349.06).

Just like the proverbial Heraclitean river, you can never step into the same stream of *Finnegans Wake* twice. "Every word [is] bound over to carry three score and ten toptypsical readings throughout the book of Doublends Jined" (20.14). The reader, like Theseus, is lost in the labyrinth of theses and antitheses fusing into new syntheses. Each pair of Heraclitean opposites form both a unity and plurality, but if Heraclitus was known as "the weeping philosopher," Joyce, "the tragic jester" (171.15) is "agush with tears of joy" (178.12), as there is "lots of fun at Finnegan's wake." (*Fun* in Japanese means "excrement"). It's "hugglebeddy fann" (616.01).

The readers of *Finnegans Wake* are of two types: those who pretend to read it and those who read it to pretend. But each time the reader turns the revolving drum of the *Finnegans Wake* prayerwheel, it sends up new revolting blasphemies.

It took Joyce seventeen years to write seventeen chapters of *Finnegans Wake*—a labour of love, a love letter, and his artistic testament—the portrait of the artist as an old man. It contains more than 50,000 different words, three times as much as in the whole of Shakespeare, and in more than seventy seven languages. That makes it easier for foreigners. "He would wipe alley english spooker, multaphoniaksikally spuking, off the face of the erse" (178.06).

Talking to the Polish writer Jan Parandowski, Joyce complained:

> the few fragments which I have published have been enough to convince many critics that I have finally lost my mind, which, by the way, they have been predicting faithfully for many years. And perhaps it is madness to grind up words in order to extract their substance, to create crossbreeds and unknown variants, to open up unsuspected possibilities for these words, to marry sounds which were not usually joined before although they were meant for one another, to allow water to speak like water, birds to chirp in the words of birds, to liberate all sounds from their servile, contemptible role and to attach them to the feelers of expressions which grope for definitions of the undefined. ... With this hash of sounds I am building the great myth of everyday life.

With a "meticulosity bordering on the insane" (173.34). There is method in his madness.

Samuel Beckett was one of the first to appreciate the mastery of the achievement. I quote: "There form *is* the content, content *is* the form.

You complain that the stuff is not written in English. It is not written at all. It is not to be read, or, rather, it is not only to be read. It is to be looked at and listened to. His writing is not *about* something: it is that something itself." One could add that, like any great work of art, the *Wake* has no goal or meaning. Like God himself, to paraphrase the God of the Jews, it is because it is.

Finnegans Wake defies the second law of thermodynamics by being in perpetual motion, while its source of energy, the writer, is dead.

By giving four sides to the *Wake* circle, Joyce achieved another impossibility: the squaring of the circle. "*Finnegans Wake* is a wheel and it's all square." "She bit his tailibout" [tail, butt] and "all hat tiffin for thea" (229.25).

And each time the wheel of *Finnegans Wake* turns, Humpty Dumpty is put together again: the egg is unscrambled.

The riverrun, the last and the first words of the river-rain cycle, is the antithesis of the raven's "nevermore." Here the dove of baptism descends with its promise of eternal life.

Finnegans Wake is about beginnings and ends, but without an end or a beginning. Tim Finnegan of the ballad, stoned by too much whiskey, and appearing stone-dead, is revived by more of the same, *uisce beatha*, whiskey, the water of life, splashed on him during a lively wake. His baptism is by fire and water of the firewater. Like the Phoenix, he rises from his ashes. A *sine qua non* of resurrection is death. His dead penis rises too—a terrible beauty is born. The mortal HCE rises and falls. The immortal ALP remains horizontal. A mountain and a river. A bobbing pile of shit on the surface of urine. A storm in a tea-pot.

The water of life in the *Wake* is also the river Liffey, described by Joyce as having the colour of tea without milk, "Tea" in slang means both "whiskey" and "urine." *Le thé* in French is "tea." But the Lethe is also the water of forgetting, the river of death.

The last word joins the first, the Lethe and the Liffey, the river of oblivion and the river of life, merge in an "obliffious" stream (317.32). Just for a moment. "Lethelulled between explosion and reexplosion" (78.04). The short lull between the last and the first word is like the 'holy hour,' the pub closure between 2.30 and 3.30 (now abolished). This bizarre by-law was described by Stephen Pile as an attempt to assist the Irishmen in their struggle to come out of the pub at some point between dawn and bedtime.

The pissed Finnegan discharges the dead water from his bladder and is revived with a fresh supply of whiskey. Pissing rain swells the Liffey again, and makes Ireland, the Urinal of the Planets, green again. This is a great country, as we say here, but they should put a roof on it.

In Italian, "riverrun" reads *riverranno*, they will come again, the Finnegans wake up again, they will revive (*rivivranno*), the river-run ends and the circular dream begins again (*rêve-rond*).

Joyce said to his friend Budgen: "the Holy Roman Catholic Apostolic Church was built upon a pun. It ought to be good enough for me": *Tu es Petrus et super hanc petram aedificabo ecclesiam meam* (Thou art Peter, and upon this rock I will build my church—*Matthew* 16:18).

Joyce's foundation of *Finnegans Wake* is a parallel pun: You are Patrick and upon this sham-rock I will build my sham-work. "Peatrick" suggests the rick of peat, the mountain, the Reek (Croagh Patrick), and "peat reek" (whiskey distilled over the smoke of peat), but also the reek of the pot, as Patrick, like Jesus, is baptised with waters of the Jordan. ("Jordan" is an obsolete term for a chamber-pot). "Tauftauf thuartpeatrick" (3.10) means "I baptise you Patrick." It's all in German, as Patrick was a disciple of St. Germanicus (*taufe*, I baptise, *Taube*, dove, *Teufel*, the Devil). Holy Joe, St. Bridget and St. Patrick! "Scentbreeched and somepotreek" (12.22)—shitty breeches and chamber-pot stink.

The pea-trick was a rigging game of itinerant sharpers, using a pea and three thimbles. A sleight-of-hand, similar to St. Patrick's demonstration of the unity of the Holy Trinity, using the three-leafed shamrock.

Finnegans Wake being written from Paris to the Liffey, is a French letter, Joyce's last "wetbed confession" (188.01). Joyce thought of it as "a French letter which does not succeed in coming off, never quite" (VI.B.12.126). It's a riverrun with a "rubberend" (144.30). "The letter that never begins to go find the latter that ever comes to end, written in smoke and blurred by mist and signed of solitude, sealed at night" (337.12). The letter is found by a hen in a heap of litter, "literatured with burst loveletters" (183.10) in the "sound seemetery which iz leebez luv" (17.35), the symmetry of uniting opposites buried in the graveyard of sounds.

An early version of the *Wake* started with "Reverend," the addressee of the letter written by ALP. In its final form, the addressee is "riverrun," i.e. the Liffey, and the letter is written by Shem. It echoes a line from Yeats's poem "A Poet to His Beloved":

I bring you with reverent hands the books of my numberless dreams.

In Irish, "riverrun" reads *ribhéar a rúin*, my darling river, a loveletter of Joyce to the Liffey. *Rún* also means "a riddle," or "mystery."

The letter ends in the middle of a sentence with the "affectionate largelooking tache of tch" (111.19), a stain of tea, the sperm drop of renewal. "Life ... is a wake, livit or krikit, and on the bunk of our breadwinning lies the cropse of our seedfather" (55.05). The sperm drop from a victim of hanging, as discussed in *Ulysses*. After all, the *Wake* is a "Suspended Sentence" (106.13).

The last sentence evaporates into nothingness, dissolves, melts into the final "thaw," the Irish sound of the affirmative *tá*, "yes," the "final breath, a nothing," as Joyce said to Gillet. The male and female opposites meet in the orgasmic little death, *la petite mort*, as the French call it. ALP, falling into oblivion, breathes *ma mort*, "mememormee" (628.14), remember me in my death. Isolde dying with the initial of Tristan on her lips—T, the. The Liebestod—the love to death.

ALP is passing out, and her daughter is taking her place, "A daughterwife from the hills ... and she is coming. Swimming in my hindmoist. Diveltaking on me tail" (627.02).

The last page is Joyce's swan song, the last leaf, the last of the Liffey, the last tea leaf. "Where there's leaf, there's hope" (227.18). "Only a leaf, just a leaf and then leaves" (619.22). "They lived und laughed ant loved end left" (18.20). And Joyce's advice to the reader is: "tare it or leaf if" (118.34)—take it or leave it.

The first and the last page of *Finnegans Wake* recall lines from Tennyson's "Dying Swan":

with an inner voice the river ran,
adown it floated a dying swan

The "great sweet mother" at the beginning of *Ulysses* appears again at the end of the *Wake*. This comes from Swinburne's "Triumph of Time":

I will go back to the great sweet mother,
mother and lover of men, the sea,
I will go down to her, I and none other,
Close with her, kiss her, and mix her with me,

5

> My lips will feast on the foam of thy lips,
> I shall rise with thy rising, with thee subside ...

Swinburne's "fair white mother" is substituted by "cold mad father" (628.02), alluding to Finn MacCool, King Lear and Mananaan MacLir. The Liffey embracing the cold sea is like Molly dreaming about Leopold in his youth, "that awful deepdown torrent O and the sea ... and his heart was going like mad and yes I said yes I will Yes."

In the poem "A Prayer," there are proleptic seeds of the end of *Finnegans Wake*.

> Cease, silent love! My doom!
> Blind me with your dark nearness, O have mercy,
>   beloved enemy of my will!
> I dare not withstand the cold touch that I dread.
> Draw from me still
> My slow life! Bend deeper on me, threatening head...
> Take me, save me, soothe me, O spare me!

The "whitespread wings like he'd come from Arkangels" (628.10) on the last page represent both Zeus descending on Leda and the Archangel Gabriel of the Annunciation, who, like Zeus, made the maid pregnant. The virgin birth will lead to death and resurrection, and Leda will lay the Humpty Dumpty egg, from which the twins, Shem and Shaun, jump out. "See what happens when your somatophage merman takes his fancy to our virgitarian swan?" (171.02).

The swan seems to like it. "As he was rising my lather" (writing me a letter) ... "I was plucking his goosybone" (424.36). "I have been lost, angel. Cuddle, ye divil ye" (147.02). "Bite my laughters, drink my tears. Pore into me, volumes, spell me stark and spill me swooning" (145.18). "When he'd prop me atlas against his goose" (626.13), he "shootst throbbst into me mouth like a bogue and arrohs" (626.05).

The Archangel Gabriel brings to mind the end of the last story in *Dubliners*: "Generous tears filled Gabriel's eyes ... the snow falling faintly through the universe and faintly falling, like the descent of their last end, upon all the living and the dead." The whiteness of the bird's wings, the silence of snow.

The swan swoons. Death is near. The white bird darkens. "You'd rush upon me, darkly roaring, like a great black shadow with a sheeny stare to perce me rawly. And I'd frozen up and pray for thawe"

(626.24). "The"—the last sound of the dying swan, "the lethest zswound" (214.10) of lethally wounded Leda. Remember me when I cross the Lethe—voice of Joyce from beyond the grave.

The last tear. "She signs her final tear. Zee End" (28.27). "To hide away the tear, the parted" (625.30). The "the" of the departed. That's the end.

The last kiss. Like Arrah na Pogue, Nora of the Kiss, freeing her lover by means of a message which she gives him with a French kiss, ALP gives us the keys to her riddle. "The keys to. Given" (628.15). "Jesus said to Peter: And I will give unto thee the keys of the kingdom of heaven" (*Matthew* 16:19). But *Finnegans Wake* is not in heaven, but in Hell. In St. John's vision, "an angel came down from heaven having the key of the bottomless pit" (*Revelations* 20:1).

The last laugh.

Finn, again! Take.
Bussoftlhee,
mememormee!
Till thousendsthee. (628.14)

...-, ...-, ...-, ...- (The Morse code for "V"; "more. So." [628.06]). It stands for "victory," and "fuck you."

The penisolate war of exiled Shem the Penman is over. Penis mightier than the sword. Isolde was reunited with Tristan. ("Pen" is the name of the female swan). The Peninsular War between Wellington and Napoleon, and other Tweedledums and Tweedledees can be re-enacted again. For the time being, as in the last sentence of Homer's *Odyssey*, a peace has been established between the two contending forces.

Like Sterne's *Sentimental Journey*, *Finnegans Wake* ends in the middle of a sentence. "The affectionate largelooking tache of tch" (111.19) is like the TUNC page with the large Tau (τ) and Chi (χ) dominating the page. TUNC is a simple anagram of the missing word in *A Sentimental Journey*. The voyage on the sea of words, full of seamen, such as Sinbad the Sailor, Noah, and Odysseus. All returning home to their Penelopes: "when all is zed and done, the penelopean patience of its last paraphe" (123.04).

After the Forty days of the Deluge, Noah's Ark lands on the top of a mountain. "And it came to pass at the end of forty days that Noah

7

opened the window of the ark" (*Genesis* 8:6) and sent out the raven and the dove. "Look, there are yours off, high on high! And cooshes, sweet good luck they're cawing you, Coole! You see, they're as white as the riven snae" (621.36). "Afartodays, afear tonights, and me as with you in thadark" (622.15). "Softmorning ... Folty and folty all the nights" (619.20). Noah was sending messages in empty bottles of Guinness, "carried in a caddy or screwed and corked" (624.01), "with a bob, bob, bottledby" (624.02) and "cast ashore" (623.30).

The first fragment of *Finnegans Wake* was about a "waterproof monarch of all Ireland" (380.34), the "pomp porteryark" (624.14), later forming the core of II.3 (309-382) in which the Norwegian Captain is in charge of a ship carrying bottled Guinness and Phoenix Stout. Guinness's barges used to leave from Kingsbridge, and Joyce had Jack Yeats's canvass depicting such a barge on the Liffey, in his Parisian flat.

It is noteworthy that this chapter opens with an acrostic of Noman. "It may not or maybe a no" (309.01).

The stout ship is also Noah's Ark, where Noah brews beer and distils whiskey by arclight ("pa's malt had Jhem or Shen brewed by arclight" [3.13]). Having taken one too many, he is sprawled across the Ark, exposing his nakedness. His alter ego, HCE, is stretched across Dublin, from Howth to Chapelizod, the Wellington monument in the Park being his protruding member. (Both Noah's Ark and the Phoenix Park are also zoos). The comatose Noah is assaulted by his sons, and he curses Ham: "And Noah awoke from his wine and knew what his younger son had done into him" (*Genesis* 9:24). Something similar happened between HCE and three soldiers in the Park, though the nature of the crime is as obscure as in *Genesis*. Other important encounters between a father figure and a young man in *Finnegans Wake* are the blinding of the drunken Cyclops by Ulysses-Noman and the shooting of the bare-arsed Russian Bear/General by the Irish private Buckley at the Crimea. This crime was precipitated by the General using a sod of turf to wipe himself and not realising that 'sod' was a metonym for Ireland, The Old Sod. All these encounters suggest sodomy. Joyce links "arse" with "Erse" and Ireland with Sodom. "Sod's brood, be me fear!" (4.06): God's blood, soda bread, and the breed of sodomites. Noman/Noah-man is also a pun on "to know a man" in the biblical sense.

In the year of Joyce's birth, 1882, another crime was committed in the park, the Phoenix Park murders, in which Lord Cavendish and his

Under-Secretary were assassinated by the Invincibles. At the trial one of the Invincibles was referred to as "No. 1," i.e. no-one, another Noman.

"*No man*, said the Nolan ..." were the first words of Joyce to be printed, in *The Day of the Rabblement*, and that word which "always sounded strangely," "gnomon," appears at the beginning of the first story in *Dubliners*. (The first word of Homer's *Odyssey* was *andra*, man.)

It was Odysseus who called himself no-one, Noman (*outis*) in the Cyclops chapter—an episode particularly near to Joyce's heart. When the drunken Cyclops was blinded by Odysseus with a burning pole driven into his eye, the giant roared so much that other Cyclopes came up to see what was happening.—What the hell is going on? Is somebody trying by treachery to murder you?—It's Noman's treachery that is killing me, screamed the giant.—Well, then, if nobody is harming you there is little we can do.

Odysseus then escaped from the blocked cave by hiding under a black ram, slipping through the giant's fingers when the Cyclops was letting his sheep out to graze, one by one. A sort of blindman's bluff. "Beerman's bluff was what begun it" (422.31). Another "beerman" is Finnegan, full of beer, stretched on a bier, bluffing his death.

There is an Irish parallel to this story. Finn MacCool got trapped in a cave of Goll, a one-eyed giant. Finn plunged a hot spit into the sleeping eye of the giant and escaped by putting a skin from a goat on himself and mingling with the giant's herd being let out.

The same motif of deceiving the blind old father by a furry disguise is Jacob fooling the dying Isaac by putting on a goatskin, to make his blind father believe that this is his firstborn, Esau, ready to receive his blessing.

Another no-man was Jesus, half-God, half-man, also known as The Lamb. He slipped out from a cave too. When his disciples came back to the cave where he was buried, he was gone. "He is not here, for he is risen" (*Matthew* 28:5). And in the *Acts of the Apostles* we read: "when we had opened, we found *no man* within" (*Acts* 5:23). But the Noman of the *Wake* is a black-sheep, or rather half-man, half-goat. A pun on the god Pan. A fauny-man, a funny man. *Finnegans Wake* is a fairytale with the furry tail and the furry head of the hairwigged Earwicker. He falls and rises. What did the earwig say when it fell off the wall again?— Earwigo again.

Finnegans Wake is full of "punns and reedles" (239.35). The answer to the central riddle of the *Wake*, Shem's riddle, when is a man not a

9

man, is easy,—when he is a noman.

Joyce divided the name of Ulysses into *outis* (Noman) and Zeus. If Homer could make a pun on Odysseus's name, Joyce, our "homerole poet" (445.32) could do the same with the name of Shem.

Shem in Hebrew means name, or God's name. As Hebrew reads backwards, *nomen* (name) gives *nemon*. *Nemo* in Latin means Noman. Noman holds the key to the *Wake*, in *Revelations* 5:3 "No man ... was able to open the book," and in the words of Noman Jesus: "I will give unto thee the keys ... then he charged his disciples that they should tell to no man" (*Matthew* 16:20).

Shem's riddle, with its solution hidden within Shem's name is modelled on the most famous riddle of all times, the riddle of the Sphinx ... "riddle a rede from the sphinxish pairc" (324.06), the Sphinx of the Phoenix Park. "There is on earth a thing which has four legs, two legs, and three legs, and one voice." The answer, provided by Oedipus, was—man: in infancy on all four, with a stick in old age, and on two in between. The answer was hidden in Oedipus's own name: *oida* (I know) and *dipous* (biped, man), i.e. "I know that the answer is man," "know-man." As Sophocles put it: "The riddling Sphinx caused us to turn our eyes to what lay at out feet."

The first key appears in the title.

FIN(d) NEG. ANSWA = KE(y).

The key word to Joyce's work. Like an abominable no-man, he says no to everything, to his country, to his church, to his family—Stephen's and Satan's *non serviam*.

"In the best manner of Shem," Joyce wrote to Miss Weaver, "I developed painful dissertation, punctuated by sighs, excuses, compliments, hypotheses, explanations, silences = no, non, nein."

Finnegans Wake follows in the wake of the "blackshape" (608.21) of *Ulysses*, Noman the Black Sheep. Joyce believed that the *Odyssey* was a Phoenician epic. "The Phoenican wakes" (608.32). *Finnegans Wake* is Phoenician Fake. It slips through our fingers like water.

CHEKA AND OGPU

It seems that even Joyce realised that the extreme right and extreme left are not antagonistic ends of a straight line. On the contrary, both ends are tied up in a "teetootomtotalitarian" (260.02) knot to form a circle whose opposite pole is "timocracy" (291.08). "Gestapose" is "to parry off cheekars" (332.07) as there is little difference between both the German and Soviet secret police. Cheka is short for the Russian *Chrezvychainaya komissiya* (*po borbe s kontrrevolutsiei i sabotazhem*) i.e. Extraordinary Commission (for Fighting Counter-Revolution and Sabotage). A similar pairing is found in "Chaka a seagull" (424.10) where "seagull" might be the German nazi greeting *Sieg heil* (cf. *Seek hells*—228.06). The Cheka was founded in December 1917 and its title was changed after its reorganisation in 1922 to another euphemism: OGPU, standing for the Russian *Ob'edinennoe gosudarstvennoe politischeskoe upravlenie* (i.e. United State Political Administration). OGPU is mentioned twice in *Finnegans Wake*: "sleuts of hogpew and cheekas" (442.35) and again in reversal "upgo, bobbycop" (338.32). However, I was unable to find an allusion to the NKVD (*Narodnaya komissiya vnutrennikh del*), i.e. National (or "nazional"? 440.05) Commission for Internal Affairs, which emerged after the OGPU was reorganised in 1934.

SLAVONIC DICTIONARY
(355.11 SLAVANSKY SLAVAR, r. SLAVYANSKII SLOVAR)

In *Finnegans Wake* there are more than 600 words and phrases of Slavonic origin and at least twice as many with Slavonic overtones or connections, all relatively evenly dispersed throughout the text, except for a massive accumulation in section II.3 ("Russian General"). To say, as Professor Tindall does in the Introduction to *A Reader's Guide to Finnegans Wake*, that there are only "a few tags from Russian" is an underestimation. It is true that *Finnegans Wake* is "basically English" (116.26) but also "wordloosed over seven seas" (219.16), the Slavonic word-pool being one of them, besides Celtic, Greek, Germanic, Iranian, Latin, and Indian branches of the Indo-European language family ("celtelleneteutoslavzendlatinsoundscript" 219.17).

The Slavonic branch is traditionally divided into three groups:

1. Eastern: Russian (R), Ukrainian (=Ruthenian) (U), Belorussian (Whiterussian) (BE)
2. Western: Czech (Cz), Slovak (Sk), Polish (P), Lusatian Wendish (=Sorbian) (W)
3. Southern: Serbo-Croatian (SC) with two written languages, Serbian and Croatian, Slovenian (Sn), Bulgarian (B), and Macedonian (M).

Russian, Ukrainian, Belorussian, Serbian, Bulgarian, and Macedonian languages are written in the Cyrillic alphabet. The first written Slavonic language was Old Church Slavonic (OCS) which survives only as a liturgical language in the Slavonic Orthodox Church (cf. 345.02 and 552.26).

At present, there are about 1260 common "panslavonic" words (PS), with similar or identical spelling or pronunciation and various shades of meaning. In about 350 cases the meaning is identical. By "panslavonic" we would consider words present at least in five Slavonic languages.

Specific use of Belorussian and Lusatian Wendish is more than doubtful. Macedonian was established as a literary language after Joyce's death. However, all the other Slavonic languages were employed by Joyce.

We encounter considerable difficulties in trying to allocate any panslavonic word used in *Finnegans Wake* to an individual Slavonic language if the context or a special spelling are not helpful. Even more complicated, or perhaps impossible, is analysis of "his root language" (424.17), i.e. of cognate words whose history is traced to proto-Indo-European forms. Let us consider, for example, the root *perd-* (to fart loudly) which appears, e.g. in 68.16, 250.03, 445.17, 447.28, or 610.34. It gives *pьrděti* in Common Slavonic (e.g. Russian *perdet*) but also Lithuanian *pérdžiu*, Latvian *perdu*, Albanian *pjerd*, Greek *pérdō*, Avesta *peredaiti*, Sanskrit *párdatē*.

Take another proto-Indo-European root *merd-* (to rub). Common Slavonic *mьrdati* (to move to and fro) underwent an obscene shift in meaning in Czech and Slovenian (to fuck). This should be kept in mind when analysing, e.g. the "Fingool Mac Kish*mard*" passage (371.22), "where obscenities abound in many tongues," as Bernard Benstock rightly writes. But his next sentence, "The Persian *mard* (=man, P.S.) merely seems to universalise the obscene directives implied" seems to be irrelevant (*Philosophical Quarterly* 44 (1965): 104).

In the present list, there will be many words missing or misinterpreted, and a few which were not meant to be Slavonic. But basically, only words relevant to the understanding of the text have been included together with selected proper names.

Standard transliteration is used in the list for Russian. Bulgarian ъ gives *u*. Ukrainian г, і, и gives *h*, *y*, *i*, respectively.

I.1

4.06	boomering*stroms*, Cz. strom (tree), cf. Du. boom
4.07	*Killykillkilly*, R. kolokol (a bell)
4.22	*struxk*, Cz. struk (a teat, udder)
4.29	**ugged*, R. uzh (adder)[1]
5.05	*Wassaily Booslaeugh*, R. Vasilii Buslaev, the hero of the Novgorod epic cycle; R. buslai (a fallen man, a drunkard)
8.19	*dux*, R. dukh (spirit, courage, heart)
10.08	*bluddle*, R.B.SC. blud (lechery, fornication)
10.15	*Hney*, Cz. hnůj, Sk.W.Be. hnoj, U. hnii (dung)

[1] N.B. Manuscript additions by the author but not incorporated in "Addenda to Slavonic List" in *AWN* 11.4 are here indicated by an asterisk. (Ed.)

10.35   *glav*, Sn.SC.B. glava (head)

11.09   *peri*, PS, e.g. Cz. peří (feather)

13.09   *mujical*, R. muzhik (peasant)

14.20   *duran*, U. duren (fool, idiot)

15.09   *pax*, R. pakh (groin), U. pakh (armhole, stink), Cz. pach (stink)

16.08   ex*check*, Czech

17.24   *swete*, R.SC. svet (light)

17.24   *brack*, R. brak (marriage), SC.B. (wedding)

19.29   *dugters*, SC. duga (rainbow)

23.01   *rudd*, PS rud- (red)

23.05   *duppy*, P. dupa (arse)

23.06   ... *gromgremmit* ..., R. grom gremit (thunder thunders)

23.16   *nicky*, Cz. nicky (nulls, zeros), PS nic (nothing)

23.16   *malo*, PS malo (a little, wee)

25.25   budd*hoch*, Cz. hoch (boy)

26.03   *kis*, U. kiz (dung)

27.26   *Fetch neahere, Pat Koy! And fetch nouyou, Pam Yates!* R. vechnyi pokoi, na vechnuyu pamyat (eternal peace, for eternal memory; R.I.P., requiescat in pace)

27.30   *So be yet!* R. sovet (soviet), cf. So vi et, 414.14

28.09   *nesters*, CS nestera (niece)

I.2

31.12   *gorban*, U. gorban, R. gorbun (hunchback)

34.27   *gaddeth*, PS gad (snake)

37.02   *Sweatogore*, R. Svyatogor (supernatural hero of Russian folklore, literally "Holy Mount," but etymologically related to St. George)[2]

37.03   *dublnotch*, PS (good night), e.g. Sn. dobro noc

37.32   *pilzenpie*, G. Pilzen (Cz. Plzeň), Cz. pivo (beer), famous Bohemian beer (i.e. pilsener)

40.07   *rusin*urbean, B. rusin (Russian), U. rusin (Ruthenian, pertaining to Western Ukrainian provinces, Galicia, Bukovina, and Carpatho-Ukraine)

40.11   *Katya*, R. nickname for Catherine

41.32   *Cujas*, R. khui (penis)

43.13   **uniates*, Russian, Ukrainian and Polish Catholics of the Eastern rite

43.33   *Mr Delaney (Mr Delacey?)*, Cz. mrdal (he fucked), i.e. fucked Annie (fucked Issy?)

---

[2] Cf. Cz. svatý (holy, saint) (Ed.)

I.3

49.04	*Zassnoch*, R. zasnut (to fall asleep), Cz. zas noc (night again)
49.15	*Horan*, Cz.U. hora (mountain)
50.16	*large* amount of the *humoresque*, two most popular musical pieces by Bohemian composer Antonín Dvořák (1841-1904; "Largo" is the second part of his Symphony *From the New World*, 1893)
51.16	*da*, R. da (yes)
52.06	*blood*athirst, R. blud (lechery, fornication)
54.08	*sobranjewomen*, B. Subranie (Bulgarian Parliament; meeting)[3]
54.09	*duma*girls, R. Duma (Russian Parliament 1906-17)[4]
54.11	*mladies*, PS mlad- (youth, young)
55.03	*Ilyam, Ilyum! Maeromor Mournomates*, R. Il'ya Muromets, a popular hero-warrior of Russian folklore
55.16	*peajagd*, SC.Cz. píča, pron. peecha (cunt)
55.24	*intourisñng*, R. Inturist (Russian Travel Agency)
55.34	*Dyas*, Cz. ďas, W. djas (devil)
56.15	*olover*, PS olovo (lead, plumbum)
56.36	panbpanungo*povengreskey*, R. vengerskii (Hungarian), R. po-vengerski (in Hungarian)
57.32	*maladik*, Cz. mladík (youngster, male teenager)
60.26	*Mr Danl*, Cz. mrdán (p.p., fucked), mrdal (he fucked)
63.06	*wodkar*, P. wodka (from "water of life," uisce beatha)
64.06	*Byelo*, PS (white), e.g. Belorussiya (White Russia)
69.14	*drema*, R. drema (somnolence)
70.21	*bulsheywigger's*, R. Bolshevik (cf. 185.34)[5]
70.29	*isbar*, R. izba (cottage), P. izba (room)
73.06	*Crumlin*, R. Kreml (the Kremlin) + Dublin district + Crumlin Road Jail in Belfast
74.11	Co*mesto*wn, PS mesto (town)
75.21	*rab, PS rab (slave)

I.4

76.31	*Bog*, PS (God)
77.13	*Oorlog*, Cz. orloj (famous orrery in Prague)
79.30	*duggies*, SC duga (rainbow), R. duga (arc)

[3] Cf. R. sobranie (meeting, collection, selection; also a name for various tobacco blends, including a well-known Russian cigarette brand) (Ed.)
[4] The Duma took its name from the old assembly of boyars; the name has again been given to the lower house of the Russian Parliament since 1993. (Ed.)
[5] Bolshevik ("of the majority"), a member of the communist faction under the leadership of V.I. Lenin which seized power in Russia during the October revolution of 1917. (Ed.)

81.15   *versts*, R. versta (3,500 feet)

81.18   *cropatkin* (Kropotkin, 1842-1921)[6] + Croagh Patrick

83.08   *porse*nal, Cz. prase (pig), R. porosenok (pig), L. porcus

84.02   *hurooshoos*, R. khorosho (okay) + Horse Show

85.02   *burral*, PS, e.g. SC bura (thunderstorm, storm)

86.10   *pussas*, Cz. pusa (mouth, kiss), cf. Ir. pus, Sw. puss

88.36   *you batt*, R. yebat (to fuck) PS, cf. 88.28 *yubeti*

89.07   *Rooskayman*, R. ruskii (Russian) + Rooskey (a village in Co. Roscommon, Ireland)

90.31   *Bladyughfoul* ..., R. blyad' (whore) + bloody awful

91.36   *Xaroshie*, *zdrst*, R. khorosho (okay), khoroshie (good ones), zdravstvuyte (be of good health; equivalent to "How are you?")

93.14   *Poser*, Cz. poser (shit it)

94.16   *mala*, PS mal- (small, wee)[7]

95.18   Go*bor*ro ... Go*bug*ga, PS bor (pine-tree), PS buk (beech-tree)

95.19   *breezes*, PS (birch-tree), e.g. Cz. bříza

96.13   *drahereen*, Cz. drahý (darling)

97.31   *orel*ode, PS orel (eagle)

98.28   *Dub*'s, PS dub (oak-tree)

99.17   inke*dup*, P. dupa (arse)

100.05   *Pozor!*, Cz.Sn.SC. pozor (attention), B.R. pozor (shame)

101.19   *yayas*, P. jaja (eggs, testes)

101.21   *da! da!*, cf. 51.16

101.26   *pratschkats*, Sk.R. prachka (washer-woman)

101.28   *zhanyzhonies*, P. zhony (wives, women)[8]

102.15   *Steploajazzyma*, R. teplaya zima (warm winter), Cz. teplo a zima (hot and cold) + Steeplechase

102.16   *piecebag*, P.R.Sk. pizda (cunt)

102.19   *Ogrowdnyk*, P. ogrodnik (gardener)

102.19   *herbata*, P. herbata (tea)[9]

102.26   *Marinka*, Cz. 1. name for a skivvy, nickname for Mary, 2. *Galium odoratum*, *Asperula odorata*, 3. a novel by Czech Romantic poet Karel Hynek Mácha (1810-36)

I.5

105.07   *Zemzem*, Cz.Sk. zem (earth)

105.10   *Nappiwenk*, P. napiwek (tip, gratuity)

---

[6]   Peter Alekseyevich Kropotkin, 1842-1921, geographer and revolutionary anarchist, the son of Prince Aleksey Petrovich Kropotkin. (Ed.)

[7]   Cf. Cz. Malá Strana ("Lesser Side" of Prague) (Ed.)

[8]   Cf. Cz. ženy (women), R. zheny (wives) (Ed.)

[9]   Cf. Hrbata (Czech surname) + Cz. hrbatý (humpbacked) (Ed.)

105.10 *Notylytl,* PS motyl (butterfly)

105.10 *Prszss,* P. przeszyć (to pierce)

105.11 *Orel* Orel the King of *Orlbrdsz,* PS orel (eagle), P. olbrzym (giant) SC brdo (mountain) + O'Reilly

106.17 *Welikin's Douchka,* R. velikan (giant) cf. 331.25, R. dochka (little daughter)

106.23 *Allolosha Popofetts,* R. Alesha Popovich, a hero of the Kiev epic cycle (+ G. Popo, Vötz)

107.36 *durn,* R. durnoi (bad)

110.22 *kuur,* PS kur, e.g. Cz. kur (fowl), Sn. kura (hen)

111.03 *biggod,* U. big (god)

114.04 *Nemzes,* R. nemtsy (the Germans)

114.05 *Bulgarad,* Bolgrad, a Bulgarian town founded in Bessarabia in 1819 (cf. 563.14)[10]

125.22 *kak, pfooi, bosh and fiety, much earny, Gus, poteen?* R. kak vy pozhivaete, moy cherny gospodin? (How are you, my black sir?)

I.6

126.03 *wodes,* PS, e.g. P. woda (water); cf. 324.18

126.06 *storehundred,* PS sto (hundred)

126.10 maxi*most,* PS most (bridge)

126.22 *boyne,* R. boinya (slaughter, massacre)

128.07 *dooms,* PS, e.g. Cz. dům (house)

130.33 *eorl,* cf. 105.11

132.35 *gorky,* R. gor'kii (bitter), R. gorkii (hot), Maxim Gorky, pseudonym of A.M. Peshkov, who was "bitter" to the ruling class

134.02 *kraal,* PS, e.g. Cz. král (king)

135.10 *Petrin,* Cz. Petřín (prominent hill in Prague)

136.08 *Ostrov,* Cz.R.Sn.B. ostrov (island)

136.32 *rep,* SC rep (tail)

137.33 *jugoslaves,* i.e. Croats, Serbians, and Slovenes, Sn.SC. jugo (south)

141.08 **Whad,* Cz.U. had (snake)

144.30 *Polk*ingtone, Cz.P. polka (Slavonic dance which originated in Prague in 1831; named to honour then suppressed Poles, polka = Polish woman), also 331.11, 557.02

145.34 *bug,* PS bog (God)

147.24 *chasta dieva,* PS, e.g. Sn. chista deva (clean maiden, immaculate virgin)

151.06 *manda*boutwoman, R. manda (cunt), Cz. manda (buttocks), cf. also 279.F31, 530.33, etc.

154.23 *orlog,* cf. 77.13

---

[10] Cf. R. gorod (city), B.SC. grad (castle), Cz. hrad (castle), R.B. grad (hailstones) (Ed.)

155.30   *vremiament*, R. vremya (time)

155.30   *tu cesses*, Cz. tucet (twelve), R. chasy (clock), PS čas (time)

155.35   *Cheekee*'s, Soviet secret police, Cheka

156.10   *sadco*ntras, R. Sadko, rich merchant from the Novgorod epic cycle

156.11   *illsobordunates*, R. sobor (National Assembly under Ivan the Terrible), R. Duma, cf. 54.09[11]

156.14   *breadchestviousness* of his *sweeatovular ducose*, R. proshestvie svyatogo dukha (Procession of the Holy Ghost)

156.17   *nepogreasymost*, R. nepogreshimost (infallibility)

156.17   *babskissed*, R. papskii (papal)

157.11   *hoch*skied, Cz. hoch (kid, boy)

159.14   *crylove fables, Ivan Andreyevich Krylov (1768/69-1844), Russian writer of satirical fables

159.28   Gnocco*vitch*, R. -ovich, -evich in patronymics (son of)

159.28   *horoseshoew*, R. khorosho (okay) + Dublin Horse Show

159.30   *curi*Λass ... slav to *methodious*ness, Cyril and Methodius, the "Apostles of Slaves"[12]

162.15   *Tobolosk*, R. Tobol'sk, old Siberian town

162.27   *mand*, cf. 151.06

I.7

170.10   *Bohemeand*, Sk.U. Boh (God) + Bohemian Brethren

170.16   *yeat*, PS, e.g. R. est (eats), Cz. jí (eats)

170.16   *abblokooken*, PS, e.g. R. yabloko (apple)

170.16   *zmear*, U. zmerti (to die), Cz. zmar (destruction)

170.17   *zhooken*, R.B.P. zhuk (beetle, bug)

170.33   *Balaclava*, Crimean town of Sevastopol, from Osmanli "bałyklava" (fish pond)

170.34   *Grex*, R. grekh (sin)

172.11   *moravar*, Cz. Morava (Moravia); Moravia and Bohemia (170.10) are the two provinces (East and West) of the Czech lands

177.12   *ryba*ld, PS, e.g. Cz.R.P. ryba (fish)

177.26   *storik*'s, R. starik (old man), PS sto (hundred)

180.25   *ycho*, R. ukho (ear) (Cyrillic *y* gives Latin *u*)

185.34   *Menschavik*, R. Menshevik[13]

---

[11] Cf. Cz. sobour (set, collection), soborný (collective) (Ed.)

[12] Cyril and Methodius were the leaders of a mission from Byzantium to Great Moravia in 863, and the codifiers of Old Church Slavonic. Constantine is attributed the creation of the first Slavonic alphabet. (Ed.)

[13] Menshevik ("of the minority"), a member of the non-Leninist wing of the Russian Social-Democratic Workers' Party. The Mensheviks were suppressed by Lenin in 1922. (Ed.)

187.36   *uterim*, R. utrom (in the morning), Cz. úterý (Tuesday)
193.14   *barishnyas*, R. baryshnya (Miss, courtesy title given to a baron's daughter in tzarist Russia)
193.17   *Iggri*, R. igry (plays, games)

I.8
196.17   *mouldaw*, the river Vltava in Prague (G. Moldau)
196.18   *dneepers*, U. Dnipro, R. Dnepr (the Dnieper)
197.04   *wiesel*, P. Wisła (the Vistula)
197.17   *Don*, R. Don (the Don)
197.21   *Sabrine*, R. Savran (tributary of the river Bug)
198.05   *Boyarka*, R. boyarka (the wife of a boyar)
198.05   *Boyana*, R. Boyan (a bard in the *Lay of Igor*)[14]
198.26   *Sure*, R. Sura (name of at least five rivers)
199.14   *dubber Dan*, Sn. dober dan, SC. dobar dan (good day)
199.16   *yayis*, P.SC. jaje (egg), + R. Yaik (a river in the Urals)
199.25   *sozh*, R. Sozh (tributary of the Dnieper)
199.27   *vistule*, cf. 197.04
200.35   *piena*, PS pěna (foam)
201.22   *ingul*, R. river Ingul
201.23   *vesles*, PS (oars)
202.02   sud*sever*, PS sever (North)
202.15   *Polist*aman, R. Polist (tributary of the Volchov and the Lovot)
202.19   *Nieman*, Niemen (in 1912 the frontier between Russia and Poland, the river Memel)
203.14   *narev*, P. Narev (tributary of the Bug)
203.26   *bog*, P. Bug (the Bug)
204.34   *oder*, P. Odra (the Oder)
205.22   *sava* (a river in the Balkans)
205.34   *Neva*, R. Neva
207.08   *Annushka Lutetiavitch Pufflovah* (pseudo-Russian name)[15]
208.01   *elb*, Cz. Labe (G. Elbe)
208.02   *Save*, cf. 205.22
208.13   haze*vaipar*, R. par (steam, vapour), Cz. výpar (haze, fume)
208.15   *blood*orange, R. blud (lechery)
208.24   *rreke*, PS reka (river)
208.36   *koros*, R. sorok in reverse (forty)
209.17   *pruth*, U. Prut

---

[14]   The *Lay of Igor's Campaign*, a 12th-century masterpiece of Russian literature.
[15]   *Annushka Lutetiavitch Pufflovah* is also an acrostic on ALP + e.g. Cz. Anežka (Agnes) + Pavlova (fem. of R, Pavlov) (Ed.)

209.19   *narrowa*, R. Narova
209.25   *sula*, five Russian rivers
209.36   *chir*, R. Chir, tributary to the Don and to the Stochod
210.06   *buch*, U. Buh
210.35   *niester*, U. Dniester
211.08   *Lena*, R. Lena
211.08   *Ludmilla*, Cz. Ludmila, a Bohemian saint-martyr, strangled in 921; grandmother of St Wenceslas [Václav], patron-saint and a famous Premyslid Prince of the Czechs (924[/5]-935)
211.13   *volgar*, R. Volga
212.01   *Yennessy*, R. Enisei
212.02   *O.B.*, R. Ob
212.31   *dvine*, R. Dvina
213.04   *isker*, B. Iskur (the river Isker)
213.08   *lovat*, R. Lovat
213.09   *moravar*, Cz. Morava, a river in Moravia, SC Morava
214.35   *draves*, Balkan river Drava
215.23   *seim*, P. Seim (Polish Parliament), R. Seim (tributary of the Dnieper)

II.1
219.12   *Pobiedo*, R. pobeda (victory), SC pobjeda
219.14   *Bratislavoff*, Sk. Bratislava (the capital of Slovakia), PS brat (brother)
219.23   *robot* (term invented by Czech writer Karel Čapek in his play *R.U.R.* [*Rossum's Universal Robots*], 1920); from Cz. robota (hard labour)
221.08   *no chee*, PS noc (night) cf. 338.21
228.10   *pagoda*, R.P. pogoda (weather)[16]
230.05   *narrowedknee domum*, Cz. Národní dům (National House, Parliament)
234.15   *zvesdals*, R. zvezda (star) + vestal priestess
239.14   *Vania*, R. Vanya, nickname for Ivan (e.g. in Chekhov's *Uncle Vanya*, 1897)
241.02   *lossassinated*, R. lososina (salmon)
242.12   *praverbs*, PS pra- (proto-)
243.10   *zoravarn*, Cz. zorav (crane, *Grus grus* Linn.)
243.10   *givnergenral*, U. givno (shit)
243.14   *Hetman*, U. het'man (cossack commander-in-chief) from G. Hauptmann
243.15   *giantar*, R. yantar (amber)
243.24   *massa*, PS maso (meat)
243.33   *Hrom*, Cz. hrom (thunder)
244.34   *loevdom*, PS, e.g. R. lev (lion)

---

[16]   Cf. R. Pogodin (surname; e.g. Nikolay F. Pogodin, 1930s Soviet film director) (Ed.)

245.09 *lissaned*, R. lisa (she-fox)
248.35 *Radouga*, R. raduga (rainbow)
251.01 *nic*, PS nic (nothing)
251.04 *Dvoinabrathran*, R. dvoinya (twins) brat'ya (brothers)
252.16 *obscind*gemeinded, R. obshchina (community, G. Gemeinde)
252.34 kata*dupe*, P. dupa (arse, also pudendum muliebre),[17] *see Brewer, 148[18]
253.03 *Russky*, R. russkii (Russian)
253.04 *suchky*, R. suchki (whores)
253.04 *slove*, PS slovo (word)
253.24 *pomelo*, R. pomelo (broom)
257.28 ... *sakroidverj* ..., R. zakroi dver' (shut the door)

II.2
264.02 *proud*, Cz. proud (stream, current, electric current)
265.21 *Vlossy*hair, Cz, vlasy (hair), R. Volos, a pagan god + Old Norse Volsi (priapus, phallus)
265.F5 *chory* P.Cz.Sk. chorý (ill)
265.F5 *szewched*, P. szewc (shoemaker)
266.07 *snoo*, Cz. snu (loc. sg., dream)
269.18 *Boreas and glib*, R. Boris and Gleb (popular pair of Russian Orthodox saints-martyrs, often depicted on Russian icons)
271.03 *da, da*, cf. 51.16
274.24 *starryk*, cf. 177.26
276.F7 *liss*, R. lis (he-fox)
277.18 *Sein*, PS, e.g. Cz.P. sen (dream)
285.11 *mand*, cf. 151.06
287.17 *odrer*, R. odr (bed), cf. also 204.34
287.31 *pizdrool*, cf. 102.16
288.18 *znikznaks*, Cz. vznik (creation), PS znak (sign)
288.19 *Mr Dane*, cf. 60.26
289.16 *ostrov*gods, cf. 136.08
289.18 *molniacs*, R. molniya (lightning)
290.16 *douche*, PS, e.g. R. dusha (soul) Cz. duše
290.F6 *dotsh*, R. doch (daughter), dozhd (rain)
290.F6 *obloquohy*, R. oblako (cloud), Cz. oblohy (firmament, nom.pl. or gen.sg.)
290.F7 *rusin*, cf. 40.07
290.F7 *Patomkin*, Prince Potemkin (1739-91), a lover of Catherine the Great

[17] Cf. e.g. Cz. Kát'a (diminutive of Kateřina, i.e. Catherine) (Ed.)
[18] Ebenezer Cobham Brewer, *Dictionary of Phrase and Fable* (1870; London: Cassell, 1970). (Ed.)

294.18   *Gorotsky Gollovar's Troubles*, R. gorodskoi golova (mayor under Catherine's rule), R. rubli (roubles)

296.02   *pervoys*, R. pervyi (the first)

296.19   *But, yaghags*, R. baba-yaga (a witch-hag in Russian folklore)

297.05   *Sibernia*, R. Sibir (Siberia) + Hibernia

297.06   *Pisk*, R. pyska (infantile penis), PS pysk (lip)

297.16   *mech*, R. mech (sword)

297.28   *cress*loggedlike, R. Cz. křeslo (arm-chair)

297.F2   *ugol*, R. ugol (angle)

297.F2   *Mi vidim mi*, R. my vidim (we see), Cz. vidím (I see) + MI (Roman numerals): i.e. we see 1001.

299.14   *palce*, Cz. *B., etc. palce (big toes)

301.01   *Spry*, B. spri (imp. stop!)

301.02   *lekar*, Cz. lékař (doctor, physician)

301.02   *Brassenaarse*, B. brusnar (barber)

301.F4   *nastilow*, B. mastilo (ink)

301.F4   *disigraible*, B.R. igra (game)

302.08   *yaggy*, cf. 296.19

302.06   *bistri*spissing, R. bystryi (fast, quick)

302.18   *aboleshquick*, R. Bolshevik, cf. 70.21

305.05   *Sim*, R. Sim (a pagan god of the ancient Russians, etymologically related to Latvian *seime*, giant)

II.3

309.10   **ruric*, Rurik (d. 879), Varangian ruler of Novgorod, the semi-legendary founder of the Rurik dynasty of Kiev Rus; allegedly the grandfather of Svyatoslav

309.12   *sweatoslaves*, R. Svyatoslav ("frommen Ruhm habend," according to Max Vasmer's Russian etymological dictionary, lit. "of the pious glory"), PS svet (world)

309.16   *duchy*, R. dukhi (spirits, perfume)

310.15   *Variagated*, R. varyag (Varangian)[19]

310.16   **Olegsonder*, Oleg, son of Rurik (d. 912), cf. 309.10 + Alexander, name of several Russian tzars, including Alexander Nevskii, a saint and prince of Novorod (1236-52) and Kiev (1246-52)[20]

310.16   **O'Keef-Rosses*, Kiev Rus

310.18   **arborised*, Boris, Rurik's descendant, cf. 309.10

310.16   *Askold*, a Russian man-of-war under the command of Vice-Admiral Richard Pierse, anchored off the Alexandria coast in 1914

---

[19] Also Virág (Hung. "flower"; surname in *Ulysses*) (Ed.)

[20] Also Alexander, the king of Serbia assassinated in 1903 (Ed.)

310.27 *orel*, cf. 105.11

313.13 *boyg*, cf. 76.31 + Nor. boyg

313.14 *pilsener ... baar*, cf. 37.32, Jindřich Šimon Baar (1869-1925) (Baar was a Bohemian writer of bucolics)

314.13 *muddies*, R. mudi (testes)

321.35 *Cheevio*, SC živio ("prosit!" a toast)

322.17 *tersey*, B. tursi (imp., search!), B. terziya (tailor)

322.30 *mhos*, Cz. mha (fog)

323.08 **portnoysers*, R. portnoi (tailor)

323.16 *pushkalsson*, R. pushka (gun, cannon), tzar-pushka (large cannon cast in 1488, housed in the Kremlin as a curiosity); "son of a gun"

323.16 *goragorridgorballyed*, R. gora (mountain), R. gorit (is on fire), R. gorb (hump, hunch), OE gor (dung)

323.17 *potchtatos*, R. pochta (post, mail)

323.19 **zirkuvs*, R. tserkov (church)

324.18 *wodhalooing*, P. woda, cf. 126.03

324.26 *chattiry*, R. chetyre (four), cf. 343.32

324.29 kokken*hoven*, Cz. hovno (shit) + L. cacare

326.02 *mard*hyr, Cz.Sn. mrd- (to fuck, i.e. "fuck her")

326.25 *Petricksburg*, R. St. Petersburg (founded by and named after Peter the Great in 1703, first Sankt-Piterburkh, later Sankt-Pitersburg, St. Petersburg, or Petrograd; Leningrad during the Soviet era)

327.34 *aasbukividdy*, R. azbuka (Cyrillic alphabet, derived from old Slavonic names for the first three letters of the alphabet, viz. A, B, V, as follows: *az*, I; *buky*, letter; *vede*, I know)

330.08 *soloweys*, R. solovei (nightingale)

331.25 *velican*, R. velikan (giant)

331.25 *karlikeevna*, R. karlik (dwarf) + -evna (in Russian patronymics: "daughter of")

332.08 *cheekars*, R. Cheka

332.19 *ribbeunuch*, R. rebenok (child)

332.32 *Sdrats ye, Gus Paudheen!*, R. zdravstvuyte gospodin (How do you do, sir?) cf. 91.36

332.36 *Check or slowback. Dvershen.* Cz. dveře pron. dverzhe (door); + "Czechoslovak version"

333.03 *n z doer*, Cz. nazdar (Hello, equivalent to R. zdravstvuyte)

333.03 *An o ... ne*, Cz. ano (yes), ne (no)

333.04 *Podomkin*, Grigor Potemkin (Russian General, lover of Catherine the Great, cf. 290.F7); Cz. podomek (man-servant)

333.04 *anni slavey*, Cz. ani slovo (hush!, softly, not a word)

333.05 *szszuszchee*, P. szczochy (piss), P. szczęść Boże (God speed you), P. szczać (to piss), P. Szczecin (Polish port)

333.05 *slowjaneska*, PS sluzh- (serve, servant), P. Slowianie (Slavs)

333.07 *katekattershin*, Cz. Kateřina (Catherine)

333.08 *darsey dobrey*, Cz. daří dobře (keeping well)

333.09 *way boy wally*, PS boi (fight, battle), Cz. bojovaly (they fought), Cz. vybojovaly (they won the battle)[21]

333.10 *cavarnan*, Cz. kavárna (coffee restaurant)

333.14 *weerpovy*, Cz. vrbový (willowy)

333.14 *dreevy*, Cz. dříví (wood, timber)

333.28 *Podushka*, Cz. poduška (pillow, literally: "below the ear"; oreiller)

333.31 *gory*, R. gora (mountain), R. gore (sorrow)

333.33 *bramborry*, Cz. brambory (potatoes)

333.34 *dorty*, Cz. dorty (cakes)

333.35 *chesty*, B. chesty (frequent)

333.35 *dauberg den*, Cz. dobrý den (good day) cf. 199.14

333.36 *noviny*, Cz. noviny (news, newspaper)

333.36 *toplots ... morrienbaths*, Bohemian spa resorts, Teplice (G. Töplitz) and Mariánské Lázně (G. Marienbad)

334.03 *melost Panny*, Cz. milost (grace), Panny (gen.sg., Virgin), Cz. milostpaní (G. gnädige Frau)

334.03 *Kostello*, Cz. kostel (church)

334.04 *Zid*, Cz. Žid (a Jew)

334.18 *prosim, prosit*, Cz. prosím (I beg, please), Cz. prosit (to beg)

334.19 *krk n*, Cz. krk (neck), Cz. krkni (imp., belch!)

335.03 *izba*, R. izba (cottage, peasant house)

335.08 *varlet*, Cz. varle (testis), varlata (testes)

335.24 *Paud the roosky*, R. po russki (in Russian) + Ignacy Paderewski (1860-1941), Polish pianist, composer and statesman

337.03 *Dupe*, P. dupa (arse), cf. 252.34

338.02 *rackushant*, Cz. Rakušan (an Austrian)

338.08 *krashning*, R. krasnyi (red), krashe (more beautiful) + Soviet icebreaker, *Krasin*, which found Nobile's expedition to the North Pole in 1928.

338.13 *da*, 338.14 *dada*, cf. 51.16

338.14 *Sea vaast a pool*, R. Sevastopol (city in the Crimea, name given by General Potemkin (333.04) in 1783, after the ancient town Sevastopolis)

338.16 *poromptly*, R. parom (ferry-boat)

338.19 *gubernier-gerenal*, R. general-gubernator (governor-general)

338.19 *Baltiskeamore*, R. Baltiiskoe more (Baltic Sea)

338.21 *nocadont*, Cz. noc a den (night and day)

338.22 *welltass*, R. TASS (acronym of Telegrafnoe agenstvo Sovetskogo

---

[21] Cf. L. Boii (Celtic tribe inhabiting the area proximate to modern Bohemia) (Ed.)

Soyuza; Telegraph Agency of the Soviet Union)

338.22 *strana*slang, R. strana (country), Cz. strana (political party)

338.22 *Malorazzias*, R. Malorossiya (Little Russia; term used formerly by Russians for the Ukraine)

338.32 *pook*, R. pukh (down)

338.32 *Upgo*, OGPU in reverse (Soviet Russian secret police)

338.32 *bobbycop*, General Bobrikov, governor of Finland, shot on Bloomsday (June 16, 1904)

339.04 *gatovit*, R. gotovit (he cooks)

339.04 *Cheloven*, R. chelovek (a man, human being)

339.05 *Povar*, R. povar (a cook)

339.05 *pitschobed*, R. pishcha (meal), R.Cz.Sk. obed (dinner)[22]

339.05 *Molodeztious*, R. molodezh (the youth)

339.06 *belaburt*, Cz. buřt (G. Wurst)

339.06 *pentschmayso*, R. pech (bake), R. myaso (meat)

339.06 *Bog*, cf. 76.31

339.09 *sobarkar*, R. sobaka (a dog)

339.11 *malako*iffed, R. moloko (milk); see Brewer *(543) for Malakoff in Crimea[23]

339.11 *varnashed*, R. verneishii (the most faithful)

339.12 *manchokuffs*, Prince Menshikov, General during the Crimean war

339.14 *Obriania's*, *P. ubranie (clothes) ~~R. oborona (defence), Cz. obr (giant)~~[24]

339.21 *Crozarktic*, R. groza (thunderstorm) + G. grossartig

339.26 *doped*, P. dupa, cf. 252.34

339.26 *jupes*, R. zhopa (arse)

340.01 *cettera*, Cz. dcera, cera (daughter)

340.01 *doubray*, PS, e.g. R. dobro (okay), Cz. dobrej (good)

340.02 *lyewdsky*, R. lyudskoi (human)

340.05 *rutene*, Ukrainian, Ruthenian (an example of Atherton's Law)[25]

340.05 *mistomist*, U. misto (town, place), mist (bridge), mistomist (town of towns)

340.06 *Lissnaluhy*, U. lis (wood, forest), lisna (woody), luh (plain overgrown with bushes), lyiss (word) *U. lyiss (word), Cz. luhy (meadows) + Ir. Lios na Luigh

340.06 *Djublian*, Sn. Ljubljana (the capital of Slovenia)

340.08 *karhag*, U. karha (hag)

340.10 *Nye?*, U. ne (no)

340.10 *Tak!*, U. tak (yes)

---

[22] Also Cz. píča (cunt) (Ed.)

[23] Brewer, *Dictionary of Phrase and Fable*, 543. (Ed.)

[24] Deleted in the typescript (Ed.)

[25] James S. Atherton, *The Books at the Wake* (London: Faber and Faber, 1959). (Ed.)

340.14   *widnows*, U. vidnova (renewing)
340.16   *selo moy*, U. selo moe (my village)
340.18   *easger*, B. Iskur (the Isker), SC uskrs (Easter)
340.18   *prolettas*, B. proletta (the spring), R. prolet (blight, bridge span)
340.20   Bruino*boroff*, R. borov (hog)
340.21   *Meideveide*, PS med (honey), PS medved (bear)[26]
340.31   *pan*, PS pan (gentleman, sir)
340.32   *pulbuties*, P. półbuty (half boots, shoes)
340.34   *Mujiksy's Zaravence*, U. muzhits'kii charivnitsya (peasant witch)
340.35   *sur*, R. tzar
340.35   *Russers*, U. Rus (ancient name of the Ukraine; Kievan State), PS ser-(shit)
341.06   *boyne*, U. boinya (fight, battle), R. boinya (slaughter, massacre)
341.07   *lubbed*, R.U. lyub- (love)
341.07   *beeyed*, U. bii (1. fight, 2. fear)
341.09   *balacleivka*, R. balalaika (three-stringed guitar-like instrument). Balykleika is the name of several rivers in the Volga and Don basins
341.09   *Trovatarovitch*, R. tovarishch (comrade), R. travit (to poison), R. tzarevich (tzar's son) + trouvère + troubadour
341.09   *I trumble*, Ivan the Terrible (Tzar of Russia [1547-84], cf. 353.24, "ivanmorinthorrorumble")
341.11   *howorodies*, U. hovoriti (to speak)
341.17   *mlachy*, R. mlechnyi (milky)
343.15   *scoopchina*, SC Skupshtina (Yugoslav Parliament)
343.25   *duhan*, U.SC. (a brand of tobacco, fr. Arabic *duhan* "smoke")
343.25   after his *obras*, PS. obraz (image; i.e. "in his own image," *Genesis* 1:27)
343.27   pulvers*porochs*, R. poroch (pulver, gun-powder)
343.30   *popes*, PS, e.g. R. pop (parish priest in Orthodox church)
343.32   *cheateary gospeds*, R. chetyre gospoda (four gentlemen), R. gospod (God, the Lord)
343.34   *Churopodvas*, ?P. (jockstrap)
344.09   *studenly*, PS studen-, e.g. Cz. studený (cold)
344.09   *drob*, Sn.R.W. (shot, i.e. lead pellets)
344.09   *led*, PS led (ice) + plumbum
344.10   *ouchyotchy*, R. ushi otchie (father's ears), PS uši (ears), PS oči (eyes)
344.14   *nitshnykopfgobknob*, R. Nizhnii Novgorod (city on the Volga, renamed Gorkii during the Soviet era, literally Lower New Town, passim, e.g. 346.02)
344.30   solongo*patom*, PS, e.g. Cz.R. potom (then, afterwards)
344.32   Dir*ouchy*, cf. 344.10

---

[26]   Also Cz. medvídě (bear cub) (Ed.)

345.02 *Gospolis fomiliours*, OCS Gospodi pomilui ny (Lord have mercy upon us, Kyrie eleison), cf. 552.26

345.08 *sopprused*, B. suprug (husband)

345.13 merz*mard*, Cz.Sn. mrd- (fuck)

345.17 *stoccan*, R. stakan (a glass, tumbler)

345.24 *oukosouso*, R. uksus (vinegar)

346.03 *ruddocks*, Cz. rudoch (Red Indian)

346.16 *dubrin din*, cf. 333.35

346.22 *az*, B. az (I)

346.24 *Sayyesik, Ballygarry*, B. ezik bulgarski (Bulgarian language)

346.28 *bog*, cf. 76.31

347.02 *sbogom*, PS, e.g. B. sbogom (farewell, literally "with God")

347.05 *krow*, R.U. krov, P. krew (blood)

347.06 blodi*dens*, PS, e.g. B. den (day)

347.06 *godinats*, B. godina (year)

347.07 *wraimy*, B. vreme (1. time, 2. weather)

347.07 *wetter*, PS, e.g. R.Sn. veter (wind)

347.09 *Krzerszonese*, P. Karkonosze (Giant Mountains)

347.13 *old stile and new style*, referring to Gregorian and Julian calendars; the Julian calendar (new style) was adopted in Europe in 1582, but not in Russia until after the revolution in 1917

347.14 *blaguadargoos*, B. blagodarya (thank you)

347.30 *topkas*, B. topka (ball)

347.31 *orussheying*, B.R.SC. oruzhie (weapon)

348.03 *bitva*like, R.Cz. bitva (battle)

348.05 *postleadeny*, PS, e.g. B. posleden (last)

348.10 *boyar*, R. boyarin (nobleman in Old Russia)

348.12 *wody*, PS, e.g. P. wody (gen.sg. or nom.pl. water)

348.16 *velligoolapnow*, R. velikolepnyi (magnificent)

348.17 *currgans*, R. kurgan (burial mound, burrow)

348.22 *plumyumnietsies*, R. plemyannitsy (nieces)

348.23 *Vjeras*, R. Vera (Faith)[27]

348.23 *Vjenaskayas*, R. venskaya (Viennese) cf. 348.36

348.23 *Djadja*, R. dyadya (uncle)

348.27 *ras*, R. raz (one time, once)

348.27 *tryracy*, P. trzy razy, R. tri raza (three times)

348.34 *Sinya*, PS sin (son), B. sinja (blue)

348.34 *Sonyavitches*, R. sonya (sleepyhead), R. son (dream), Sonia (Sophia)

348.35 *raday*, PS, e.g. R. rady (are glad)

349.15 *nichilite*, Cz. ničil (destroyed)

---

[27] Cf. Cz. Věra (fem. forename) (Ed.)

349.23   *the latchet of Jan of Nepomuk*, Czech saint-martyr (1340-93) from the village of Nepomuk near Prague, drowned in the river Vltava on the orders of Wencelsas IV when he refused to disclose secrets of the confession of the king's wife. In 1719, 330 years after his death, his tomb was opened and his tongue alone was found fresh.

349.27   *notnoys*, R. notnyi (adj. music)

350.06   *olyovyover*, Cz. olovo (lead, plumbum), Cz. olivový olej (olive oil)

350.16   *Prostatates, pujealousties!*, R. prostite pozhaluista (excuse me, please), Cz. pyje (penis)

350.16   *Dovolnoisers, prayshyous!*, R. dovol'no, proshus (that's enough, thanks)

350.17   **chaste daffs*, cf. 147.24

350.20   *prace*, Cz. práce (work), P. pracie (penis)

350.20   *cossakes*, R.U. kozaki (Cossacks, a free people who established themselves in the Dnieper basin during the 17th century and were feared for their plundering expeditions. Their strongholds were destroyed by Catherine the Great)

350.23   *pukny*, Cz. pěkný (nice)

350.27   *troupkers*, R. trubka (tobacco-pipe)

350.29   *Slobabogue*, R. slava bogu (Glory to God), i.e. Timotheos

350.34   *komnate*, R. komnata (room)

351.12   *popiular*, P. popiół (ashes)

351.13   *poppyrossies*, R. papirosy (cigarettes with black tobacco)

351.13   *Chorney*, PS, e.g. U. chornyi (black)

351.14   *Pivorandbowl*, PS pivo (beer) + Peter and Paul

351.18   *strest*, R. strast (passion)

351.24   *sunpictorsbosk*, cf. 326.25

351.27   *reptrograd leanins*, Petrograd + Lenin (Leningrad), cf. 326.25

351.36   *rasky wolk*, R. russkii volk (Russian wolf)

352.02   *nemcon*, cf. 114.04

352.05   *brich*ashert, Cz. břich (belly, abdomen)

352.16   *bron a*, R. bronya (armour), P. broń (weapons)

352.16   **nuhlan*, P. ulan (uhlan, member of light cavalry)

352.17   *volkar boastsung*, The song of the boatmen on the Volga

352.18   *unzemlianess*, R. zemlya (land, earth)

352.23   *bragadore*, R. braga (home-brewed beer)

352.34   *O'Khorwan*, PS. e.g. P. kurwa (whore)

352.24   **Vonn*, R. vonj (stink)

352.35   *bluzzid*, B. blazhen (blessed)

352.36   *maikar*, B. maika (mother)

353.02   *Trisseme*, B. tursi me (search me), see 322.17

353.03   *sobber ... souber*, R. sobor (cathedral, synod), cf. 156.11

353.10   *nyet*, R. nyet (not, no)

353.14   *knout*, R. knut (Russian whip)

353.19   *dobblenotch*, cf. 37.03

353.22   *grosning*, R. groza (thunder-storm), groznyi (terrible)[28]

354.03   *doorak*, R. durak (idiot)

354.22   *gadden*, PS gad (snake), cf. 34.27

354.33   *usses*, PS uši (ears)

355.11   *Slavansky Slavar*, R. slavyanskii slovar (Slavonic dictionary)

357.07   *Brassey's*, B. brusnat (shaved)

361.09   *promissly*, R. promysl (providence), cf. 590.12

361.16   **Killykelly*, cf. 4.07

367.34   *vode's*, PS voda (water), cf. 348.12

367.35   *dupest dupes*, cf. 252.34

370.20   *drob*, B. drob (liver)

371.22   Kishg*mard*, Sn.Cz. mrd- (fuck-)

372.25   *bruk*, PS, e.g. R. bryukho (belly)

373.28   *hray*, Cz. hra (play, game), hraj (imp., play!)

II.4

392.25   *Navellicky Kamen*, Cz. na veliký kámen (on a big stone)

396.24   *mhost*, Cz. mha (mist)

397.21   *xmell*, R. khmel (1. drunkenness, 2. hops)

397.30   *old style*, R. (before 1917), cf. 347.13

III.1

404.24   *krasnapoppsky*, R. krasnopopskii (papal red)

408.30   *hownow*, PS, e.g. W. howno, Cz. hovno (shit)

409.29   *sabotag*, PS sobota (Saturday) + sabbath + G. tag (day)

411.17   *mat*, PS, e.g. R.Sk. mat (mother)

411.18   *Hek domov muj*, Cz. Kde domov můj (Where is my home; the first line of the Czech national anthem)

414.14   *So vi et*, R. sovet (soviet), cf. So be yet! 27.30

414.20   ... *cashl* ..., PS kašel (cough)

415.03   *diva*, U. diva (virgin, girl), Cz. diva (wild)

415.10   *rockcoach*, R. rogach (stag-beetle) + cockroach

415.14   *pszozlers*, P. pszczolar (bee-keeper)

415.24   *zeemliangly*, R. zemlya (earth, land), cf. 352.18

415.26   *Pschla*, PS, e.g. R. pchela (bee), P. pchła (flea)

415.34   *voida*, PS voda (water)

416.07   *mouche*, PS, e.g. Cz. moucha (a fly)

416.07   *muravyingly*, R. muravei (an ant)

---

[28]   Also Grozny (capital of Chechnia, founded 1818) (Ed.)

416.14   *vosch*, PS, e.g. R. vosh (a louse)
416.15   *gnit*, PS gnida (a nit; cf. Old and Modern Icelandic gnit=a nit)
416.15   *Bruko*, R. bryuki (trousers)
416.16   *osa ... osi*, PS osa, vosa (wasp)
416.17   *pikopeck*, R. kopeyka (kopeck)
416.19   *O moy Bog*, PS O moi bog (O my God)
416.35   *blohablasting*, PS, e.g. R. blokha (a flea)
417.10   *motolucky*, R.Cz. motýlek (butterfly)
417.12   *babooshkees*, R. babochka (butterfly), Cz. babočka (red admiral, *Vanessa Atalanta*)[29]
417.12   *smalking*, R. smolkat (to fall silent)
417.23   *ptchjelasys*, cf. 415.26
418.15   *Luse polkas*, Luisa's polka, a popular composition by Czech composer Bedřich Smetana (1824-84)
419.13   *velk*tingeling, PS velk-, e.g. Cz. velký (big)
422.07   *brach*, Cz. brach (comrade, mate)
423.16   *bog*orror, cf. 76.31
423.20   *switchedupes*, R. svishch (knot hole), P. dupa (arse, cunt)
423.36   *Fran Czeschs*, Cz. František (Francis, Frank, e.g. František Schaurek, Joyce's brother-in-law) + France + Bohemian Brethren (Frères tchèques)
424.01   *Brat Slavos*, Sk. Bratislava, cf. 219.14, PS brat (brother, i.e. Slavic brothers)
424.09   *Prost bitten!*, Cz. prosit (G. bitten)
424.09   Ti*beria*, Lavrentii Pavlovich Beria, chief of the NKVD from November 1938
424.10   *Chaka*, R. Cheka (Soviet Russian secret police) + Anton Pavlovich Chekhov (1860-1904), Russian playwright and prose-writer + *R. chaika (seagull; also a play by Chekhov)
424.35   *sto*lentelling, PS sto (hundred)
425.18   *go braz*, PS obraz (picture, image)
425.22   *bolshy*, R. bol'shoi (great, big), Bolshevik (cf. 70.21)
427.27   *Moy*, R. moi (my)

III.2

429.22   *kozydozy*, PS kozy (she-goats, female breasts)
437.29   *Mazourikawitch*, P. mazurek (mazurka, Masovian dance), cf. 159.28[30]
437.29   *sukinsin*, R. sukin syn (son of a bitch)

---

[29]   Also R. babushka (grandmother) (Ed.)
[30]   Also Cz. surname, Masaryk, e.g. Tomáš Garrigue Masaryk (first president of the Czechoslovak Republic, 1918-35) (Ed.)

442.11	*Peterborough*, cf. 326.25
442.35	*hogpew*, OGPU
442.35	*cheekars*, Cheka
445.34	*rumilie*, Rumelia (since 1885 part of Bulgaria)
451.19	*divy*, U. divy (virgins), PS, e.g. Cz. divy (wonders)
457.11	*to*, Cz. to (it)
457.11	*my*, Cz. my (we)
457.11	*onus*, Cz. on (he)
457.11	*yan*, Cz. ja (I)
457.12	*tyan*, Cz. ty (you)
457.26	*drewher*, Cz. drahý (darling), cf. 96.13
459.05	*dutch*, R. doch (daughter)
463.24	*Rossya*, R. Rossiya (Russia)
463.32	Geesy*hus*, Cz. husa (goose)[31]
466.20	*diva devoucha*, PS, e.g. Cz. divá děvucha (mad girl), U. diva (girl)
466.20	*Dauber Dan*, PS (good day), cf. 333.35
471.04	*Mirra! Myrha!*, PS, e.g. R. mir (peace), U. myr (peace)

III.3

475.35	*kapr*, Cz. kapr (carp) + L. caper (goat)
477.30	*indo*, PS, e.g. Cz. do (in)
480.31	*vuk vuk*, SC vuk (wolf)
482.11	*weslarias*, PS veslo (oar), cf. 201.23
485.06	*Moy Bog*, cf. 416.19
487.22	*Roma now*, Romanov (last dynasty of the Russian Tzars)[32]
489.09	*Tass*, cf. 338.22
491.06	*sokolist*, PS sokol (falkon)[33]
491.06	*besoops*, PS sup (vulture)
492.09	*diva*, cf. 415.03
492.10	*Wolossay*, cf. 265.21
492.10	*Crasnian* Sea, R. krasnyi (red)
492.18	*pilsens*, cf. 37.32
497.16	*lodes*, Cz. lodě (ships)
497.19	*Boyards*, cf. 348.10
497.28	*Rinseky Poppakork*, Russian composer Nikolay Andreyevich Rimskii-Korsakov (1844-1908)
497.28	*Piowtor the Grape*, Peter the Great (Russian Tzar, 1682-1725)
498.02	*Cesarevitch*, R. tzarevich (heir-apparent)

[31] Also Jan Hus (Czech martyr, burned as a heretic in Konstanz in 1415) (Ed.)
[32] Also Roma (gypsies) (Ed.)
[33] Cf. Sokol (Czechoslovak patriotic organisation based upon a doctrine of physical education, founded in 1862) (Ed.)

498.12   *Catchering*, Catherine the Great (married to Peter, heir to the Tzarist throne; erotic literature describes her as a fellatrix)
498.14   grand*dauch*ter, R. doch (daughter)
498.15   *Liubokovksva*, R. lyubov (love), + R. lyubok (kitsch) + Moskva[34]
498.19   *pani*, PS, e.g. Cz. paní (mistress, lady)
498.23   *Ogonoch*, R. ogonek (light, ignis fatuus)
499.01   *bogey*, cf. 76.31
499.07   *Smirtsch*, P. śmierć (death)
499.08   *Smertz*, R.U. smert (death)
499.09   *Umartir*, OCS umerti (to die)
499.10   *Ser*, PS ser- (shit)
500.17   *slog*, R. slog (syllable)
502.03   *jesse*, Cz.Sk.Sn.SC. jesen (autumn)
502.04   *snaachtha*, PS, e.g. Cz. sníh (snow), snacha (daughter-in-law)
502.05   *zimalayars*, PS zima (winter), Sk. jar (spring)
502.06   *westnass*, R. vesna (spring)
502.06   *ostscent*, R. osen (autumn)
502.10   *lieto*, PS, e.g. R. leto (summer)
502.19   *voda*shouts, PS voda (water)
502.26   *derevatov*, R. dereva (trees)
509.03   *vechers*, PS večer (evening)
509.05   *Tomsky*, R. Tomsk (Siberian town named after the river Tom)
509.13   *rooshiamarodnimad*, R. rossiya moya rodnaya mat (Russia, my native mother)
513.11   *kniejinksky*, PS kněži (priests), + Vaslav Nijinsky (1890-1950; famous Russian-born ballet dancer)
513.11   *choro*episcopally, B. choro (national round-dance)
513.12   *cola*nder, Cz. kolo (round-dance)
513.13   *polkat*, polka, cf. 144.30
514.22   *Hora*, Cz.U. hora (mountain)
516.04   *wesz*, P. wesz (louse)
516.09   *plushkwadded*, U. plyuskva (bed-bug)
516.25   *bog*, cf. 76.31
516.10   *mrowkas*, P. mrowka (ant)
517.11   *mard*red, Cz.Sn. mrd- (fuck)
518.21   *mere*, PS mir (peace)
518.21   *woiney*, e.g. P. wojna (war) PS; L.N. Tolstoy, *Voina i mir* (*War and Peace*)
518.28   *mujic*, R. muzhik (peasant)
518.31   *voina*, PS, e.g. R. voina (war)
525.20   *vesh*, PS, e.g. Cz. veš (louse), cf. 416.14

---

[34] Cf. Lobkowitz (Czech noble family) (Ed.)

528.23 *liryc and themodius*, cf. 159.30

531.19 *juppettes*, R. zhupa (arse), cf. 339.26

531.36 *Kovno-*, PS (shit) + Lithuanian Kaunas, cf. 408.30, 624.08

534.01 *Godnotch*, good night, cf. 37.03

534.02 *Tak*, PS, e.g. U. tak (yes), P. tak (so)

534.22 **Belgradia*, SC Beograd (Belgrade), the capital of Serbia

536.16 *dhymful*, PS dym (smoke)

536.18 *divane*, SC divan (beautiful)

536.22 *voyce*, Cz. vejce (sg. and pl., egg, testicle)

536.33 *jurats*, U. dzhura, chura (orderly of a cossack officer), e.g. Sn. cureti (to piss) PS

537.24 *Cherna Djamja*, B. cherna dzhamiya (Black Mosque) in Sofia?

540.11 *suke*, P.U.R. suka (bitch, whore)

540.31 *glovars*, R. glovar (leader)

541.04 *chort*, PS, e.g. R. chert (devil)

541.23 *warschouw*, P. Warszawa (Warsaw)

541.24 *praharfeast*, Cz. Praha (Prague)

541.26 *slobodens*, Sn. sloboden (unmarried, single), PS (free)

547.36 *zivios*, SC. zhivio (prosit, your health)

549.23 *sankt piotersbarq*, cf. 326.25

551.31 *Hibernska Ulitzas*, Cz. Hybernská ulice (a street in Prague where the former College of the Irish Franciscans stands, founded in 1629, from whom the street takes its name)

551.35 *kolossa*, U. kolossya (ears of cereal plants), PS kolesa (wheels)

552.26 *gospelly pewmillieu, christous pewmillieu*, OCS gospodi pomilui ny, khriste pomilui ny (Kyrie eleison), cf. 345.02

554.09 *Joahanahanahana*, Cz. hana (shame), cf. "Thrice shame!" 618.10 + Hannahannas (Sumerian goddess figuring in the myth of Telepinus)

III.4

555.20 bad*brat*, PS brat (brother)

558.07 *nepmen*, R. N.E.P. (Novaya ekonomicheskaya politika, New Economic policy announced by Lenin in 1921)

560.14 *Boggey*, cf. 76.31

561.01 hoy*hra*, Cz. hra (play, game), cf. 372.28

561.10 *pes*name, Cz. pes (dog)

563.07 *sobrat*, R. sobrat (fellow, brother), cf. 555.20

563.14 *bulgar*, Volga Bulgars were Turkish-speaking people who merged with the Slavs; Bulgarus was a Bulgarian heretic accused of sexual perversions; E. *bugger* is derived from the latter

563.22 *blizky*, PS, e.g. Cz. blízký (close, intimate)

563.34 *Vellicate nyche!*, Sn. Velika noc (Easter), Cz. Velikonoce (Easter)

564.24   *Listneth!* 'Tis, Cz. list (a leaf), Cz. tis (yew-tree)
565.06   *Whervolk*, R. volk (wolf)
565.10   *Niet*, R. net (isn't it; no)
565.13   *boyazhness*, R. bojazn (fear)
565.15   *Putshameyu!*, R. pochemu (why)
565.20   *muy malinchily malchick*, R. moi malen'kii malchik (my little boy)
565.21   *Gothgorod*, R. gorod (town), R. god (year)
566.11   *Katya*, cf. 40.11
566.35   *verst*, cf. 81.15
567.06   *O my bog*, cf. 416.19
567.08   *glover's*, cf. 540.31
567.34   *troykakyls*, R. troika (3 horses harnessed abreast), Cz. trojkolka (tricar, three-wheeled bike)
568.31   *Serenemost*, Cz. sere na most (he shits on the bridge)
568.33   *youghta*, R. yuft (Russian leather)
569.09   *Weslen*, PS veslo (oar), cf. 482.11
572.22   *Dar*, PS dar (gift)
578.22   *steptojazyma's*, cf. 102.15
580.01   *voda*valls, PS voda (water)
589.33   *hussites*, followers of the heretic Jan Hus of Prague
590.11   *plemyums*, cf. 348.22
590.12   *promishles*, R. promysl (providence), Cz. průmysl (industry)[35]
590.20   *mand*, cf. 151.06

IV
593.03   *bludyn*, B. bluden (lecherous), SC. bludan
593.06   *Tass*, cf. 338.22
601.21   *Veslandrua*, PS veslo (oar) + Westland Row
602.21   civareke, cf. 208.24
604.03   *bog*, PS bog (god)
605.02   *douche*, cf. 290.16
605.07   *praviloge*, R. pravilo (rule, regulation)
607.08   *smolking*, cf. 417.12
607.18   *Ni, gnid mig*, R. ni na mig (not for a moment)
608.16   *Stena*, R.Cz.Sk.B. stena (wall)
608.21   *nyets*, cf. 353.10
609.24   *Domoyno*, R. domoi (home)
610.14   *Skulkasloot*, Cz. s kulkou (with a bullet), cf. "Sgunoshooto" 160.29
614.25   *Deva*, PS deva (girl)

---

[35] Also Cz. Přemysl, mythical founder of the Premyslid ruling dynasty of the Bohemian lands (Ed.)

616.21   *Skulksman,* cf. 610.14

619.02   *pan,* PS pan (mister, gentleman)

620.32   *hospodch,* Cz. hospoda (pub)

621.24   *glave,* PS glava (head), cf. 10.35

623.07   *newera,* PS nevera (unfaithfulness)

624.08   *Gowans,* PS, e.g. P. gowno (shit)

624.08   *Ser,* PS ser- (shit)

625.21   *dim in dym,* U. dim (house), dym (smoke)

628.10   *Arkangels,* R. Arkhangel'sk (city named after the Monastery of Archangel Michael)

IMAGINABLE ITINERARY THROUGH THE
PARTICULAR UNIVERSAL (260.R3)

Whence. Quick lunch by our left, wheel, to where. Long Livius Lane, mid Mezzofanti Mall, diagonising Lavatery Square, up Tycho Brache Crescent, shouldering Berkeley Alley, querfixing Gainsborough Carfax, under Guido d'Arezzo's Gadeway, by New Livius Lane till where we whiled while we whithered. Old Vico Roundpoint. (260.08)

Let us take a map of Dublin and set off on an imaginary itinerary through Dublin 7. After having a quick lunch in one of the pubs at Arran Quay, we shall start walking along the Liffey downstream ("Long Livius Lane" to the Custom House where we shall then take the left turn into Amiens Street to get on to the North Circular Road (NCR). After a fifteen-minute walk along the NCR we shall pass the Mater Misericordiae Hospital (260.F2)[1] "shouldering Berkeley" Road and two hundred yards further up we shall cross Phibsborough Road ("querfixing Gainsborough"). Having reached the zenith of our circular journey we shall start to descend along the NCR down towards the main gate ("Gadeway") of Phoenix Park and back along the Liffey again ("New Livius Lane") "till where we whiled while we whithered" at Arran Quay.

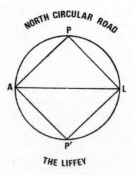

<hr />

[1] "Mater Mary Mercerycordial" in the footnote comprises the Mater Hospital in Eccles Street, St. Mary's Hospital in Phoenix Park, and Mercer's Hospital in Mercer Street. These three hospitals form an isosceles triangle with the Liffey running through its apex

After this walk which would take us about one and a half hours in reality (five miles), let us sit down to rest our feet and do our homework in geometry.

If *AP'L* is the left bank of the Liffey (*AP'* = New Livius Lane; *P'L* = Long Livius Lane) and *LPA* is *NCR*, then *LP* is Tycho Brache Crescent, and *PA* is Guido d'Arezzo's Gadeway.

In the diagram on the page 293, the parallelogram *aπλP* is the part of the mother's bottom exposed to the lavatory bowl:

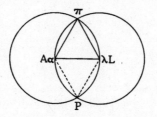

Hence *APLP'* in our diagram is Lavatery Square and the diagonal *AL* ("the forest" 294.3) must be "mid Mezzofanti Mall."[2] *P* is the point where Phibsborough Road crosses the NCR, and *P'* was our starting point at Arran Quay.

and base as the perpendicular.
2 Is this another Magazine Wall? (Cf. also "magmasine fall" 294.25.)

WASSAILY BOOSLAEUGH (OF RIESENGEBORG) (5.05)

Vasilii Buslaev is a hero-warrior of the Novgorod cycle of *byliny* (epic poems) from the fifteenth century, a Russian equivalent of Finn MacCool (Fionn MacCumhaill). The name *Booslaeugh of Riesengeborg* also anticipates Buckley and "rising gianerant" (368.08) (G. Riese = giant).

The Christian name *Vasilii* is of Greek origin, being from *basileus* (king) (cf. e.g. "baislisk glorious with his weeniequeenie" [577.02]), which, incidentally, we might hear also in *Booslaeugh*. *Buslaev* comes from *buslai*, which is shortened form the name *Boguslav* ("glory to God"). *Buslai*, however, means also "fallen man (heruntergekommener Mensch)" or "drunkard" (Vasmer's *Russisches Etymologisches Wörterbuch*). The latter meaning ties well with an English reading of *Booslaeugh* as "boose-love" (... with a love of liquor Tim was born ...).

Wassaily, incorrectly etymologised by Brewer as "water of life" (AS waes hoel)[1] and perpetuated by Joyce (see e.g. "wassailhorn tot of iskybaush" [91.27]) combines with death in *Booslaeugh* (Ir. bás) to be immediately counterpointed with life (*-laeugh*). Similar combinations are found, e.g. in "a viv baselgia" (243.29) or "a live ... baas" (608.14-15). Basil Finnegan is brought back from death to life with water of life.

Vassal is cognate with Irish "uasal" now standing for "Mr" in a title. A complete Irish version could be constructed as *Uasal Buadh-Sliabh*, where *Buadh-* means triumphant or joyous, and *Sliabh* means "a mountain," or "a range of mountains" (= G. Gebirge), "the Mountain of Joy" (76.04).

There are several other less relevant allusions, e.g. Dan. *Bøsseløb* (gun-barrel), Fr. *bosse* (knoll, hillock), *bossu* (hunchback), or *bouse* (dung). *Boos-* alludes to "Bous Stephanoumenos" and to the supernatural bull Finnbhennach "Whitehorned" from the *Táin Bó Cuailnge*.

The place-name *Riesengeborg* refers to *Riesengebirge*, the Giant Mountains, the tertiary mountain range forming a natural border between Bohemia and Poland. The German name was used by Sudetic German inhabitants before 1945. The Czechs call them "Krkonoše" and the Poles, "Karkonosze." Hence, "Krzerszonese" (347.09),

---

[1] Ebenezer Cobham Brewer, *Dictionary of Phrase and Fable* (1870; London: Cassell, 1970). (Ed.)

"mountains from his old continece" (462.32), the abode of the bearded giant Krakonoš (G. Rübezahl).

In *Riesen-* we also have the Latin root *ris-* (laugh). *Booslaeugh* splits into the derisive "boo" and "laugh." Buckley-Burrus-Shaun kills the laughable father-giant-general, thus committing "a risicide" (161.17). Could we read *Riesengeborg* also as "born (G. geboren) in laugh" or "born laughing," as some prophets?

HAVVAH-BAN-ANNAH (38.30)*

The seemingly illogical *ban* for "son" instead of the expected *bat* for "daughter" not only serves a purpose in "have a banana" but also refers to a minor controversy flourishing among the biblical exegetes of the nineteenth century.

In the Massoretic text of *Genesis* 36:2, one of Esau's wives is named "aholibamah *bat-anah* bat Sibeon hahivvi"; the Vulgate has "Oolibama filiam Anae filiam Sebeon Evei." In the same chapter of *Genesis*, verse 24 and also in 1 *Chronicles* 1:40, however, Anah appears as a *son* of Sibeon. To bring these lines into harmony, the Samaritan Septuagint and Syriac Peshitta and some modern biblical scholars (and Joyce) read "bat-anah," in *Genesis* 36:2 as "*ben-anah.*"

The trans-sexualism of the passage is further elaborated by the mention in the adjacent line of the book of *Ecclesiastes*, the author of which calls himself "a son of David" though in fact the name of the book in Hebrew, "qohelet," is a feminine. (Joyce uses the Hebrew name at 29.16, "cohalething.") The feminine authorship is alluded to by "writress" (38.30). "Ruah of Ecclectiastes" (38.29) may hide another biblical book and woman, Ruth, but "ruah" means literally "a puff" played upon by Joyce in "outpuffs" (38.30).

* N.B. For typographical reasons, the transliteration of Hebrew is only approximate.

O QUANTA VIRTUS EST INTERSECATIONIBUS CIRCULORUM

Joyce, not unlike a Cabbalist, is preoccupied with numbers and haunted with names. Not unlike Bruno, he is obsessed with Egyptian mythology and his interest in Bruno cannot be brushed off by pretending that he just borrowed one trivial idea of "the identity of opposites."

Giordano Bruno belonged to the Hermetic-Cabbalist tradition and differed from other Renaissance Magi by his rejection of the Christian interpretation of the Hermetic lore, substituting for it his total sun-centred "Egyptianism."[1] He would be a genuine heretic even in 1973 and the scholarly account by Miss Yates opens the eyes of everybody who still believes in Bruno-the-revolutionary.

The tenth chapter of *Finnegans Wake* is crammed with hermetic and Cabbalist references. Some numerical problems are tackled by Danis Rose in *AWN* 10.3 and by Fritz Scheele in *AWN* (old series) 11.7-8. This chapter is not only on geometry, but also on Gematria, most complicated method of the Cabbala by which words can be calculated into numbers and numbers into words. It is by the method of Gematria that we obtain the number 111 for our geomater (297.01), ALP.

The tenth chapter ends with 10 sephiroth. To invoke the sephiroth through which God (Ainsoph) manifests himself to the Cabbalist, one can contemplate the 22 letters of the Hebrew alphabet which contain the Name of God or recite Hebrew names of 72 angels which constitute the Name of God.

The Cabbala was introduced into Renaissance magic and thus to Bruno by Giovanni Pico della Mirandolla who wrote 72 *Conclusiones Magicae*.[2] The 56th conclusion reads: "Qui sciuerit explicare quaternarium in denarium, habebit modum si sit paritus Cabalae deducendi ex nomine ineffabili nomen 72 literarum."

The tetragrammaton was dealt with elsewhere by Adaline Glasheen (*AWD* 73-4).

---

[1] Frances A. Yates, *Giordano Bruno and the Hermetic Tradition* (London: Routledge & Kegan, 1964).
[2] Giovanni Pico della Mirandola, *Opera Omnia* (1557; Hildesheim: Reproduction anastatique, 1969).

Another of God's numbers is 1001 as exemplified in the number of letters in ten thunders or in "Ainsoph, this upright one, with that noughty besighed him zeroine" (261.23). Similarly, "Only caul [= God] knows his thousandfirst name" (254.19); "thoughtsendyures and a day ... Great Shapesphere" (= Sephiroth, 295.03); "I yam as I yam [cf. *Exodus* 3:14] ... onebut thousand insels ... Osthern Approaches" (= A+Ω, 604.23); "unthowsent and wonst ... livesliving being the one substrance of a streamsbecoming. Totalled in toldteld and teldtold in tittletell tattle. Why?" (597.05). "Why" could stand for the Tetragrammaton; cf. Glasheen, v.s.

The last sentence recalls the beginning of the tenth chapter: "... tomtittot to teetootomtotalitarian. Tea tea too ..." "From tomtittot to teetootomtotalitarian" means from water of life to waters of death, from the beginning to the end, from zero to infinity (284.11), from aab to zoo (263.F1), from ardent Ares to zealous Zeus (269.17), from aleph to taw (553.04), i.e. the 22 letters of the Hebrew alphabet, Oo! Ah! Augs (= ALP) and ohrs (= HCE, 90.28), A and Ω (*Revelations* 21:5-6), etc.

Now, let us apply Gematria to the first paragraph, page 260, as "Every letter is a godsend" (269.11). The first sentence has 70 letters. Seventy is a God's number in Christian numerology (*Genesis* 10; 46:27; *Numbers* 11:16; *Jeremiah* 25:11; 29:10; *Deuteronomy* 9:24; *Luke* 10:1; *Matthew* 18:22). But the next sentence invites: "Tea tea too" (= tot two, add up two) to get "oo" (= infinity, ∞). The name Ainsoph (261.23) consists of 72 letters according to the Cabbala of Pico and others. Ainsoph means literally "without end" and in modern Hebrew is used for "infinity." If we add up A + Ω (in Hebrew, aleph and ayin) we get 1 + 70 = 71. To prove by our pseudo-Cabbala Mrs Glasheen's intuitive point (v.s.) in the passage "is he ... is he?" (261.28-31), let us count those "broken heaventalk" letters: it gives 71; and 7 and 1 are God's numbers.

But back to 72, Ainsoph (∞), 1001, and Bruno's stretching Christian 70 in a Procrustean manner to fit Cabbalist 72[3]: *Op. lat.* I.ii.427: "Et notandum, a Christo etiam in numero septuaginta duorum servatam

---

[3] *Jordani Bruni Nolani Opera Latine Conscripta*, ed. F. Fiorentino *et al.* (Napoli: 1879-91; facsimile reprint Stuttgart-Bad Cannstatt: F. Frommann Verlag Gunther Holzboog, 1962) (op. cit. is *De Monade Numero et Figura, Secretioris Nempe Physicae, Mathematicae et Metaphysicae Elementa*).

fuisse senarii virtutem ...," and I.ii.428: "Idem praeceptione servavit Deus, qui a Mose diffudit spiritum in septuaginta duos seniores." We find this 70 *vs* 72 controversy also in the problem of authorship of the Septuagint, allegedly translated by 72 elders in 72 days, but nevertheless called LXX.

In *De monade* (ed. cit., 349) Bruno draws two intersecting circles which he calls the Diadis Figura and explains that the monas contains its opposite (e.g. "Immo bonum atque malum prima est ab origine fusum"). And, on page 466, ed. cit., we read: "Decem circulis sphaera tum visibilis tum invisibilis definitur. Horizon Apollonio in libro de tribunalibus, spirituum est duplex illorum. ... Hi, ut dicit Astaphon, in libro Mineralium constellatorium, et in tetradis scala notavimus, in intersectionibus circulorum contemplantur. O quanta (inquit) virtus est intersecationibus circulorum, et quam sensibus hominum occulta!"

After this, the figure on page 293 of *Finnegans Wake* gets its Cabbalist meaning, being identical with Bruno's Diadis Figura except for Joyce's ALP triangles with their anatomical and geographical connotations.

Intersecting circles are a sign of infinity and Ainsoph. Let us test the newly acquired knowledge on the passage: "Wins won is nought, twigs too is nil, tricks trees makes nix, fairs fears stoops at nothing" (361.01). Obligatory counting of the letters gives 72. The sentence also reads: 110 + 220 + 330 + 440 = 1000. But that does not make sense. We know that 72 corresponds to 1001. But, fortunately, the next sentence starts "And till" which can be read "and tilly" and Arthur (Artist, God, HCE) can come again and against us. Now, "spose we try it promissly" (361.09). (Russian "promysl" means "Providence.") "Love all" (361.09) is O:O, or ∞ or intersecting circles, Ainsoph, zeroic couple (284.10), Gyre O, gyre O (295.23); O.O. (54.17), etc., etc.

Similarly, "Foughty Unn, Enoch Thortig" (283.01) gives 41 + 31 = 72, alias Ainsoph ("endso"), alias "one" (283.01), alias 10 sephiroth (zipher, 283.04), plus other numbers as discussed by Danis Rose (v.s.). By the way, Hermes Trismegistus is Triplex because there were three Hermes: Noah, Enoch, and Thoth (Unn, Enoch Thortig).

Also, 283.F1 gives 12 + 28 + 40 + 2 twins = 72, alias 111, i.e. God's Trinity. (There are three Names of God within the Tetragrammaton according to Pico's sixth conclusion (*Opera omnia*); cf. also Glasheen's comment on combining IHS with YHWH.)

Or, "lex, nex and the mores" (273.05) = LXX and two more. This passage combines life and death, God's numbers 7 (in preceding sentences) and 72, and perhaps ALP's 111.

MORE HEBREW

The following transliteration of Hebrew characters is used: aleph ', beth b, gimel g, daleth d, he h, waw w, zayin z, ḥeth ḥ, teth ṭ, yodh y, kaph k, lamedh l, mem m, nun a, samekh s, ayin ,' pe p, ṣadhe ṣ, qoph q, reš r, śin ś, šin š, taw t. Consonants b, g, d, k, p, t pronounced as spirants (i.e. without dagheš) are transliterated as bh, gh, kh, ph, th. For typographical reasons a simplified transliteration of vowels has been accepted: qameṣ and pathaḥ give a, ṣere, seghol and vocal šewa give e, ḥireq gives i, ḥolam gives o, šureq and qibbuṣ give u; silent šewa is disregarded.

Many important entries were supplied by Roland McHugh and Matthew Hodgart.

3.09	mishe mishe	moše(h) moše(h)	Moses, Moses (*Exodus* 3:4)
13.27	Marchessvan	marḥešwan	8th month
25.24	sedeq	ṣedeq	justice[1]
29.13	Eset	yesod	9th sephirah (Foundation)
.13	Artsa	ereṣ	Earth
.16	cohalething	qoheleth	Book of Ecclesiastes
.17	sherif	śaraph	venomous serpent
.17	Toragh	tora(h)	Law, i.e. Pentateuch
.18	Mapqiq	mappiq	a dot in the letter he
.18	Humme	ḥamma(h)	sun; its apparent orbit around the Earth
.20	paroqial	raqia'	firmament
.26	shebi	šebi	captivity
.27	adi and aid	'ade 'ad	for evermore
.29	batin	beṭen	belly; bosom
		hibheṭin	to get pregnant
.32	lashons	lašon	language
.32	honnein	ḥanneni	pity me (in *Psalms* 9:14, starting with "I will praise thee")

---

[1] But Cz. zadek (buttocks, arse) makes better sense.

.33	hamissim of himashim	ḥamiša(h) ḥumše	five fifths, i.e. Pentateuch
.34	sober	sepher	book
		śebher	hope
.35	hubbub	ḥibbubh	love
30.04	enos	enoš	man
31.12	gorban	qarban	offering, corban (Webster)
32.01	Mulachy	? malkhuth	10th sephirah (Kingdom)
.04	Hokmah	ḥakma(h)	2nd sephirah (Wisdom)
.04	metheg	methegh	a pause mark in the Hebrew script, lit. "bridle"
33.16	Mohorat	maḥarath	morrow
.17	Athma	ethmol	yesterday
34.16	shomers	šomer	watchman
38.03	zaynith	zaith	olive
.29	ruah	ruaḥ	spirit; wind; puff
71.19	Gibbering	gibbor	giant (*Job* 16:14)
.19	Bayamouth	behemoth	great beast (*Job* 40:15)
75.02	Ariuz	ari	lion
		'oz	strength
77.25	Mac Pelah	makpelah	burial place of Abraham and Sara, Isaac and Rebecca, and Jacob
78.10	sheol om sheol	šeol im šeol	sheol by sheol
83.08	sheol		
107.34	oxhousehumper	aleph, beth, gimel	
112.07	targum	targhum	interpretation (of Old Test. in Aramaic)
116.32	ichabod	i khabhodh	where is the glory? (1 *Samuel* 4:21)
118.16	baccbuccus	baqbuq	flask
.18	Soferim	sopherim	scribes
136.08	Mabbul	mabbul	Flood
177.10	sheols	[see 78.10]	
.10	chems	ḥem	hot
.10	divans	diyun	judgement
194.17	blzb	ba 'al zebhubh	Lord of the Flies
198.31	nera	ner	candle, lamp
213.08	gihon	giḥon	a river in *Genesis* 2:13

228.14	Mischnary	mišna(h)	a part of Talmud
.15	shimach	śimḥa(h)	joy
		śamaḥ	to rejoice
.15/17	Mum's ...	m, b, d, h supplied	joyous (perhaps pun on
	hedgehung[2]	with vowels gives	Joyce's name)
		mebhadeah	
.33	mullmud	melammedh	teacher in Hebrew school
241.19	ozeone	ozen	ear
.22	Milchku	malkhuth	kingdom
.27	begeds	beghedh	clothes
.27	nahar	na'ar	young man
		nahar	river
.27	koldbethizzdryel	kol beth yiśrael	all the house of Israel
241.28	zouz	zuz	ancient coin
242.28	Avenlith	ebhen	stone
244.05	Ceder	sedher	Seder; Passover Feast
.08	hag	ḥagh	feast
.36	behemuth	[see 71.19]	
245.01	Salamsalaim	šalom 'aleikem	peace (be) with you
.10	simwhat toran	śimḥath tora(h)	Rejoicing in Law
.10	antargumens	[see 112.07]	
246.05	Hushkah	ḥošekh	darkness
.05	Gadolmagtog	ghadhol	big
256.11	Halome	ḥalom	dream
258.09	Yarrah	yareah	moon
.11	Immi	emi	my mother
.11	ammi	'ami	my nation
.11	Semmi	šemi	my name
		šemeš	sun
.12	Lebab	lebhabh	heart
266.04	Hod	hodh	8th sephirah (Majesty)
267.71	shibboleth	šibboleth	flood (see *Judges* 12:6)
278.F7	Eddems	adhama(h)	clay
283.01	endso	en soph	infinity, lit. "without end;"
			God in Cabbala
296.F3	Thargam	[see 112.07]	
	goeligum	goel	Saviour, Redeemer
301.24	shittim	šiṭṭim	acacias (e.g. *Exodus* 25:10)

---

[2] The sentence ends with "sheolmastress." She appears as "skillmistress" later (571.07), again with an alphabetical pun.

306.07	mizpah	mișpe(h)	watchtower
310.15	Barringoy	(Aramaic) bar	son
	Bnibrthirhd	goy	a gentile; nation
		Ben berith	son of Covenant (= Jew)
343.33	haftara	hephṭara(h)	haftara (an excerpt from Prophets read in synagogue)
350.01	catz	first letters of kohen ședheq (priest of justice)	common Jewish name
365.13	eres	ereș	Earth
371.25	eres	[see 29.13]	
380.02	Sherratt	šereth	to serve
		mešaretheth	servant girl
404.13	shaddo	šaddai	Almighty
410.26	benison	ben	son
413.29	Queer	qebhira(h)	funeral
		qebher	grave
413.29	gaon	gaon	a head of mediaeval Jewish Academy in Babylonia; honorary title of a rabbi
415.04	deborah	debhora(h)	bee
423.01	shemish	šemeš	sun
471.05	Solyma Solemita	šalom	peace
480.30	dob dob	dobh	bear
.31	zeebs	zeebh	wolf
499.07	Mahmato	memith	death
588.24	Mizpah	[see 306.07]	
.28	Esh	eš	fire
619.34	Yawhawaw	YHWH	Tetragrammaton

A AND AA AB AD ABU ABIAD (254.16)

On page 254, the water of the Liffey rehearses her meeting with her husband-son-father Manannán. This is also the cryptic meaning of "A and aa ab ad abu abiad."

The key can be found in, for example, a revised edition of the World Atlas of *Everyman's Encyclopaedia* (1940), page 28, where in one column of geographical terms the following expressions are clustered:

A, aa (Swedish and Dano-Norwegian) river

ab (Persian) water, river

abu (Arabic) father

abiad (Arabic) white

And and *ad*, however, are not listed, but there is the And Fjord in Norway and *ad*, perhaps, has its Latin face value.

For a good measure, the same column gives Bab-el-Mandeb "the gate of tears." Cf. "A babbel men dub gulch of tears" (254.17).

STRUCTURE AND MOTIF IN THUNDERWORDS:
A PROPOSAL

It is surprising that the thunderwords in *Finnegans Wake* have received so little attention considering their rich symbolic significance. It is usually the first Cletter (to use the neat term of Adaline Glasheen) dominating page three which puts the potential reader off turning to page four. (You can hear him mumbling, "enough, however, have I read of it ... slopbang, whizzcrash, boomarattling.")

Before attempting a detailed letter-by-letter explication of the thunderwords we have to know their structure and motif, the grammar and lexicon of thunderese. The rules of *Finnegans Wake* exegesis have been well laid down by Clive Hart in "The Elephant in the Belly" (*AWD* 3-12). The first rule (sounding like a proposition from Wittgenstein's *Tractatus*) reads: "Every syllable is meaningful." Fair enough, but let us not lose sight of the wood for the trees. The consequence of syllabification is amply demonstrated by Wiggin's attempt to chop the first thunder (*JJR* 3: 56-59). The arbitrary syllabification leads to arbitrary reading and over-reading until "meaning dissolves because everything corresponds to everything else." Also, to start with the assumption that the thunderwords are about everything will result in trying to find and finding anything. This characterises the method of Adaline Glasheen's elaborate letterification of Cletters (*Analyst* 23, Nov. 1964), which, though entertaining and brave, is wide open to criticism.

By arranging the thunderwords into a cryptogrammatic matrix and reading the letters vertically or horizontally (and why not diagonally?) as anagrams, anything goes. For example, column 19 (which gives the 19th letter of each thunder in their order) is an anagram of "Greek and Hindu," the straight downward reading of column 83 gives "oldsorlusn" (? Sorley boy 499.22), and the following matrix picked out by random will give material for another PhD thesis:

	67	68	69	70	71
H	H	E	R	D	E
I	A	T	O	U	X
J	D	O	D	R	R

(Consider, e.g., Mutter Erde; ex-rex HCE; river Dodder; HAD = the root in Sanskrit for "cacare" and "snake" in Ukrainian; rod dur = phallus in Bog Latin; DEUX is lurking in H70-H71-I70-I71 and the significance of the numbers 70 and 71 in "the broken heaventalk" was discussed by both Adaline Glasheen and myself before, etc., etc.).

I believe together with Gerry O'Flaherty that *Finnegans Wake* is a simple book (with some reservations). I totally accept Clive Hart's structural theory of *Finnegans Wake* based on Viconian cycles. Thunder is important for Vico, so is for Joyce. Thus, thunders are markers of Viconian cycles in *Finnegans Wake*.

There are nine 100-letter thunders. The tenth thunder is a *ricorso* thunder, a *Götterdämmerung* of Norse gods. The first nine thunders form three Viconian triads. They do not follow a quadripartite scheme; there is no thunder in Book IV. The first three triads belong to HCE, his birth, whoring, and fall. The tenth thunder is Shaun's. The king is dead, long live the king. I cannot find any resurrection theme in the first nine thunders.

	BIRTH	MARRIAGE	DEATH
	I	IV	VII
BIRTH	THUNDERWORD	WHORE	FALL
	II	V	VIII
MARRIAGE	THUNDERSENTENCE	LETTER	WAKE
	III	VI	IX
DEATH	CLAP	DOOR	FUNERAL

Triad I: *Birth, language, shit*
I. first thunder, the birth of language (words)
II. birth of sentence as a marriage of the subject and predicate
III. dissolution of thunderclap and sentence, only clap and onomatopoeia remain

Triad II: *marriage, sex, shut*
IV.   first sex with a whore; sex is sin
V.   marriage of HCE and ALP; their correspondence
VI.   close the [bedroom] door, death of sexual life

Triad III: *death, shot*
VII.   fall at the Magazine wall of the bad old character with whores; mortal sin
VIII. A ballad sung at the wake of Persse O'Reilly
IX.   Coughin' in the coffin, death-rattle ("his poor old dying boosy cough")

Comments, suggestions, and queries:

I. The first thunderword starts with babe's babbling and ends with Babel's confusion of words for thunder in various languages. According to Vico (*Scienza Nuova* §448), thunder gives birth to human speech, first as monosyllable, which is then doubled. The first monosyllable is "ba" (or "pa" in the example given by Vico), as labials belong to the first layer of the consonants acquired by children. But here "syllabification" ends. *Bhā- happens to be the proto-Into-European root for "to speak." Benveniste puts it as follows: "the whole family of forms clustering around the root *bhā-, which in the vocabulary of Indo-European expressed the strange, extrahuman power of the word, from its first awakening in the human infant to its collective manifestations, which were non-human in virtue of their being depersonalised and were regarded as the expression of a divine voice" (*Indo-European Language and Society* (London: Faber, 1973): 413). Also compare "Baaboo" (191.35), the first word of Giorgio.

Thunders are Japanese *kaminari* (Graham), Gk. *Brontē*, Fr. *tonnerre*, Ital. *tuono*,? Old Roumanian *tun*, Port. *trovaō* (trovarrhoun), Sw. *ăskan* (awnskawn), Dano-Norw. *tordenen* (toohoohoordenen), and Ir. *toirneach* (thurnuk). What is missing at the beginning are most likely further words for thunder. I do not believe that Varuṇa is meant to be there. He is not a thunder-god and there are no other gods mentioned, at least not in the primary plane of meaning which concerns me at present.

II. The second thunder is again composed from expressions for "thunder" in various languages and also in simple sentences of the type "thunder thunders" appears. The first word is possibly the Lithuanian thunder-god *Perkunas* or Lettish *pĕrkuons* (thunder). The next is Breton *kurun* (thunder), then "lightning" in Hebrew (*baraq*), Arabic (*el barq*), or Persian (*berg*; Benstock). "Gruauya" is Lithuanian *griauja* (it thunders). Turkish *gök* (sky) *gürliyor* means "thundering sky," Russian *grom gremit* "thunder thunders," Malay *guntur* (thunder; Knuth), Old Norse *pruma* (thunder), Anglo-Saxon *thunar* (thunder), Swahili *radi* (thunder; Dalton); cf. Arabic *el rad* (thunder), ... and finished in Finnish *ukkonen* (thunder). Until thunders in other languages are exhausted temptation should be resisted to syllabify "... dillifaititillibumullun ..."

III. (VI.B.18,19) This thunder is composed from words for "applaud" or "clap." Fr. *claque*, G. *Klatsch*, Rus. *khlopat*, Ital. *battere*, Fr. *battre*, Sw. *applåd*, Ir. *greadadh*. Before descending to the intricacies of "... semmihsammihnouith ..." look into various dictionaries under "applause," "beat," and "clap." "There's where. First." Scatological elements in the first triad of "shit-thunders" are obvious. The language degenerates to onomatopoeic noise. From cletter (Thunder I) to clatter. From God's *flatus vocis* to HCE's diarrhoea. Note the symmetry of onomatopoeic thunders III, VI, and IX in my table.

IV. (VI.B.18:3) The fourth thunder consists of words for prostitute, starting with Russian *blyad'* and Dublin "bloody awful Mecklenburgh whore." I suspect that the unconventional spelling "moeck ..." as used in the thunder may hide another Greco-Latin word *moechus*, mentioned in *Stephen Hero*. "Whura" and "whora" blend English *whore* and Swedish *hora* or German *Hure*, "scorta" is Latin *scortum*, "strumpa" is *strumpet*, "porna" is Greek *pornē*, "neny" is perhaps *nanny* (whore; Partridge), "kocksa" is Lithuanian *kekše*, "pastippatappatupper" = ???, "strippach" is Irish *striopach*, and "puttanach" is Italian *puttana*.

V. Although in plain English, the content of this central thunder is as elusive for detailed explication as is the Letter juxtaposed. The theme of the second half is the sexual union of "him around her," kankan of the maggies and him, the kinky voyeur, not minding looking at it. In the table it is the cross-section of Marriages.

VI. This onomatopoeic word for slamming the bedroom door consists of imperatives "close the door" in various languages. "Shut" is the preterite of the superstrong verb "shit" in Joycean scatological root declension. The first three (i.e. Danish, Irish, and French) are given in Tindall's *Guide* (page 165). "Kappakkapuk" is not "the hen's cackle that also follows the fifth thunder" but Turkish for "close the door." The correct Turkish spelling is *kapiyi kapat* (*kapi* = door, *yi* = the, *kapat* = close, imp.). "Sakroidverj" is Russian (*AWN* 9.4 (1972): 57). The rest will require diligent, but rather mechanical, effort of a dictionary-maniac.

VII. This thunderword is a phonetic echo and dissolution of the first one. There is nothing hopeful in the terminal "up" as it reflects "thurnuk" of the first thunder. Turnup (whore), *strum* (*coire*), and *thrum* (*coire*) (all in Partridge) further specify the medium of the fall. The general meaning of thunder VII is the fall of "bothallchoractor" ("badoldkarakter") at the Magazine Wall.

VIII. O Hehir's analysis (*Gaelic Lexicon*) of this thunder is correct. There is a burial place of O'Reilly of Breifne in Cavan. The thunder breaks into a ballad. The stutterer Pierce O'Reilly "horrhorrd his name in thuthunder" (378.07). The stuttering "pappappa" also echoes the beginning of the first thunder. According to Vico (*Scienza Nuova* §228), stutterers used songs for overcoming their defect, but this thunder is not sung by O'Reilly but rather by his sons who imitate his hesitancy to have fun at his wake; "our fathers oft' were naughty boys, whack fol the the diddle lol the di da day" ("Whack fol the diddle," by Paedar Kearney, is a parody of the relationship of Ireland and England). "Peace, O wiley" (332.09) also suggests R.I.P. and wailing. The thunder gives the location of the grave and the inscription on the tombstone.

IX. (VI.B.21:181) The death-rattle of this thunder is composed of words for "cough" in various languages, e.g. Ger. *Husten*, Lat. *tussis*, Ital. *tosse*, Ir. *casacht*, Fr. *toux*, Welsh *peswch*, Gk. *bēchós* (gen. of *bēx*), panslavonic root *kashl-*.

X. In the "last word of perfect language," "rackinarockar" (Ragnarøkr) is announced. There is no more recrimination against HCE, who is dead and buried. The language is pure, god-like, and monoglot. *Ull* is the archer-god of Asgard, *Hoder* is the blind god, *Thord* is the priest of Freyr, *Andvari* is the dwarf, *Midgard* is the World of men, *gringnir* = ?, *Urdr* is one of the guardians of the World Tree, *Mjollnir* is the hammer of Thor, *Fenrir* is the wolf, son of *Loki*, *Baugi* is the giant who held the mead (*mand*??) of inspiration in the cauldron *odreri* (Atherton). There are two other possible readings of "odrrerin": 1) *Odr* is the husband of Freyja and *Rerin* is a king in the *Vǫlsunga Saga*, 2) *Otter* (*Otr*) and *Regin*, sons of Hreidmar, who killed their father. The last reading, though not the closest phonetically, gives the best sense in the context of *Finnegans Wake* and the tenth thunder. *Surt* is the fire giant and *krinmgern* = ?. I found all these characters in H.E. Ellis Davidson, *Gods and Myths of Northern Europe* (London: Penguin, 1964), which gives a good word list in traditional and Old Icelandic spelling. A similar treatment of the tenth thunder is given by Atherton in *A Conceptual Guide to Finnegans Wake*, ed. Michael Begnal and Fritz Senn (Pittsburgh: Pennsylvania State University Press, 1974) 168.

A NOTE ON "POLISH IN *FINNEGANS WAKE*"*

The entry **platschpails** (101.27) contains a German interjection *platsch!* and, perhaps, Polish *płuczka* (pronounced "pluchka") meaning "a washing machine." The entry **ubranje: suit** is wrongly allocated to "ubanjees" (205.32). The latter is a river in Central Africa (Ubangi or Oubangui) blended with banshees and banjos. The correct place is in 339.14 (Obriania's). **Nuhlan** (352.16) is not an invention *ab nihilo* but a contamination of the Polish uhlan (*ulan*, a lancer) and Irish Nolan.

* Cf. "Polish in *Finnegans Wake*," *AWN* 11.4 (1974), 65-67.

294.F4

On the first day of May [1170] ... Robert Fitz Stephens ... with thirty Knights, threescore Esquires well mounted and three hundred foot, being Archers well appointed, of his own kindred, and trayning up in feates of armes, and the choice souldiers of all Wales, landed at the Bann, not farre from Wexford; hereupon the rime runneth:

At the Creeke of Bagganbun
Ireland was lost and wonne.

—*The Chronicle of Ireland, Collected by Meredith Hanmer in the Year 1571* (Dublin: Society of Stationers, 1683; rpr. Hibernia Press, 1809) 224.

INFINITE VARIETY

The recently published book by Eugene Watters and Matthew Murtagh[*] is a gold mine for music-hall memorabilia of the Dublin of Joyce. Tracing the history of Dan Lowrey's "Star of Erin" Variety Theatre in Dublin, the authors have collected a wealth of material on high kickers, lions comiques, blacked-out knockabouts, mystagogues, turks, missing links, idols, characters comédiennes, magnetic ladies, chicks, christmas shows (such as *Lalla Rookh* on Monday, 29th December 1884— "Tremendous & Unprecedented Hit!"), the Great Vance (211.32), Little Tich (465.29), Vesta Tilley (526.30), catch-phrases, songs, photographs, and cartoons. Lowrey's competitors in the Rotunda, Mechanics, Leinster Hall, Gunn's Gaiety, Grafton Theatre, Harp Music Hall, Queen's are also mentioned, together with Adam S. Findlater's financial involvement in the war of the halls.

Daniel Lowrey appears in *Finnegans Wake* as "Damyouwell Lover" (93.34) to herald allusions on pages 94-95. "Sycomore Lane" (95.21) refers to 1 Sycamore Street, Lowrey's address and back entrance to the Star. The main entrance was from the Crampton Court off Dame Street.

The comic singer W.J. Ashcroft was always referred to as the Solid Man because of his famous rendering of "Muldoon the Solid Man" (3.20; 94.04). White-Eyed Kaffir ("Whiteside Kaffir" 95.15), the stage name of G.H. Chirgwin, made his first appearance in Lowrey's music hall in the year of Joyce's birth. In the same year, 1882, the Ghost of Paganini, Paganini Redivivus, played Irish melodies on violin, lying on his back.

"Since the Levey who might have been Langley may have really been a redivivus of paganinism or a volunteer Vousden" (50.14) refers to the uncertainty of the time as to the identity of the Maestro's impersonator who visited Dan Lowrey's on thirteen different occasions. He was said to be the grandson of the bagpipe player Giant O'Shaughnessy and others claimed that he was R.M. Levey.

Watters and Murtagh have solved the puzzle by suggesting that R.M.

[*] Eugene Watters and Matthew Murtagh, *Infinite Variety, Dan Lowrey's Music Hall 1879-97* (Dublin: Gill and Macmillan, 1975 [quarto, 176 pages]).

Levey was a son of Giant O'Shaughnessy but changed his name to Levey on the grounds that it was more musical. One of his sons, Richard Michael Levey, played the part of the Ghost of Paganini in London and lived the role until his death in 1904.

Joyce complicated the matter further by suggesting that he might have been "Langley" or "a volunteer Vousden." Dublin-born "Professor" Valentine Vousden also played violin but was more known for singing, dancing, and playing various national characters as "the Polynational Character Actor." Perhaps Langley was also a violinist.

The Serio-Comic Minnie Cunningham came to the scene in 1895 and acted as Male Impersonator (cf. "Minxy Cunningham" 96.09 and "Minxy ... wor a Man" 433.19).

"Kathleen May Vernon" (93.31) hides another actress and singer of the period, Harriet Vernon. "May" is complementary to the Latin *ver*, *verno* and *Kathleen Mavourneen* by F.N. Crough is easily recognisable.

"Whirligigmagees" (27.20) was a song from the repertoire of George Beauchamp, *The Ball of Whirligig Magee*, now forgotten in Dublin.

A troupe of American Christy Minstrels ("christian minstrelsy" 3.18) arrived to Lowrey's in 1887. This may strengthen the case for the identification of "erse solid man" as W.J. Ashcroft, American-Irish comedian, who sang at the height of his career:

> *I am a man of great influence*
> *And eddicated to a high degree,*
> *Came here when small from Donegal*
> *With my cousin Tim across the sea.*
> *In the Alton Road we were situated*
> *In a lodging-house with my brother Dan;*
> *By perseverance I elevated*
> *And came to the front like a solid man!*
> *All together now—*
> *Come with me and I'll treat you dacent*
> *I'll set you down and fill your can.*
> *As I walk the street each friend I meet*
> *Says, there goes Muldoon the Solid Man!*

The Solid Man fell, his marriage with Kitty Brookes broke up, he went bankrupt, attempted suicide, and died in a mental asylum.

ANGLO-IRISH IN FINNEGANS WAKE

In Dublin, you will often hear "the best English is spoken in Dublin," which is an example of an Irish bull. Irish English, or as it is also called, Hiberno-English or Anglo-Irish, differs from the "standard" English in phonology, spelling, syntax, and lexicon. However, it is more often the brogue than syntax or words that makes Anglo-Irish difficult to follow (or even distinguish from Irish) for foreign visitors, particularly in rural districts.

Many phonological and lexical peculiarities of Anglo-Irish can be traced to the seventeenth-century English, but basically Anglo-Irish is English planted on the Irish cultural and linguistic substrates. Words for various agricultural implements and their parts, types of bog, kinds and sizes of potatoes or domestic animals, and similar expressions important in everyday life of a farming community, for which there are no suitable or known equivalents in the standard English, are retained in Irish (and suitably modified into Anglo-Irish), while hosts of emotional expressions, particularly of derogatory nature describing nuances of foolish, idiotic, or impudent behaviour, curses, and expletives are kept for the sheer joy and luxury of it. There are many dialects of Anglo-Irish. Often the boundary between Anglo-Irish dialect and slang is difficult to make or arbitrary.

It is a perverse situation that we have Basque and Bulgarian glossaries for *Finnegans Wake* but no Anglo-Irish. O Hehir's *Gaelic Lexicon* does not even acknowledge the distinction between Irish and Anglo-Irish. Thus, for example, Professor O Hehir wonders in the Preface how much Irish Joyce knew when he spelled e.g. *siubhal* as *shool*. The difference between *siubhal* and *shool* is not the difference between the "right" and "wrong" spelling, but the difference between Irish and Anglo-Irish. The spelling *shool* is well attested and there is also a difference in meaning as in the following excerpt from Samuel Lover: "Troth, you do me wrong, said the beggar, if you think I came shooling." Just one more random example from the *Lexicon: jackeen* is glossed as half-translation of *Seáinín* or *Seóinín* (112, 326, 336). Now, *jackeen* is not a half-translation of *Seáinín*. *Seáinín* means "little Seán" or "a thornback." Anglo-Irish *shoneen* means "an aper of English ways"

60

(from *Seon* = John, esp. John Bull). On the other hand, Anglo-Irish *jackeen* (more often *Dublin jackeen*) means "a loud-mouthed, ignorant youth" (Gerry O Flaherty), "a nickname for a conceited Dublin citizen of the lower classes,"[1] or "a self-assertive but worthless fellow, esp. a Dublin rough."[2] To complicate it further, *Seóinín* can stand for either *shoneen* or *jackeen*, beside other meanings, such as "a small farmer," or "a poor Protestant." Since Joyce's English is Anglo-Irish, we should try to rectify our neglect and paradoxical omission of Anglo-Irish from Wakean studies. The present glossary of one hundred Anglo-Irish words and phrases is intended only to stimulate to action and provoke those better qualified for the task.

The list does not contain Anglo-Irish words listed in *Webster's Third* or in O Hehir's *Lexicon* (with one or two exceptions).

5.03	clittering	"the great noise of hurrying feet, esp. on a stone"[3] (Ir. *cliotar*)
9.24	Bullsear	a clown (Ir. *ballséir*)[4]
19.33	signs on it!	therefore, consequently, as a result; (translation of Ir. *tá a shliocht air* or *tá a rian air*)[5]: P.W. Joyce gives a following example: "Tom Kelly never sent his children to school, and sign's on, they are growing up like savages."
23.12	Betoun	between; e.g. "The Lord betune us and harm" (Le Fanu), "God be betune uz and harm" (S. Lover)
26.18	metherjar	*mether* (or *medher*) is a wooden drinking vessel (Ir. *meadar*); cf. U 325.23: "the medher of dark strong foamy ale"; *jar* = a pint of stout, or a drink in general; "he is on the jar" (i.e. on the booze); jarred = drunk (heard in speech)
31.12	gorban	gorb = a ravenous eater, a glutton[6]; cf. 31.12 "ceasing to swallow" (Ir. *gorb*)

1 Patrick W. Joyce, *English as We Speak It in Ireland* (1910; Dublin: Wolfhound Press, 1997).

2 Eric Partridge, *A Dictionary of Slang and Unconventional English,* 5th ed. (London: Routledge and Kegan, 1961).

3 Diarmuid Ó hÉaluighte, "Irish Words in Cork Speech," *Journal of the Cork Historical and Archeological Society* 49 (1944): 33-48.

4 É. Mhac an Fhailigh, "A Westmeath Word-List," *Éigse* 5 (1945-1947): 256-66.

5 Patrick S. Dinneen, *An Irish-English Dictionary* (Dublin: Educational Company of Ireland [for Irish Texts Society], 1927).

6 Joyce, *English as We Speak It in Ireland.*

33.09	clawhammers	in Dublin lingo, "a Dublin type who is a bit of an eejit" (John Kilduff, *Irish Times*, 25 Nov., 1974)
35.13	bamer	a straw hat[7]
39.33	red biddy	a drink of Dublin winos, a cheap wine (occasionally fortified with methylated spirits)
46.01	E'erawan	combines Butler's Erewhon and the end of the phrase *Have you e'er a wan*; "wan" is Anglo-Irish spelling for "one"; cf. 510.27
50.30	snob of the dunhill	snob = a snot (snuff) of a candle[8] (Ir. *snab de'n choinnil*); perhaps also "snuff of Dunhill tobacco"; cf. non-Anglo-Irish "to die dunghill" and "to snuff it"[9]
51.02	possing	flooding; *possing-wet* = saturated, wringing wet[10]
72.03	*Ban*	Lord-Lieutenant of Ireland[11]; jocularly from Serbo-Croatian *ban* (a provincial governor)?
77.15	blaetther	variation of *blather, blether, blither, bladdher* (all Anglo-Irish) for "boastful or nonsensical talk" (Ir. *Bladar*, flattery)
79.30	moggies'	*moggy* = a fat lazy person[12]
87.31	bank from Banagher	from the phrase "that bangs Banagher and Banagher beats the Devil," i.e. out-blarneying blarney, a super-lie; also in Partridge; there is a village Banagher off Birr in Co. Offaly
93.15	hames	a mess; usually in the phrase "to make a hames of (something)" (heard in speech)
93.24	plause	i.e. *plausy* (Ir. *plás*, flattery); e.g. "he is a good hand at the plausy"[13]
97.30	libber	"a flipper, an untidy person careless about his dress and appearance; an easy-going ould sthreel of a

---

[7] Eilís Brady: *All in! All in!: A Selection of Dublin Childrens' Traditional Street-games with Rhymes and Music* (Dublin: Comhairle Bhéaloideas Éireann, 1975).

[8] D. Ó Conchubhair, "Focail ghaedhilge ó Dharmhagh Ua nDuach," *Éigse* 5 (1945-1947): 267-82.

[9] Partridge, *A Dictionary of Slang and Unconventional English*.

[10] L. Ua Broin, "A South-West Dublin Glossary," *Béaloideas* 14 (1944): 162-86.

[11] Partridge, *A Dictionary of Slang and Unconventional English*.

[12] P.C. O Neill, "A North-County Dublin Glossary," *Béaloideas* 17 (1947): 262-83.

[13] Ua Broin, "A South-West Dublin Glossary."

man"[14]

102.33	Goo	"a useless person, a fool"[15] (Ir. *guag*, silly, vain, or light-headed person[16]); cf. 381.06
122.10	within an aim's ace	very near, almost[17]; Partridge has "within ambsace"[18]
127.32	mausey	having large hips or heavy buttocks[19] (Ir. *más*, buttock); cf. 284.F4
128.02	mouldystoned	mouldy = stoned, i.e. drunk (Dublin slang)
134.03	laveries	Irish pound notes with the portrait of Lady Lavery posing as an Irish colleen
138.08	motts	girls (from Romani *mort*)[20]
140.34	*more* power to you	originally used to approvingly encourage a piper or fiddler; "more power to your elbow"; now used as encouragement of any kind; see 274.10
153.36	jackasses all within bawl	i.e. too near; "I wouldn't go within the bawl of an ass of him"[21]
156.23	botheared	partially deaf (Ir. *bodhar*)
179.07	creased	beaten[22]; cf. Scottish *creese, creesh*
179.08	gayboys	*go-boy* = a sly fellow who goes about doing harm in secret[23]
190.08	more grease to your elbow	a combination of "put more elbow grease into it" or "use a bit more elbow grease" (i.e. try harder; don't be lazy) with "more power to your elbow" cf. 140.34
191.04	Afferyank	"a massman," "a crawthumper" (Ir. *aifreannach*)
191.11	on his keeping	on the run (from the gardaí) (Ir. *ar a choimhéad*)

---

[14] Joyce, *English as We Speak It in Ireland.*
[15] O Neill, "A North-County Dublin Glossary."
[16] Dinneen, *An Irish-English Dictionary.*
[17] Joyce, *English as We Speak It in Ireland.*
[18] Partridge, *A Dictionary of Slang and Unconventional English.*
[19] Ó hÉaluighte, "Irish words in Cork Speech."
[20] Partridge, *A Dictionary of Slang and Unconventional English.*
[21] "OMURETHI": Book notice for Patrick W. Joyce, *English as We Speak It in Ireland*, in the *Journal of the County Kildare Archeological Society* 6 (1909-1911): 524-39.
[22] O Neill, "A North-County Dublin Glossary."
[23] O Neill, "A North-County Dublin Glossary."

193.02	crawsick	sick from the *craw* (= stomach); e.g. "he has a raging confusion in his craw" (F. O'Brien, *The Dalkey Archive*); "ill in the morning after a drinkin bout"[24]; perhaps originally from Ir. *craosach* (gluttonous) and folk-etymologised (Mrs E. Jeffries from Ballask, Co. Wexford records in her unpublished MS on Wexford Anglo-Irish, *crasheac* for "morning-after," "hangover")
195.03	sloothering	soft-soap, blarney; "this fellow would coax the birds off the bushes with his sloother"[25]; cf. 195.04 "gossipaceous"
196.09	hike!	go back!, stop! (call to a horse)[26]; cf. 377.23
199.32	not a mag	not a sound (Ir. *meig*, bleat of the goat); also in the phrase "not a meg or geg," i.e. not a sound or stir (Ir. *gíog ná míog*)
203.09	sarthin suir	confident, "sarthin shure" (i.e. certain sure); Joyce deviates from Anglo-Irish spelling because of the context of rivers (Ir. *súir*, water, a river)
209.06	twigged	to twig = to understand, know, notice, catch the point; "When I hinted at what I wanted, he twigged me at once"[27] (Ir. *tuigim*, I understand)
215.12	old skeowsha	old friend, usually "me ould s.," always with "old," other spellings are "sagowsha," "skidosha"[28]; very common, but origin unknown
215.14	foostherfather	fooster = bungler[29]; confusion[30]; flurry, fluster, great fuss[31]; "What are you foostering at?"[32] "when a boy went to see a girl he was said he went foostering" (E. Jeffries) (Ir. *fústar*, fussiness, etc.[33])
215.31	chittering	constantly complaining[34]
222.06	betune	see 23.12

[24] Joyce, *English as We Speak It in Ireland.*
[25] Ua Broin, "A South-West Dublin Glossary."
[26] Pádraig Ó Conchubhair, "An Offaly Glossary," *Béaloideas* 20 (1950): 188-91.
[27] Joyce, *English as We Speak It in Ireland.*
[28] O Neill, "A North-County Dublin Glossary."
[29] Ua Broin, "A South-West Dublin Glossary."
[30] Mhac an Fhailigh, "A Westmeath Word-List."
[31] Joyce, *English as We Speak It in Ireland.*
[32] Mhac an Fhailigh, "A Westmeath Word-List."
[33] Dinneen, *An Irish-English Dictionary.*
[34] Joyce, *English as We Speak It in Ireland.*

239.30	mearing	a boundary between two farms, bogs, or fields[35] (ME *mere*, boundary)
248.29	twig	see 209.06
253.16	Noodynaddy's	hesitant in speech[36]; an ignorant, incapable person[37] (Ir. *niúdar-neádar*, hesitancy[38]; *niúdaimí-neádaimí*, a hesitant person, in S. MacClúin, *Réilthíní óir*, 1922); obviously an important word
253.27	fecking	here not in the usual Anglo-Irish meaning "stealing," but "throwing"; "He was fecked out of the class" (thrown out by the teacher) (heard in speech)
257.17	fecking	as above
269.22	Cookcook!	"Hide-and-seek is often called Cook, because Cook! is sometimes the signal given that everyone is in hiding and the search may begin"[39]
271.18	Gam	a soft fool of a fellow[40]; more often spelt *gom*, e.g., in The Peeler and Peadar; "Don't think I am a fool or a gom or a gawk" (Ir *gam*, fool)
274.10	more livepower elbow him!	see 140.34
275.09	signs is on	see 19.33
284.F4	Massach	one with large hips, thighs, or buttocks (Ir. *másach*)[41]; cf. 127.32
288.F7	gatch	"affected gesture or movement of limb, body, or face"[42]; showing off (Ir. *gáitse*, a showy gesture, a swagger[43])
303.04	Fourth power to her illpogue!	see 140.34
304.26	delph	any crockery; it is often heard in "wash the delph," i.e. wash up after meal

[35] Joyce, *English as We Speak It in Ireland*.
[36] Ó hÉaluighte, "Irish Words in Cork Speech."
[37] P.L. Henry, *An Anglo-Irish Dialect of North Roscommon: Phonology, Accidence, Syntax* (Dublin: Department of English, University College, 1957).
[38] Dinneen, *An Irish-English Dictionary*.
[39] Brady, *All in! All in!*
[40] N. Breathnach, "Focail Ghaedhilge atá le clos sa Bhéarla a labhartar i gceanntar an Chaisleáin Nua, Co. Luimnigh," *Éigse* 7 (1953): 45-51.
[41] Dinneen, *An Irish-English Dictionary*.
[42] Joyce, *English as We Speak It in Ireland*.
[43] Dinneen, *An Irish-English Dictionary*.

304.31	cog	to crib (in school); P.W. Joyce[44] gives the following example: "You cogged that sum," which could suggest to Joyce the pun on "cogito ergo sum"
313.29	gauger	"a kind of half-way between bowsie and a louser; a disagreeable ne'er-do-well" (E. Anderson in *Signature*, New York, March 1972); very current in Dublin, usually spelled *gouger* or *gowger* (Ir. *gabhadaire*, a cunning fellow)
321.01	no more powers to their elbow	a further elaboration on 140.34
328.05	Andraws Meltons	see 392.03
338.16	*furry*	= furzy
351.16	Bonhamme	combines Fr. *bonhomme* and Anglo-Irish *bonham* (suckling pig) (Ir. *banbh*, piglet); cf. 459.24
356.17	sowansopper	*sowan* or *sowens* is a traditional dish eaten on Hallowe'en (Ir. *Samhain*), the recipe for which is given by Joyce as "gudhe rudhe brodhe with swedhe medhe," i.e. a kind of flummery
375.36	moya!	interjection implying doubt or irony (Ir. *mar bhéadh*, as if it were so[45]); often spelled *moy-yah* or *mor-yah*
377.23	hike	see 196.09
381.05	mouldy	see 128.02
381.06	googs	P.W. Joyce gives a diminutive form *googeen*;[46] (Ir. *guag*, light-headed person); in Anglo-Irish also *googaw* or *goo*;[47] *gug* or *guggy* is childish word for egg[48]
388.02	gink	a small nose[49]; the opposite to *conk* (388.01); (Ir. *geannc*, a snub nose)
390.14	wangles	"a tall, lanky, weak, young fellow"[50]
392.03	andrewmartins	pranks, tricks, shenanigans; e.g., "We're used to Oliver's (i.e. Oliver Flanagan, T.D.) Andrew Martins," said by an opposition spokesman in a political debate (*Irish Times*, 30 July, 1974); also

---

[44] Joyce, *English as We Speak It in Ireland.*
[45] Dinneen, *An Irish-English Dictionary.*
[46] Joyce, *English as We Speak It in Ireland.*
[47] O Neill, "A North-County Dublin Glossary."
[48] Ó hÉaluighte, "Irish Words in Cork Speech"; Ua Broin, "A South-West Dublin Glossary"; O Neill, "A North-County Dublin Glossary"; Henry, *An Anglo-Irish Dialect of North Roscommon.*
[49] Ó hÉaluighte, "Irish Words in Cork Speech."
[50] Joyce, *English as We Speak It in Ireland.*

spelled as *andramartins* or *anthramartins*[51]

393.02	signs on	see 19.33
393.05	Andrew Martin	see above
397.25	johnny magories	haws or hips[52] (Ir. *mucóirí*, haws or hips[53])
409.15	meeow	misfortune[54]; "he is a great *meeaw*" (i.e. an unfortunate person)[55]; "the *meeah* is on you" (i.e. you are unfortunate)[56]; *myaw*[57]; (Ir. *mí-ádh*, ill-luck, misfortune[58])
426.25	betune	see 23.12
435.04	tony	shoneen, anglicised in speech and manners; "he is very tony in his speech" (= he has a distinct English accent) (in Dinneen[59] under "gallda")
436.26	gab	chatter, prattle[60]; one gets "a gift of the gab" after kissing the Blarney stone; "listen to all the old gab he goes on with" (i.e. she subjected him to her small talk)[61]; (Ir. *geab*, chat)
454.15	jolly magorios	see 397.25
456.03	protestants	potatoes, jocularly from Ir. *prátaí* (potatoes)
459.24	bonhom	bonham, cf. 351.16; pet pig (cf. 459.25 "Pip pet," i.e. Swift's childish talk to Stella and "pet pig")
463.07	aimer's ace	see 122.10
467.10	twig	see 209.06
472.02	googoos	see 381.06
475.34	within the bawl of a mascot	see 154.01
488.06	ere yesterweek	the week before last; "I met him e'er yesterday" = day before yesterday[62]; (Ir. *arbhú i ndé*, day before

---

[51] Ua Broin, "A South-West Dublin Glossary."

[52] Dinneen, *An Irish-English Dictionary*; Joyce, *English as We Speak It in Ireland*; Brady, *All in! All in!*

[53] Dinneen, *An Irish-English Dictionary*.

[54] Joyce, *English as We Speak It in Ireland*.

[55] Breathnach, "Focail Chaedhilge atá le clos sa Bhéarla a labhartar i gceanntar an Chaisleáin Nua, Co. Luimnigh," *Éigse* 6 (1950): 169-79.

[56] O Neill, "A North-County Dublin Glossary."

[57] P. Martin, "Some Peculiarities of Speech Heard in Breifny," *Breifny Antiquities Society Journal* 1 (1921): 174-91.

[58] Dinneen, *An Irish-English Dictionary*.

[59] Dinneen, *An Irish-English Dictionary*.

[60] Henry, *An Anglo-Irish Dialect of North Roscommon*.

[61] Henry, *An Anglo-Irish Dialect of North Roscommon*.

[62] "OMURETHI."

		yesterday[63])
504.02	crans	little tricks or dodges[64]; as in Irish always in plural (Ir. *cranna*, antics)
508.32	leg a bail	"to take leg bail" means "to run away, to abscond"; e.g. "He took leg bail on the spot like a deer"[65]
510.27	e'er a one	"Have you e'er a one" is a common phrase in which "one" is presumed to be understood from the context or gesture. It means "have you got a …?" The negative answer to this is "I have ne'er a one." (Ir. *earra*, article, goods, and *arra*, an equivalent.)?
516.03	gag	"a conceited foppish young fellow who tries to figure as a swell"[66]
521.23	freckened	frightened
524.36	doodah	a fool[67] (Ir. *dúdálaidhe*, a dunce, an awkward person[68])
532.01	eirenarch's	"herenach," a historical term for a church official (Ir. *airchinneach*, steward of church lands[69])
536.18	redden	to light (a fire or a pipe)[70]
557.07	googoo	see 381.06
577.07	great gas	fun; e.g., a Dublin mother coming home from a hen party would say: "We had great gas" (i.e. lot of good-humoured fun and laugh); "He is a gas man" means "there is lot of fun with him" or "he is a bit of a character"
581.07	betune	see 23.12
584.12	hooley pooley	a hubbub, a great din (Ir. *húille búille*)[71]
608.26	Signs are on	see 19.33
615.29	cafflers	caffler = "a contemptible little fellow who gives saucy cheeky foolish talk"[72]; one who plays pranks[73]

63 Dinneen, *An Irish-English Dictionary.*
64 Joyce, *English as We Speak It in Ireland.*
65 Joyce, *English as We Speak It in Ireland.*
66 Joyce, *English as We Speak It in Ireland.*
67 O Neill, "A North-County Dublin Glossary."
68 Dinneen, *An Irish-English Dictionary.*
69 Dinneen, *An Irish-English Dictionary.*
70 Joyce, *English as We Speak It in Ireland.*
71 Henry, *An Anglo-Irish Dialect of North Roscommon.*
72 Joyce, *English as We Speak It in Ireland.*
73 Breathnach, "Focail Chaedhilge atá le clos sa Bhéarla a labhartar i gceanntar an Chaisleáin Nua, Co. Luimnigh," *Éigse* 6 (1950): 169-79.

(Ir. *cafaire*, a prater; cf. German student slang *koffern*, to prattle)

618.11 waxy   "a cobbler, because he uses wax-end for stitching. Up to about 1890 the waxies of Dublin held an annual gathering called Waxies' Dargle"[74]

[74] Brady, *All in! All in!*

THE PETER THE PAINTER (85.05)

Professor Liam O'Briain recalling Countess Markievicz's military outfit during the Easter Rising, mentions that she carried "a big revolver which used to be called *the* Peter the Painter" (W.R. Rodgers, *Irish Literary Portraits* (London: B.B.C., 1972) 222).

How many of "the many Joyceans who were astonished by the publication" (*AWN* 9.6 (1972): 115) of Mrs von Phul's query (*AWN* 9.3 (1972): 46) would now swallow copies of their indignant letters to the Editor?

THE KEY No. ONE TO NO-ONE

FIN(D) NEG. ANSWA = KE(Y).
The key of Two-tongue Common ... To be continued.

—ANON

SIGNS ON IT! (II)

I am glad that Victory Pomeranz (*AWN* 14.4 (1977): 62) has given me an opportunity to expand on my gloss on *signs on it* in *AWN* 13.5 (1976): 80.[1] She questions the equation of "sign's on" with "sings on" and she suspects that it may be a curse, though she could not find it in any dictionary.

I gave a reference to Dinneen's dictionary, where the phrase *signs on it* is quoted twice (237, 895) and once in the singular form *sign is on it* (1058). P.W. Joyce has *sign's on it*, and Traynor, *The English Dialect of Donegal* (Dublin: Royal Irish Academy, 1953) 258, lists the form "*signs on it, him* etc." The apostrophe in "sign's" has no special significance but merely reflects an orthographic convention. The explanation for the dual usage of "sign's" and signs' is found in Irish original forms from which this Anglo-Irish phrase is translated, namely, *tá a rian air* and *tá a shliocht air*, both of which mean literally "its sign (or mark, sg. or pl.) is on it," i.e. "it bears the consequence of the preceding action referred to," "as a result of which can be seen," or simply, "consequently." *Rian* and *sliocht* have identical forms in the singular and plural, which answers Miss Pomeranz's question whether "sign's" and "signs" may be equated or not.

In *Finnegans Wake*, the phrase is used four times: *signs on it!* (19.33), *signs is on* (275.09), *signs on* (393.01), and *Signs are on* (608.26). The usage is perfectly clear. Thus, *You gave me a boot (signs on it!) and I ate the wind* (19.33) means "You refused to lend me money, you kicked me out, and as a result, I was hungry." In another example, *acid and alkolic; signs on the salt* (393.01) the meaning is "mix acid and alkali and the result will be salt," or in alchemistic terms, "conjugation of two opposites gives the salt" (salt = sexual intercourse, see e.g. Partridge).

Miss Pomeranz has been misled by the phrase in U 430: *Signs on you, hairy arse*, probably because of an obsolete meaning of "sign" as "omen." Virago speaks Anglo-Irish (note *More power the Cavan girl* in the same line, and the relevant gloss in *AWN* 13.5 (1976): 81) and in Anglo-Irish *signs on you* is a translation of Irish *tá a rian ort* (there is a sign(s) of it on you) meaning "your previous conduct has left its mark

---

[1] Petr Škrabánek, "Anglo-Irish in *Finnegans Wake*," *AWN* 13.5 (1976): 79-85.

on you," "you show the effect of it," "you show it." What Virago says to Cissy Caffrey could be rendered into English—if it is necessary—as, "You have a look of it, you hairy arse, go on, keep singing, good luck to you." *More power* is always used approvingly and thus cannot be preceded by a curse as suggested by Miss Pomeranz.

Nathan Halper (*AWN* 14.4 (1977): 61) suggests that *cabbageblad* (56.25) is "a bit of female pudenda," *ergo* Virgo. Roland McHugh (*AWN* 13.4 (1976): 75), on the other hand, identified *cabbageblad* as Aquarius. I believe that McHugh is right for wrong reasons. It is true, as Halper points out, that the constellation of Aquarius does not look at all as cabbageblad. However, the symbol of Aquarius is two wavy lines which look very much like a crumpled cabbage leaf. In Ireland children are not brought by the stork but they are found under a cabbage leaf. Joyce was born under the sign of Aquarius. True, he was born through the female pudenda but he was also told that he was found under a cabbage leaf. These two statements are not contradictory. On the contrary, they are perhaps the key to the slang meaning of "cabbage." The symbol of Aquarius represents prophetically the stream of water, i.e. *Finnegans Wake*. And Joyce is the waterbaby. Don't you know he was kaldt a bairn of the brine, Wasserbourne the waterbaby? (198.07). He is the *Waterman the Brayned* (104.13). Naturally, these expressions also refer to Noah with whom Joyce identified himself (*L* III.364). The *zooteach* is also Noah's ark and the seven signs of the zodiac allude to the seven colours of iris which the weeping exiled Joyce Traveller (*maundering pote* with *snobsic eyes*) sees through his teary glaucomatous eyes.

The shemming serpent Joyce made this semisemitic pun nickname by translating Stephen's "silence, exile, and cunning" into the Hebrew in a reversed order as follows: *nasha* (to deceive), *gur* (to be in exile), and *hasha* (to keep silence). Nash of Girahash is, in other words, the schemer of the silent exile. He is not deceiving Eve and Adam, but us. He is silent because the answer is "noanswa." He is an exile *ex île* of Eire because he carries the light (Lucifer). "His Nile" (75.01) is both the symbol of the resurrection and the salvation through the annual Flood (note "Boghas the baregams" 75.02; i.e. Turkish Boghazköy and Bergama with the archives containing accounts of the Hittite Flood, etc.) and a symbol of negation, *nil*, "in the best manner of Shem ... silences = no, non, nein" (*L* I.237). He is Cain, because *kein* = no. (Shem-Cain = ⊏, *L* I.231, where ⊏ stands for C). He is nomened Nash of Girahash, because his nomen is Nemon-Demon.

THE WHOLE GAMMAT (492.04)

This is the *Finnegans Wake* ballad of seven bars as sung by "Annie Delittle" (492.08), HCE's accomplice (It. *delitto*, crime) in handpicked Russian and other tongues-in-cheek. When Yawn renders the lunatic crescendo to the Four, they are astounded: "Dias domnas! Dolled to dolthood? ... his daintree diva ... singing him henpecked rusish through the bars?" (492.08) But they asked for it: "How voice you that, nice Sandy man?" (492.01) He gave them the "voice of jokeup" through the gamut of the wake week (492.05-07):

Loonacied!
Spanish *lunes* (Monday) is derived from *lunae dies*. Irish Luan (the moon, Monday). In the *Wake* Latin, *lunae dies* could also mean the moon is dead, lunacide. The crescent moon is dead, long live the new nascent moon. Joyce made this Monday the *Lunacy Day* (Anglo-Irish for the commemoration feast of Lugh who blinded Balor-Cyclops).[1]

Marterdyed!!
Italian *martedi* (Tuesday), i.e. *Martis dies*. God is martyred and dead. Blood flows from the eye of Balor-Polyphemus-HCE to form the *madder-dyed* Red Sea. He sees red. Cf. "Crasnian Sea" (492.10) = Red Sea (Russian, *Krasnoe more*).

Madwakemiherculossed!!!
German Mittwoch (Wednesday, literally *midweek*) + Spanish *miércoles* (Wednesday, from *Mercuri dies*). Hercules's madness in which he killed his children was recalled annually in funeral games in Thebes. Hercules also ties up with the hircos-hairy theme on the page. Cf. "Wolossay" (492.10), Polish *włosy*, Russian *volosy*, hair.

Judascessed!!!!
French *jeudi* (Thursday, i.e. *Jovis dies*). Maundy Thursday is called on the Continent "Green Thursday" (cf. 491.27). God is betrayed after he died in this Holy Week in reverse. Judas's kiss was Judas's cess (Anglo-Irish,

---

[1] Cf. *Lughnasa*, Irish harvest festival devoted to the Celtic god Lugh. (Ed.)

bad cess to you), which led to his low death. He fell like Humpty Dumpty and "burst asunder" (*Acts* 1:18).

Pairaskivvymenassed!!!!!
Greek *paraskeué* (Good Friday, *Matthew* 15:42; "Paraskivee" 192.21) + Greek *ménás*, the moon. On Friday, HCE was menaced by a pair of skivvies, "little curls" (kerls or girls) from "drary lane" (491.30, 31) (drury lane ague = syphilis; "Phyllis ..." 491.30). Friday in *Veneris dies*, i.e. syphilis death.

Luredogged!!!!!!
Dano-Norwegian *lørdag* (Saturday). The Saturday of "holinight ... twixt a sleep and a wake" (192.19).

And, needatellye,
Old Church Slavonic *nedelya* (Sunday)

faulscrescendied!!!!!!!
Old Church Slavonic *voskresenie* (Resurrection) and Russian *voskresen'e* (Sunday). The resurrection of the "fellow that fell foul of the county de Loona" (465.20), the false Christian under the banner of the crescent, who fell from the cross and became crescent again. It's lunatic. It's mad week. Joyce—"God has jest" (486.10) of "cruelfiction" (192.19).

Dias domnas! = God damn us! + Irish *Dia Domhnaigh* (the Day of Lord, i.e. Sunday).

Structurally, in Viconian terms, the whole *Wake*-week song is squeezed in between ABC (aleph-alpha "allaughed," beth-beta "baited," gamma "gammat" 492.04) and D (daleth-delta "dolthood" 492.08).

THE CHESS ELEPHANT IN THE BELLY

Apropos the explication of "slomtime" (228.34; *AWN* 15.1 (1978): 8), *slom* is not Russian for "bishop." *Slom* is not a Russian word. The Russian for "bishop" is *episkop*. However, Russian for "elephant" is *slon*, as in other Slavonic languages. In Russian, *slon* is also used for the bishop in chess since in the original Arabic the name for this piece was *al-fil* (elephant). Dr MacArthur suggests that "bishop" is a large cundum used to contain others and as such seems to appear in a number of places, and he uses as an example "piawn to bishop's forthe" (377.14) which happens to be the opening chess move in the Queen's Gambit. Did Joyce really mean that "bishop" is an elephant condom or a condom for an elephant and to make it more difficult he misspelt the Russian *slon*?

BASQUE BEGINNING

On page 109 of *Scribbledehobble*, there is the following entry: Adam and Eve spoke Basque. The source for this statement could be Abbé Dominique Lahetjuzan (1799-1818) who claimed that "Le basque est un langue original" (*Essai de Quelques Notes sur la Langue Basque par un Vicaire de Campagne, Sauvage d'Origine*). The Basque *ur*-nationality of Eve and Adam (3.01) is established by oranges (3.23). Basque *laranja* (orange) was derived by folk etymology from Basque elements meaning "the fruit which was first eaten." After Adam and Eve there was nobody to pluck them and the oranges became over-ripe (rusty in colour) and fell to the ground "to be laid to rust" (rest+rot) on the place where the first Tempter laid Eve (cf. orange = female pudend; greens = sexual sport; knock out = coitus; Partridge gives e.g. "to knock out an apple" = to beget a child; and knock means also the penis). The half-translation of Dano-Norwegian *appelsin* (orange) or German *sine* (orange) gives "the apple of sin," an incidental pun.

EPSCENE LICENCE (523.34)

"It is strange that on the day I sent off to you a picture of an epicene professor ... I received a paper from Dublin containing news of the death ... of an old school fellow of mine ... his name (which he used to say, was an Irish (Celtic) variant of mine own) is in English an epicene name being made up of the feminine an masculine personal pronouns—Sheehy" (Joyce to Miss Weaver in 1923, *L* I.205). The word "epicene" is a grammatical term which Joyce used rather loosely.

Joyce also joked that his name somewhat mispronounced by Slavonic people sounded like one of their expressions for "eggs" (see *JJI* 396), e.g. *jajce* in Slovenian. (Ellmann missed the pun when Joyce said to his sister that marrying Schaurek she was not really changing her name. In Czech, *šourek* means "scrotum," so that the marriage was in the bag.) "Eggs" could belong, as ova or testes, to either sex, and in this sense they again support the "epicene" nature of the name Joyce.

The third "epicene" coincidence in Joyce's baptismal names was the birth registration of Joyce as James Augusta (see *JJI* 20). Augusta was a honorary title of Livia, a suitable name for the author of "riverrun." Moreover, August is the name for a mocking fellow, a clown, and the Irish form of Joyce's name is *Seoighe*, which could be derived from Irish *seó* (mocking, funny). The womanly man in Joyce's writings is a well known theme. Bloom is named Leopold Paula and in *Finnegans Wake* we find numerous similar examples of "epicene" names, e.g. Mr Himmyshimmy (173.27), O'Shea (Shem, but also "she"; 182.30), Sheehohem (188.18), Mrs Shemans (397.31), sexmosaic (107.11), Kevin Mary (555.16), etc.

The last association between Joyce and the merging of sexes comes through his tenor voice and the popular belief that the height of the voice pitch is inversely proportional to manliness. The large size of the larynx with consequently longer vocal cords in men is epitomised by the term "Adam's apple," but in tenors this becomes "his madam's apple" (436.07). Several tenor castrati are mentioned: Moreshi ("mareschalled" 132.24), Grossi ("grossed" 132.25; cf. "his conversion" line 25, and "that grand old voice" line 27), Farinelli ("mandaboutwoman type ... Fairynelly" 151.06), Tenducci (541.32, see *Census III*) or castration is jokingly implied, "ambiamphions ... Joan MockComic, male soprano" (222.07) or indicated in general terms: "He is too audorable really, eunique!" (562.32); "Treble" (i.e. boy soprano), "formerly Swordmeat" (see Partridge for "sword" and "meat"), "I'd be better off without." (490.20); "Kevin Mary ... chief of the choirboys" (555.16). In Book III, Shaun has "a high voice and O" (= female genital) (404.08), he is "Irish ferrier" (castrato Ferri?) (404.19), he "looked a young chapplie of sixtine" (430.31) (note the castration allusions abound; castrati were first admitted to the Sistine Chapel Choir in 1559), or "like a woman" (454.20), is impotent ("Esterelles, be not on your weeping what though Shaunathaun is in his fail!" (462.07), and signs himself/herself as "Ann Posht the Shorn" (454.06). (For details on castrati singers see M.M. Melicow and S. Pulrang, "Castrati Choir and Opera Singers," *Urology* 3 (1974): 663f.

The bisexual self-reproductive phoenix is the emblematic bird of *Finnegans Wake*. In Japanese, the word for "phoenix" is an "epicene" compound of two Chinese characters, transcribed as *ho* and *wo*, where *ho* means "a male phoenix fowl" and *wo* "a female phoenix fowl." Combined in *howo*, they stand for the mythical Phoenix. This word appears in the pseudo-Japanese sentence: "Hovobovo hafogate hokidimatzi in kamicha" (234.01) with the following Japanese elements—*hovobovo*, plural of *hovo*, the reduplication of *hovo* requires in Japanese *bovo* in the second half, i.e. double phoenix, *ha* = yes, *fo* = sail, *gaten* = riddle, *hokka* = setting out on a journey; *hokki* = arise, *demidzu* = flood, *ina* = no, *ine* = to sleep, *kami* = 1. god; 2. hair, *cha* = man. The meaning of the sentence could be approximately: Noman / Godman / Hairyman has a dream about the Flood and he sails in the Noah's Ark in the Phoenix Park.

In Chinese, the same characters as in Japanese are used to represent Phoenix, but the transcription is quite different: *feng*[4] (male phoenix bird) and *huang*[2] (female Phoenix bird) give *feng-huang* (mythical Phoenix). See e.g. "fungopark" (51.20, for Phoenix Park) and "Fung Yang" (109.06, for Finnegan).

The epicene theme is closely related to the themes of the change of sex and of the union of the opposites.

A BORN GENTLEMAN IS (?) (116.25)

James Otis, born in West Barnstable, Massachusetts ("bornstable ghentleman" 10.17), a descendant from John Otis of Barnstable (!), Devon, England, *deus ex machina*, with a "tomestome of Barnstaple" (253.34). James Otis fought William Howe ("Howe?" 18.12) at Bunker's Hill ("bunkersheels" 9.29). He was killed by—all give up?—lightning at Andover, Mass. On 23 May, 1783 ("Oye am thonthorstrok" 18.16). James Otis was the author of the anonymous letter "Considerations on Behalf of the Colonists in a Letter to a Noble Lord" (cf. "reverend" of earlier *Finnegans Wake* drafts), published in London in 1765. The publication was prefaced with: "The following pamphlet was sent to the Publisher, by an unknown Person, from Boston, ..." and signed "humble servant, F.A." ("F... A..." 59.04). James Otis took part in the Boston Tea Party. And "lastly when all is zed and done, the penelopean patience of its last paraphe" (123.04), the letter came from a noman (*outis* in the *Odyssey*).

THE TURNING OF THE Ш

Luigi Schenoni (*AWN* 13.3 (1976): 54) explained ingeniously the origin of "the turning of the E" from Snellen's optotypes. The "sign ᴟ" which turned "contrawatchwise" to represent "his title in sigla" (119.17) hides the name of Shem in the Cyrillic alphabet: ШЕМ, i.e. ᴟ turned anticlockwise and written backwards.

Note that in *Finnegans Wake*, ᴟ appears in the following order: Ш (6.32), Ǝ (36.17), Е (51.19), and ᴟ (119.17), giving ШƎЕᴟ, i.e. SHEEM when read from the left to the right, and also upside down (the Cyrillic alphabet has two Es: Э, Е). "But by writing thithaways end to end and turning, turning and end to end hithaways writing and with lines of litters slittering up and louds of latters slettering down, the old semetomyplace and jupetbackagain" (114.16). The old same Shem's trick ("I advise you to conceal yourself ... Sheem" 188.05), Japhet-Jacob's trick (Russian *sheemy* = tangled hair), and St Patrick's trick of conjuring Unity from the Trinity ("seme ... jupet ... tham" 114.18) of the shamrock ("Meesh, meesh" 457.25).

SLAVONICISMS IN *FINNEGANS WAKE*

Out of 217,937 words in *Finnegans Wake*, 49,200 occur only once.[1] This unprecedented crop of *hapax legomena* would be a stumbling block for an average reader even if all the words were to be found in an English dictionary. Unfortunately, this is not so. *Finnegans Wake* is assembled from seventy-odd languages, or, as Joyce puts it in an understatement: "wordloosed over seven seas crowdblast in cellelleneteutoslavzendlatinsoundscript" (219.16), i.e. Celtic, Hellenic, Teutonic, Slavic, Zend (= Iranian), Latin and Sanskrit.

One often hears a naïve question: "and where did Joyce learn all these languages?" He did not learn all of them, but he dipped into dictionaries and freely misspelt, inflated into portmanteaux, chopped in fragments, wrote backwards and otherwise mutilated words to suit his artistic plan of a riverrun of multiple meanings, euphony ("soundscript"), pun, riddle or allusion. The resulting mesh of Indo-European ("earopen") and other languages has become a fluid word-stream shimmering on the surface with multiple facets of intended *and* fortuitous semantic puns, paradoxes and inner conflicts of meaning and, like the proverbial river of Heraclitus, the same *Finnegans Wake* cannot be stepped into twice. This method of "superfecundation" of words, which is the basis of *Finnegans Wake* construction, adds a "living" quality to the apotheosis of Anna Livia, the river alive with words. At the same time, paradoxically, this method both enhances and destroys the meaning. It comes as no surprise that, for many, *Finnegans Wake* is gibberish. If "gibberish" is to mean "lacking intelligibility or meaning," it does not follow that the text is to blame: the fault could well lie in the reader. Conversely, the Golden Calf of meaning is not worshipped by everybody: "any work of art which can be understood is the product of a journalist" (Marcel Duchamp). *Finnegans Wake* is certainly not a hoax, since one of the best writers of the 20th century, James Joyce, devoted seventeen years of his mature life to the completion of this literary experiment and his artistic testament.

One of the first translations of *Ulysses* was into Czech in 1930 by

---

[1] Clive Hart, *A Concordance to Finnegans Wake*, corrected ed. (New York: Paul Appel, 1974) iii.

Ladislav Vymětal and Jarmila Fastrová. *Ulysses* was brought to the attention of Czech *literati* by Tomáš G. Masaryk, philosopher and first President of the Czechoslovak Republic, at a time when in the West the book was banned in many countries as obscene. In the communist East-European bloc, perhaps with the exception of Poland, an interest in Joyce beyond *Dubliners* and *A Portrait of the Artist as a Young Man* was positively discouraged. The first translation of *A Portrait* into Russian appeared as late as 1976 (not as a book, but in a literary magazine).[2] Slavonic studies of *Finnegans Wake* in Eastern Europe do not exist and Western commentators usually lack a knowledge of Slavonic languages sufficient to unearth and savour Joyce's puns.

Joyce's knowledge of Slavonic languages was superficial, but he was able to cook a rich meal from a few ingredients. Joyce was more interested in words than Slavonic literary style, so that Russian literature gets only scanty attention in *Finnegans Wake*—usually in the form of allusions to an author's or hero's name or to a book's title. Atherton, who listed these allusions systematically, included Chekhov, Dostoyevsky, Gogol, Gorky, Krylov, Kropotkin and Pushkin.[3] Joyce read Russian authors in English, French, German or Italian translations. A surviving portion of Joyce's inventory of his books in Trieste in 1919 contains: *Pensieri di saggi per ogni giorno, Scritti* and *Der Roman der Ehr* by Tolstoy, *La grande rivoluzione* by Kropotkin, eleven volumes of Turgenev's novels and Bakunin's *God and the State* (*JJI* 794). About Tolstoy Joyce wrote to his brother Stanislaus:

> He is head and shoulders over the others. I don't take him very seriously as a Christian saint. I think he has a very genuine spiritual nature, but I suspect that he speaks the very best Russian with a St Petersburg accent and remembers the Christian name of his great-great-grandfather (this, I find, is at the bottom of the essentially feudal art of Russia). [*JJI* 217]

Although Tolstoy is not listed by Atherton, "mere and woiney" (518.21) refers to *Voina i mir* (*War and Peace*), where battles are bottles of beer ("mere") and wine ("woiney"). *Mere* is also a Maori war club (to enhance the battle context) and Latin *merum*, of course, is unadulterated wine. Later on the page, wine becomes war in "in voina viritas"

---

2 Dzheyms Dzhoys, "Portret khudozhnika v yunosti," *Inostrannaya Literatura* 10 (1976): 171-98; 11 (1976): 119-74; 12 (1976): 139-82.
3 James S. Atherton, *The Books at the Wake* (London: Faber and Faber, 1959) *passim*.

(518.31), i.e. *in vino veritas*, but also "in war virility is a virtue." Anna Karenina hides probably in "nana karlikeevna" (331.25), where Greek *nanos* and Russian *karlik* mean "dwarf."

Joyce's first encounter with a Slavonic culture was in Pola (then in Austria, now in Yugoslavia), where he taught English in a Berlitz school. A large proportion of the working class in Pola were Croatian. One of Joyce's informants in Pola in 1905 was Miss Globočnik, a Slovene teacher of Croatian in the same Berlitz school. Later in Trieste, Joyce met more Yugoslavs from whom he collected scraps of words and snippets of phrases. One of his Triestine friends, Alois Skrivenich,[4] appears as "Shem Skrivenitch, always cutting my prhose to please his phrase, bogorror, I declare I get the jawache!" (423.15), obviously a self-disparaging comment on difficulties in mastering Slavonic pronunciation.

In 1915, Joyce's sister, Eileen, married in Trieste the local Czech bank official, František Schaurek, who supplied Joyce with Czech words during their joint stay in Trieste in 1918-1920. According to Ellmann, Joyce joked that Triestine Slavs mispronounced his name as "yoyce" which "meant 'eggs' in Czech" and he consoled Eileen at her wedding, saying that by marrying Schaurek she was not changing her name at all.[5] Since Ellmann interviewed Eileen 40 years after the wedding and since the excitement of the occasion and the lapse of time did not help Eileen's memory, the Ellmann version is garbled and the joke lost. In fact, *jajce* means "eggs" or "testicles" in Slovene and not in Czech, and the Czech form of the name Schaurek (*šourek*) does not mean "eggs," but their container—scrotum.[6] Joyce was surely aware that *Ei* in Eileen means also "egg" in German. All this augured well for fertility.

Still later, in Paris, Joyce took Russian lessons from Alex Ponisovsky, a Russian *émigré* and one of the suitors of Joyce's daughter, Lucia. Another Russian *émigré* and a friend of Joyce was Paul Léon, his Parisian secretary.

Finnegans Wake contains about 1000 Slavonicisms.[7] Their analysis and language allocation is impeded by the fact that about 1260 words

---

[4] I. Vidan, "Joyce and the South Slavs," *Studia Romanica and Anglica Zagrebiensia* 33-36 (1972/1973): 265-277.

[5] *JJI* 396.

[6] Petr Škrabánek, "Epscene licence," *AWN* 15.5 (1978): 74.

[7] Petr Škrabánek, "Slavansky slavar, R. Slavyanskii slovar (Slavonic dictionary)," *AWN* 9.4 (1972): 5-68.

are common to most Slavonic languages.[8] In view of the way in which words are transcribed and isolated in *Finnegans Wake*, it is more accurate to list them as "panslavonic,"[9] when characteristic features of the individual language are lost. Occasionally, though, Joyce exploited semantic shifts occurring in these "panslavonic" words in individual Slavonic languages. For example, in a blasphemous passage on the Easter week in 492.04f.,[10] Joyce used the word "faulscrescendied" to mean "Sunday" (in Russian *voskresen'e*) to follow after "Loonacied" (Spanish *lunes*, Irish *Luan*, "Monday"), "Marterdyed" (Italian *martedi*, "Tuesday"), "Madwakemiherculossed" (German *Mittwoch*, Spanish *miercoles*, "Wednesday"), "Judascessed" (French *jeudi*, "Thursday"), "Pairaskivvymenassed" (Greek *paraskevé*, "Good Friday"), and "Luredogged" (Dano-Norwegian *lørdag*, "Saturday"). However, "faulscrescendied" also contains Church Slavonic *voskresenie* (Resurrection) to tie up the mad wake-week with the main theme of the ballad "Finnegan's Wake" ("Bedad he revives, see how he rises, and Timothy rising from the bed"). The word "faulscrescendied" is purposely (and typically) ambiguous: while "resurrection" is clearly conveyed, it also implies a fall ("faul ...") and a false death ("fauls ... died") with a further ambiguity of the middle part "... crescen ..." which could be both a growing crescent between new moon and first quarter and a receding crescent between last quarter and new moon.

Old Church Slavonic appears again in "Gospolis fomiliours" (345.02), i.e. *Gospodi pomilui ny* (Lord have mercy upon us) with "paterfamilias" included, and in "gospelly pewmillieu, christous pwemillieu" (552.26), i.e. *Gospodi pomilui ny, Khriste pomilui ny* (= Kyrie eleison, Christe eleison) of the Orthodox liturgy, punning on the superstitious atmosphere of muttered spells in gospel halls.

Russian history gets a sweeping cover from Kiev Rus' ("O'Keef-Rosses and Rhosso-Keevers" 310.16) to the rule of hammer and sickle ("hummer enville and cstorrap" 310.19) (Russian *serp* "sickle"). Early Russian rulers and tzars walk over the page.[11] Russian epic heroes are also revived, such as the Hellenised Ilya Muromets in the Trojan lament for the dead: "Ilyam, Ilyum! Mearomor Mournomates!" (55.03) or the fat arsed *bogatyr'* Alyosha Popovich in "Allolosha Popofetts" (106.23)

---

8   František Kopečný, *Základní všeslovanská slovní zásoba* (1964; Prague: Academia, 1981) 4.
9   Škrabánek, "Slavansky slavar," *passim*.
10 Petr Škrabánek, "The Whole Gammat," *AWN* 14.6 (1977): 100-101.
11 Fritz Senn, "Early Russian History of *Finnegans Wake*," *JJR* 2.1-2 (1958): 63-64.

(German *Popo* + *fett*). Another hero is "Wassaily Booslaeugh" (5.05), i.e. Vasiliy Buslayev from the Novgorod epic cycle. "Booslaeugh" is both the princely God-praising Boguslav and a boozing *buslai* (a fallen man, drunkard).[12]

Russian words and phrases generally appear with an Irish flavour, e.g. "Fetch neahere, Pat Koy! And fetch nouyou, Pam Yates!" (27.26), i.e. *"vechnyy pokoy, na vechuyu pamyat,"* "eternal peace, for eternal memory." Russian *khorosho* stands once for a Horse Show in the Royal Dublin Society "horoseshoew" (159.28) with a horse-shoe for good luck, and another time it signifies "Roman Godhelic" Christ in "Xaroshie, zdrst!" (91.36) with another Christ in *zdravstvuy* for a good measure. The Orthodox "breadchestviousness of his sweeatovular ducose" (156.14) (*proshestviye svyatogo dukha*, "Procession of the Holy Ghost") has overtones of the sweaty smell of the breeches, and papal infallibility can be deciphered in "babskissed nepogreasymost" (*papskiyaya nepogreshimost'* 156.17).

A number of Russian words can be found in II.3 where there are about 20 pages elaborating on an anecdote Joyce heard from his father about a battlefield encounter between a Russian general and an Irish private named Buckley during the Crimean war. The Russian general was caught with his pants down and Buckley hesitated to take aim at the defenseless target. However, when the general wiped himself with a sod of turf ("Another insult to Ireland," interjected Samuel Beckett at this point when Joyce was retelling him the story[13]), Buckley finished him off. The prototype of the story can be traced back to *Táin Bó Cuailnge*[14]:

> Then Medb got her gush of blood.
> "Fergus," she said, "take over the shelter of shields at the rear of the men of Ireland until I relieve myself."
> "By God," Fergus said, "you have picked a bad time for this."
> "I can't help it," Medb said. "I'll die if I can't do it."
> So Fergus took over the shelter of shields at the rear of the channels, each big enough to take a household. The place is called Fual Medba, Medb's Foul Place [literally: Medb's urine] ever since. Cúchulainn found her like this but he held his hand. He wouldn't strike her from behind.

---

[12] Petr Škrabánek, "Wassaily Booslaeugh (of Riesengeborg)," *AWN* 10.3 (1973): 42-43.
[13] *JJI* 411.
[14] *The Táin*, trans. Thomas Kinsella (Oxford: Oxford University Press, 1970) 250.

Hiberno-Slavonic puns abound. The Battle of the Boyne is also "bloodstained boyne" (Ukrainian *boinya*, "battle," Russian *boinya* "massacre"). The Russian Kremlin is Dublin Crumlin, and Dublin could be "Petricksburg" (326.26) (St. Petersburg named after St. Patrick), or Polish Lublin in "lucky load to Lublin" (565.22), all located in Hibernian Siberia "Sibernia" (297.05). The Crimean Balaclava merges in "balacleivka" (341.09) with Baile Átha Cliath (the Irish name for Dublin) and Russian *balalaika*.

"Prostatates, pujealousties! Dovolnoisers, prayshyous!" (350.16) reads in Russian as *prostite pozhaluyista, dovol'no, proshus'* (excuse me, please, that's enough, thanks) with sexual overtones of prostitutes and prostatic leaders (Greek *prostátes*, "chief," "president"), penis jealousy (Czech *pyje*, "penis") and lousy lust. A Iagonian greeting: "How are you, my black sir?" becomes hardly recognisable in "kak, pfooi, bosh and fiety, much earny, Gus, poteen?" (125.22) (*kak vy pozhivayete, moy chyornyy gospodin?*).

The insect-incest section on pages 414-19 opens with a Soviet *imprimatur* "So vi et!," i.e. "so be it." The section contains a number of Slavonic words for insects, such as "pszozlers" (Polish *pszczoła*, "bee"), "Pschla" (Russian *pchela*, "bee"), "muravyigly" (Russian *muravey*, "ant"), "vosh" (Russian *vosh'*, "louse"), "motylucky" (Czech *motýlek*, "butterfly"), "babooshkees" (Russian *babochka*, "butterfly" + *babushka*, Czech *babočka*, "red admiral"), "jukely" (Russian *zhuk*, "beetle," German *jucken*, "to itch"), etc.[15]

In the late thirties (*Finnegans Wake* was published in 1939), the future of Europe was bleak and Joyce wrote in a premonitory paragraph: "Noo err historyend goody" (332.01). In this paragraph, it is for "Gestapose to parry off cheekars," where "cheekars" alludes to the Soviet equivalent of the Gestapo, the feared Cheka (*Chrezvychaynaya komissiya po bor'be s kontrarevolyutsiey i sabotazhem*) which in 1922 became the OGPU (*Ob'edinyonnoye gosudarstvennoye politicheskoye upravleniye*). OGPU is mentioned together with Cheka in "sleuts of hogpew and cheekas" (442.35) and again in reversal as "upgo, bobbycop" (338.32),[16] where "bobbycop" refers to the Russian governor of Finland,

---

15 Petr Škrabánek, "Arthroposophic Glossary for Ondt and Gracehoper (414.16-419.10)" [this article was accepted for publication in *AWN* just prior to the time of the journal's discontinuation, but has not been located among the author's papers (Ed.)].

16 Petr Škrabánek, "Cheka and OGPU," *AWN* 8.1 (1971): 13-14.

Bobrikoff, shot on Bloomsday, 16 June, 1904.[17] In "Chaka a seagull" (424.10), Cheka is greeted with a Nazi *Sieg Heil*, with a double pun on Chekhov: *Chayka (The Seagull)*. The sentence immediately preceding warns: "Tiberia is waiting on you, arestocrank!," spelling the Siberian exile for aristocrats and dissident cranks. Had Lavrentiy Pavlovich Beriya become the chief of the OGPU successor, NKVD (*Narodnaya komissiya vnutrennikh del*), earlier than he did (November 1938) his name could have been added to glosses on "Tiberia."

Slavonic languages other than Russian and Czech appear infrequently. There is a small cluster of Ukrainian on pages 340-41 and of Bulgarian on pages 346-47. The Polish material in *Finnegans Wake* amounts to about 50 entries.[18] For instance, "Prszss Orel Orel the King of Orlbrdsz" (105.11) contains a Polish pun on the name of the main protagonist named Earwicker or Pierce O'Reilly (French *perce-oreille*, "earwig"), here "Prszss Orel," where *przeszyć* = "pierce," and *orzeł* = "eagle" (found in the Polish national emblem). The whole phrase is another version of "The wren, the wren, the king of all birds." In another Polish example, the Dublin bookseller firm Browne & Nolan appear in the Polish armour: "given a bron a nuhlan" (352.16), where *broń* is "weapon," "arms" and *ułan* is a Polish lancer called uhlan.[19]

---

[17] *Census III* 34.

[18] W. Swinson, "Polish in *Finnegans Wake*," *AWN* 11.4 (1974): 65-67; Petr Škrabánek, "Addenda to Slavonic List," *AWN* 11.2 (1974): 32-33; Petr Škrabánek, "A Note on 'Polish in *Finnegans Wake*,'" *AWN* 12.6 (1975): 111.

[19] Those readers whose appetite has been whetted by these random dips into the *Finnegans Wake* treasure-house are strongly recommended to the *Annotations to Finnegans Wake*, in which most known glosses have been intelligently collated and brought up to date. Roland McHugh, *Annotations to Finnegans Wake* (Baltimore: Johns Hopkins University Press, 1980).

GAMBARISTE DELLA PORCA! (II)

Nathan Halper (*AWN* 14.1 (1977): 14) discovered the telescopic link of Giambattista de la Porta and Wellington with the jinnies' sexual warfare. This could be brought a step further. In Italian, "pig" is often used in curses, e.g. *porca Madonna!* or *porco Dio!* and also in expressions for "prostitute," e.g. also in expressions for "prostitute," e.g. *porcella.* Already in Latin *porcus* also meant *cunnus* (cunt).

"Gambariste della porca!" (9.35) contains Italian *gamba* (leg), *bariste* (barmaids), *arista* (chine of pork) and *porca* (pig, cunt). In other words, the "rinnaway jinnies" showed their legs (which is a slang expression for "running away"); they are whores of Napoleon's "royal divorsion." Pork-leg barmaids also allude to the park temptresses aiding and abetting in the erection of the phallic Wellington's "marmorial tallowscoop" in the Park. Since the Phoenix Park is also Noah's ark, they are Noah's birds: "The jinnies is a cooing her hand and the jinnies is a ravin her hair" (8.33).

Joyce used the obscene meaning of *porca* in several places, e.g. "What's pork to you means meat to me" (411.36) ("meat" = woman, whore, female pudend, coitus); "to break the porkbarrel seal" (212.23) (i.e. to deflower); "the porker barrel" (304.13) (i.e. vagina); or "this little pink into porker" (368.10) for coitus. In "Figura Porca, Lictor Magnaffica" (463.05), which possibly refers also to the figure on page 293 (which itself is a figure of a "fig"), "magnaffica" means "fig-eater" (Italian *mangiare*, "to eat"[1]; *fica*, "cunt") and "lictor" has here an appropriate meaning besides the official bearing the fasces. Joyce combines "pig" and "fig" also in 303.R3 "FIG AND THISTLE PLOT A PIG AND WHISTLE." and in "Phig Streat" (169.23) with obvious sexual connotations.

A well known Mediterranean obscene gesture (Italian *far la fica*, French *faire la figue*) appears in "Figtreeyou!" (9.13), also alluding to the cursed tree on which the traitor Judas hanged himself (*Matthew* 21:18-24; *Mark* 9:12-14, 20-24), to the victory at Vittoria, and to the Peninsular Marshal Victor.

Halper also suggests that for the meaning of the curse which follows

---

[1] Also L. *magna*, fem. "great" (Ed.)

the first: "Dalaveras fimmieras!" (9.36) one should look into the Iberian languages, because Talavera de la Reina is in Spain and Vimeiro in Portugal. In Spanish *fimo* = shit and *mierda* = arse. Perhaps the curse means something like *Del vera fimo mierda!*, i.e. "of the really shitty arse!," which would fit into the diarrhoeal context of the battles at Orthez and Toulouse: "Arthiz too loose!" (9.26), i.e. arse is too loose; and also with Cambronnian "Brum! Brum! Cumbrum!" (9.26). "Dalaveras fimmieras!" is probably the riposte of the runaway jinnies to the insult of "Gambariste della porca!"

THE CONDOM CUNUNDRUM OF A FRENCH LETTER

You're a nice third degree witness, faith! But this is no laughing matter. (522.27)

Joyce wrote *Finnegans Wake* to the Liffey from Paris for seventeen years. In a notebook, Joyce jotted down: "W.P. = a French letter which does not succeed in coming off, never quite"[1]. A French letter packed with seamen, such as Odysseus, Noah, Tristram and St. Patrick. The ancient mariners are navigating the flood of the Liffey in "Dublin's capital, Kongdam Coombe" (255.22).

As *Ulysses* was a day-book, so *Finnegans Wake* is a night book, a wet dream, "his last wetbed confession" (188.01). Joyce's death-bed artistic testament. Why should we "condone every evil by practical justification and condam any good to its own gratification" (142.22)? *Finnegans Wake* is a condemnation of con-domination of art, issued from France, the "condom-nation" (362.03). No art and part in anything short of l'art-pour-l'artism. *Finnegans Wake* is the climax of Joyce's *non serviam*. Molly's "yes" becomes Noman's "no." However, there is no "no" at the end of *Finnegans Wake*. "We may come, touch and go, from atoms and ifs, but we're presurely destined to be odd's without ends." (455.16). The book ends (and starts) in the middle of a sentence. "The letter that never begins to find the latter that ever comes to end" (337.10). We are hoping "for the latter to turn up with a cupital tea before her ephumeral comes off" (369.32) but it "comes to nullum in the endth" (298.21)— the end "the."

The last "the" is the dead end, oblivion, the waters of the Lethe (French *Le thé*, the tea. The "obliffious" (317.32) river of Death, the Lethe, meets the water of Life, *uisce beatha*, the Liffey, in the gap between the last "the" and the opening "riverrun." "What a neanderthalltale to unfurl and with what an end" (12.25).

In slang, "tea" means "urine" or "whiskey"—the dead water of live water, the Lethe and the Liffey. In the ballad "Finnegan's Wake," pissed Finnegan is revived by a drop of whiskey. The dual function of 'tea' in the circular design of *Finnegans Wake* is shown in this diagram:

---

[1] VI.B.12.126. Cf. *JJA* 31.

THE .... RIVERRUN

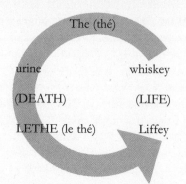

The (thé)

urine   whiskey

(DEATH)   (LIFE)

LETHE (le thé)   Liffey

The French letter of *Finnegans Wake* is signed by a stain of the bed-sheets. A tea-coloured stain instead of a signature. "The teatime stained terminal ... whether it be thumbprint ... or just a poor trait of the art less" (114.29). The last sentence of *Finnegans Wake* dissolves, thaws, melts (melt = semen). It is the end of the love-to-death song. Joyce's swan song. "If I seen him bearing down on me now under whitespread wings" (628.09) is an allusion to Leda and the swan. (French *cygne* "swan" reflected in "seen"). But the last "the," the capital "T" is also the initial of Tristan's name, when Isolde sings in the final bars of *Tristan und Isolde*: "in des Welt Atemswehendem All ertrinken," wishing to melt and drown in the breath (*Atem*) of the universe. She dies with the initial of her lover on her lips.

Joyce said to his friend, Louis Gillet, Member of the French Academy, that the last word of *Finnegans Wake* is "le mot le plus glissant, le moins accentué, le plus faible de la langue anglaise, un mot qui n'est même pas un mot, qui sonne à peine entre les dents, un souffle, un rien, l'article *the*."[2] Perhaps it also echoes the "yes" from *Ulysses*. "Thaw! The last word in stolentelling! ... Yes." (424.35-36). Strictly speaking, there is no "yes" in Irish, but the Irish tá melts nicely.

The stain of Capitol tea is also the sign and signature of Cain, whose sign was "tau," the last letter of the Hebrew alphabet. Cain is homophonous with German *kein* (nobody). To call himself "Nobody" was one of Odysseus's tricks. "When all is zed and done, the penelopean patience of its last paraphe" (123.04) weaves (Penelope =

2 Louis Gillet, *Stèle pour James Joyce* (Marseilles: Editions du Sagittaire, 1941) 164-165.

weaver) into the last word the Homeric allusion—Penelope's patient waiting for the homecoming of Odysseus.

Tea-coloured whiskey and urine are important ingredients in the central pun of *Finnegans Wake*. Joyce said to Frank Budgen: "The Holy Roman Catholic Apostolic Church was built on a pun. It ought to be good enough for me."[3] The pun, of course, was Jesus's play upon the name of Peter. "Tu es Petrus ..." (*Matthew* 16:18): "Thou art Peter: and upon this rock I will build my church." In *Finnegans Wake* it becomes something like this: You are Patrick and upon this sham-rock I will build my Sham-work.

In the second paragraph of *Finnegans Wake* we come across the words "tauftauf thuartpeatrick," a baptismal phrase (German *taufe* "I baptise"; *Taube* "dove"; also alluding to the baptism of Jesus by John the Baptist, with the dove of the Holy Spirit). In Irish it reads *Is tú art Pádraig*.

Note that in Irish, *art* means "stone," "rock." You are rock Patrick, a heap of stones, Croagh Patrick, The Reek, dead as a stone, stoned drunk. Drunk with peat-reek. ("Peat-reek" = whiskey distilled over peat smoke.) I baptise you with whiskey. I baptise you from the chamber pot. You reek with urine, pot-reek Patrick. Like Jesus you are being baptised in the Jordan (*Matthew* 3:5). ("Jordan" = chamber-pot.) The pea-trick is a sharping sleight of hand, using one pea and three thimbles. "A penny for him who finds the pea" (pee?). Using the three-leafed shamrock, St. Patrick demonstrated the Unity of the Holy Trinity. A pea-rigging trick! He is verily a Trick-Pat, "Trichepatte" (228.06), Nimble Fingers.

One of the models for *Finnegans Wake* was *The Book of Kells* edited by Edward Sullivan in 1914. Joyce always carried *The Book of Kells* with him on his peregrinations and he liked to compare *Finnegans Wake* to its intricate arabesques. Both books deal with the Resurrection—of Finnegan and of Jesus Christ. Both books have four parts. Both books end in the middle of the 17th chapter. *The Book of Kells* tapers off with the word "Tui" the first word of the 6th verse of the 17th chapter of John's Gospel (Latin *tui* "thine"). The last word of *Finnegans Wake* is "the," the end of the letter, "thine," "yours sincerely." "T" is the 17th letter of the Irish alphabet. Joyce wrote *Finnegans Wake* from 1922 to

---

3 Frank Budgen, *James Joyce and the Making of Ulysses and Other Writings* (1934; London: Oxford University Press, 1972) 347.

1939, i.e. for 17 years. He published 17 excerpts in *transition*. The 17th (March) is St. Patrick's Day. Bloomsday was 16th June, the Doomsday of *Finnegans Wake* is the night after, the 17th of June. June 17 = John 17. Go to the john and pick a sweet pea. "I have finished the work which thou gavest me to do" (*John* 17:6), "for I have given unto them the words" (*John* 17:8), "and the world hath hated them" (*John* 17:14).

When you look at the "Tunc" page of *The Book of Kells* (*Matthew* 27:38), you will see a monster biting its own tail and squarely framing the page. The epitome of *Finnegans Wake*. "She bit his tailibout all hat tiffin for thea" (229.25). As at the end of every good story, they put the kettle on and they all had tea. In this sense, *Finnegans Wake* is a storm in a teacup, or rather a pot, whether a chamber pot, whiskey pot, or a tea pot. The brown Liffey is the Goddess (*thea*) in Resurrection. "The affectionate largelooking tache of tch" (11.19) is also the pair of illuminated letters on the *Tunc* page: *tau* and *chi*, "tch." (Hiberno-English *cha* = tea.)

The tea-like Liffey runs to the sea and the water recirculates back as rain. "Riverrun" = river-rain. In French, *rêver/rond* and *rêve/errant* subtitles the book as a circular, recurrent dream of an exile, Wandering Jews, wandering Joyce. Joyce dreaming about the Liffey, starting his French letter with *ribhear a rún* (my darling river), river who are a secret, riddle, conundrum (Irish *rún*, secret, riddle). In Italian, Joyce's household language, Finnegans are coming back to life (*riveranno*, "they will return again"), Finnegans are waking up (*riviveranno*) "they will revive"? *Finnegans Wake* is based on such puns and riddles.

The most famous riddle in history was the riddle of the Sphinx. This becomes in *Finnegans Wake* a riddle from the "Sphinxish pairc" (324.07), the Sphinx of the Phoenix Park. The Sphinx, like *Finnegans Wake*, throttled those who could not find the correct answer. "There is on earth a thing which has 4 legs, 3 legs, 2 legs, and has one voice. What is it?" 432? The date of St. Patrick's coming. Unity in Trinity? Three persons in one is the shamrock trick.

Oedipus got it right. The answer was—man. On all fours as a child, on two legs as an adult, with a stick as an old man. Oedipus should have known because his name contained the answer in Greek: *oida* (I know) and *dipus* (Two legs = man), i.e. "known-man." Ulysses was another "noman." This trick name was also contained in his name: Odysseus = Outis (Noman) + Zeus, according to Joyce's interpretation. When Odysseus blinded the one-eyed giant Cyclops, the giant roared for help, and when the other cyclopes arrived on the scene and asked who was murdering him, the Cyclops answered "Outis" (nobody, noman).

There is a parallel to the Noman and Cyclops story in Irish folklore. Curtin in his *Myth and Folklore of Ireland* (1890) narrated how Finn MacCool (the hero of *Finnegans Wake*) blinded the one-eyed giant Goll and then escaped from the cave between the giant's legs, on all fours, pretending to be a goat. Another noman was Jesus, who was a God-man. Jesus also escaped from a cave as a white Lamb. (Ulysses hid under a black ram). When Mary Magdalene and the other Mary came to the tomb sealed with a stone, an angel rolled the stone back and said: "He is not here, for he is risen." (*Matthew* 28:5). "Bedad, he revives, see how he rises, thanam o'n dhoul, do you think I'm dead?" asked Finnegan of the ballad.

In *Finnegans Wake* the Noman motif is incorporated into the Sphinx riddle, which is turned inside out. "The first and last rittlerattle of the anniverse" (607.11) is: "when is a man not a man?" (170.05). Obviously, when he is a "noman." The *nomen omen* becomes *nemo nemon*. The answer to the riddle was contained in the backward reading of Shem's name. "Shem ... went backwards," says *Genesis* 9.23. *Shem* in Hebrew means "nomen." Hebrew reads backwards, hence "nemon" (Noman).

The title itself contains the key to its riddle. Fin.neg.answa.ke. = find the negative answa, that is the key. The answa is "no." No! I will not return to Ireland. I will not come, says the French letter. "I will not serve whether it calls itself my home, my fatherland, or my church; and I will try to express myself in ... art as freely as I can ... using for my defence the only arms I allow myself to use—silence, exile and cunning" proclaims Dedalus proudly in *A Portrait of the Artist as a Young Man*. The Old Man did not change.

The beginning of the central pivotal chapter of *Finnegans Wake* opens with the cryptic words: "It may not or maybe a no" (309.01), hiding an acronym of I'M NOMAN. Why "noman"? Because Joyce was nobody's man. He was not going to prostitute his art in the name of anything.

Stephen Dedalus was James Joyce. The Greek Daedalus was a genial inventor and smith. "Smith" is the commonest English surname. "Smith" could stand for "anybody" or "nobody." *Daidalos* in Greek means "the cunning worker, the artist." Daedalus, like Joyce, was an exile and in the exile he built the Labyrinth (French *dédale*) to house Minotaur, a noman because Minotaur was a half man and half bull. "The neoliffic smith" (576.36), the "connundurumchuff" (352.34) (i.e. the Commander-in-Chief of Conan Doyle's conundrums) built another labyrinth. In the smithy of his soul, he built a sound labyrinth to be read and listened to, "the lubberendth of his otological life" (310.21), forged by "Smith onamatterpoetic" (468.10).

The pregnant Irish bull, "cunningly hidden in its maze" (120.05), is waiting for you within the *Finnegans Wake* labyrinthine condoms. You have been warned!

ST. PATRICK'S NIGHTMARE CONFESSION (483.15-485.07)*

In the preceding paragraph (482.29-483.14) we hear Mark Lyons from Munster playing Noble the Lion ("Le Père Noble" 184.34) from Caxton's *Reynard the Fox*,[1] as he presides over the animal court at which the cunning fox is accused of a number of crimes and murders ("the point of eschatology our book of kills reaches for now" 482.33). The smell of the fox still hangs over the farm ("He is our sent [scent] on the firm [farm]" 483.11). Before the Lion is "to twist the penman's [in charge of animal pens] tale [tail] posterwise" (483.02), another witness is called—the leopard ("Leap, pard!" 483.14). Before Firapeel the Leopard (Old French *fier a pel*, proud of pelt) can open his mouth, the Goodman Fox-Patrick-Tristram-Yawn-Jacob-Cain (Æ) makes a false confession to save his skin, because he is in a "wrynecky fix"[2] (480.23) and defuses the accusation by diffusing the issue. The lion mentioned his "post" (483.13), which the fox takes to be the letter he received as St. Patrick from the Irish and delivered to him in a dream by a certain Victoricus,[3] an angelic postman. The letter opened with "The voice of the Irish" ("the gist is the gist of Shawm" 483.03. i.e. "the voice is the voice of Jacob" *Genesis* 27:22). As he read the letter he thought that at the same moment he heard their voice in the Wood of Voclut (Patrick's *Confession*, 23), the voice of the wild Irish men, "the wolves of Fochlut" (479.13; Irish *faolchú*, wolf). The swineherd or shepherd (authorities disagree here) Patrick called "wolf! wolf!" once too often ("Folchu! Folchu!" 480.04; "Vulva! Vulva!" 480.07; "vuk, vuk" 480.31: Serbo-Croatian *vuk*, wolf).

"Fierappel" (483.15) also contains Italian *fiera*, wild beast, and *pelo*, hair. The appeal of the Irish is the appel of the wolves: "In his final

---

* I owe a special debt of gratitude to my friend, Professor Ken'ichi Matsumura of the Chuo University, Tokyo, for his help in deciphering Patrick's Nippon English.
1 Cf. "Caxton and Pollock" [Castor and Pollux]; Isegrim the Wolf (480 *passim*), Curtois the Hound ("courteous" 480.30), Cuwart the Hare ("couard," 480.27), Grimbert the Dasse ("Grimbarb," 480.24), Bruin the Bear ("Misha, 485.05, Russian *misha*, bear; "Bruin goes to Noble," 488.14 [Browne & Nolan]), etc.
2 *Reinecke Fuchs* by Wolfgang v. Goethe ("Wolfgang?" 480.36).
3 "Victoricus" in earlier drafts of this paragraph (Hayman, *A First Draft Version of Finnegans Wake*, 235.31) but later deleted.

desperate appeal to his countrymen, he begged them not to throw him as a sop to the English wolves … They did not throw him to the English wolves, they tore him in pieces themselves" ("The Shade of Parnell" *CW* 228). The fear of a furry beast. Jacob's fear of Esau. Cain's fear of Abel [fier appel]. "Fierappel putting years on me!" (483.15) alludes to the Four (Matthew, Mark, Luke and John), (German *vier*, four), whose querulousness, (Hiberno-Yiddish *feribel*, quarrel, trouble) makes him old. (St. Patrick wrote his confession at the end of his life.) And the leopard should stop pulling fox's ears!

"Nwo, nwo! This bolt in my hand be my worder" (483.15) is the first of several Japanese allusions inserted in the galley stage of the final version of *Finnegans Wake* (BM 47487.192v), setting the stage for the combat between the Japanese Patrick and Chinese arch-druid at Tara, further elaborated on pages 605-6 ("Barkeley the arch-druid and his pidgin speech and Patrick the arch-priest and his Nippon English" *L* I.406). Patrick's Book of Kells against Bulkely's[4] Book of Kills. St Patrick is a missionary bringing "gold tidings to all that are in the bonze age" (483.09), anteceding the Jesuits in Japan (*bonze*, a Buddhist monk). In his hand he wields a crozier, which is his warder, i.e. a symbol of authority. It is a dangerous weapon, which pierced the foot of the king Oengus ("luckat your sore toe" 485.09) during his baptism in Cashel. (The Buffalo Notebook VI.B.30.73 gives "spear in hand"). Since Patrick's answer revolves around the pun on I-eye, the spear also introduces the motive of blinding by spear (noman's motive from *Ulysses*, the blinding of the Cyclops), such as the blinding of Cormac mac Airt in Tara by Óengus Gaíbuaibhtech (= of the poisonous spear).[5] The bolt in hand is also the thunderbolt of Thor and the spear of Odin. The bolt in hand could likewise be the *digitus impudicus* gesture (thrusting the thumb between two fingers) or the real thing (Elizabethan *bolt*, penis). In Japanese, the character for "writing," "document," "book," "worder" (483.16) is 書, interpreted as a hand holding a brush writing on a piece of paper.[6] The Japanese reading of this character, *fumi*, appears as "fumiform" (413.31), "Nwo, nwo'" (483.15), besides imitating the West Munster pronunciation of "no, no" is Japanese *nao-*

---

4 Adaline Glasheen (*Census III* lxviii) quotes an unpublished letter by Joyce to Budgen, mentioning a Chinese Archdruid Bulkely meeting a Japanese St. Patrick.

5 John Francis Byrne, *Irish Kings and High-Kings* (London: Batsford, 1973) 55.

6 Len Walsh, *Read Japanese Today* (Tokyo: Tuttle, 1969) 64.

nao (more and more).

"I'll see you moved farther, blarneying Marcantonio'" (483.16). The threat was effective and Mark took a step back. Milliken's "The Groves of Blarney" served as a model for "The Bells of Shandon" ("bells of scandal" 483.06) by Father ("farther" 483.16) Prout ("prouts" 482.31; French *prout*, a noisy fart), and both are sung to the same air. Scatology from "eschatology" (482.33). The farting *marc an ton* (Irish, Mark the Arse) is another Irishman, Marcan mac Tomaini, the proto-Mark of the Tristan tale,[7] and the triumvir Marcus Antonius (Octavius appears as "octopods" 484.02 and Lepidus as "leposett" 484.33). However, in *Finnegans Wake*, Tom, Dick, and Harry ("Thugg, Dirke and Hacker" 485.11) are the ABC "Antonius-Burrus-Caseous grouptriad" (167.04) as well; the three sons threatening the old man Noe ("Nwo, nwo!"). Thus, not surprisingly, Brutus and Cassius lay lower down ("buttyr" 483.24; "fromming" 483.28, French *fromage*, cheese). The grandfather of Marcus Antonius was Marcus Antonius, one of the most distinguished Roman orators ("blarneying" 483.16; "worder" 483.16, "a verbose person" according to Webster's *Dictionary*). Marcantonio, *mercatus Antonius*, the merchant Antonio, of *The Merchant of Venice* by Shakespeare. The foxy Patrick shakes the spear against Mark the Lion, as in the Shakespearian essay by Wyndham Lewis: "*The Lion and the Fox.*" The next sentence, "What can such wretch [Russian *rech'*, speech] to say to I [me, Japanese *me*, I ("eye")] or how have My [Russian *my*, we; Japanese *mi*, self] to doom with?" (483.17) is also a galley addition (BM 47487.192v).

"We were wombful of mischief" (483.18) brings us to the beginning of the quarrel between the twins, Esau and Jacob ("hairytop on heeltipper" 483.19; hairy Esau and Jacob clutching Esau's heel of *Genesis* 25.25-26) who struggled in Rebecca's ("alpybecca's" 483.19) womb ("And the children struggled together within her" *Genesis* 25:22). The twins were much alike ("everliking a liked" 483.19; one "Sameas" [same as] the other, "an ikeson am ikeson" 483.20—Japanese *aniki*, elder brother, i.e. Esau), both Ike's (Isaac's) sons, and although one was good (am ik ... = St. Michael) and the other bad (an ik ... = Nick the Devil), they were exchangeable ("unwachsibles" 483.18; German *umwechseln*, to exchange) enough to fool the blind old Isaac. Jacob had to be Patrick's ancestor, because Patrick's baptismal name was Sucat, by which he signs himself off (485.07) and Jacob, the white sheep, on the

---

[7] Byrne, *Irish Kings and High-Kings*, 243.

run from the black wolf Esau, settled in Succoth (*Genesis* 33:17).

Rebecca, the "mother of thousands of millions" (*Genesis* 24:60), the mother of deception (*Genesis* 27:5-17), is one of the springs of ALP ("alpybecca" 483.19; *beck*, a small stream) in which dirty linen of all races is washed (Italian *becca*, garter; "unwachsibles" 483.19 [unwashable unmentionable underwear] the beginning of the alphabet. Various beginnings are alluded to by Patrick: birth, the alpha (and omega) of J.C., the beginning of the Roman Empire, the beginning of the Gospels ("initiumwise" 483.18; "Initium evangelii" *Mark* 1:1; "inprincipially" 483.20; "In principio creavit Deus" *Genesis* 1:1; "In principio erat Verbum" *John* 1:1; I'm *princeps* [abbot] = I am the alpha, the beginning).

Defending himself, Patrick-Fox accuses the animals of blasphemy by comparing them to leopards (the beast of blasphemy of John's *Apocalypse* "was like unto a leopard" *Revelation* 13:1-2) and lepers ("my leperd brethern" 483.21), more cunning than himself (Dutch *leperd*, cunning fellow). Patrick arrived in Ireland with a leper,[8] increasing later his leper retinue to twelve,[9] Lepers are unclean, but he is pure ("puer" 483.21), although he hastens to add that, as a boy of fifteen springs ("Puer ... of but fifteen primes" 483.21) he committed a sin of sins in his innocence ("ens innocens" 483.21; Latin *ens innocens*, innocent being)[10]. The "pure" boy was a stinker (French *puer*, to stink; "the evilsmeller" 182.17 [the Devil], the sheep in wolf's clothing), a counterfeit J.C. Another beginning, this time from Suetonius's *The Twelve Caesars*, suggests that another J.C. is meant here, too: "Gaius Julius Caesar lost his father at the age of fifteen. During the next consulship, after being nominated to the priesthood ..." In the Roman context, the "leperd brethren" could also be the Roman priests "leapers," who danced on the Ides of March. Further pagan practices are indicated by the word "trilustriously" (483.22; *lustrum* = a purification of the whole Roman people after the quinquennial census; note that 3 x 5 = 15) and by a pagan baptismal ritual: "to be upright as his match [his twin], healtheous [heal-Theos] as is egg [Isaac], saviour so [German *so*, as] the salt ["salt has lost his savour" *Matthew* 5:13, *Luke*

---

8 Whitley Stokes, *The Tripartite Life of Patrick* (London: 1887) 448.
9 Stokes, *The Tripartite Life of Patrick*, 228. Stokes comments that the devotion bestowed on lepers in Irish hagiography was possibly due to the belief current in the Middle Ages that Christ himself was a leper.
10 Patrick's *Confession*, 27: "*in pueritia mea ... annos quindecim ...*"

14:34] and good as wee braod" (483.22)[11] [German *wie*, as; wee brat; Dutch *brood*, bread].

Patrick is innocent of introducing pork to innocent Jews. "That innocent did I alter [altar] him towards hogfat?"[12] It was Abel who sacrificed the fat from the firstlings of his flock (*Genesis* 4:4). "Been ike hins kindergardien? I know not" (483.25) identifies Patrick clearly as Cain ("I know not. Am I my brother's keeper?" *Genesis* 4:9.) (Dutch *ben ik*, am I). Hogs also allude to Patrick's miracle on the pirate ship, when in an attempt to convert the hungry crew, Patrick conjured up a herd of pigs (*Confession*, 19). "Hogsfat" (483.25) is of course "the real school" (483.22), i.e. Oxford, but it is not clear who is from Oxford, the four accusers ("Ya all" 483.22; Anglo-Irish *ye*, you, Japanese *yo*, four) or Patrick-Cain (Russian *ya*, I). The phrase "a flare insiding hogsfat" (483.25) is a tautology, as "flare" = "fat inside the hog." Pig's lard is acceptable to the Christian Lord.

"O cashla" (483.26): Cashel, the capital of Mark's province, Munster, echoes Patrick's "O lord," in Japanese (*okashira*, chief, boss; o-honorific prefix) and the Anglo-Irish term of endearment *acushla*. Since *kashl-* is a Panslavonic root for "cough," (cf. "ahem" 484.36; "hastan" 484.06; German *Husten*, cough), Patrick appears to parody John's coughing ("coughan" 482.10; "plucher" 482.14).[13]

Patrick does not pretend to be God ("the first mover" 483.27; "father" 483.28), he is an inhabitant of this earth ("I am sure oft habitand [a candidate for the habit] this undered heaven" 483.26). "This undered heaven" is a literal translation of the Japanese *tenka* 天下 i.e. "heaven + under" meaning "the world." In the original Chinese, this expression (*tien-hia*) was used for "China" (cf. "under heaven" 110.04, among other names for China).

Still a child ("childehide" 483.31), in his infancy ("meis enfins" 483.27; echoing *mea infantis* from *Confession* 27), the little Patrick already thinks of the esc(h)atological ("scatological past" 483.36) end (French *mais enfin*, finally) when addressing his incredulous audience (French *mes enfants*, my children). First an altar-boy, he became a candidate for novitiate (postulant), before becoming a monk and receiving the habit

---

[11] "present at birth, match-upright, salt-pure, egg-healthy, bread-good" (VI.B.17.12); see Roland McHugh, *AWN* 15.6 (1978): 89.

[12] David Hayman, *A First Draft Version of Finnegans Wake* (Austin: Texas University Press, 1963) 235.25.

[13] "plucher (cough)" VI.B.6.46. (language not identified).

("I received the habit." 483.32) after he dropped the sinful habit ("I am sure oft habitand" 483.26 [I am off the habit]). His postulancy, however, was imposture. He continued to kiss pilgrims ("embracing a palegrim" 483.33), having no clothes on ("removed my clothes" 483.33; "sum a fame et nudate" *Confession* 27), showing his emaciated arse ("means minimas culpads" 483.35, French *cul*, arse). He baptised the palegrims (pale green is the colour of baptism) and he "verted" (483.32; French *vert*, green) them, making conversion cum perversion a virtue (French *vertu*, virtue, chastity).

This pious fraud Patrick stinks. "I ascend [scent] fromming [from me (Anglo-Irish for "my"); German *fromm*, pious; French *fromage*, cheese] knows [nose] as I think [stink]" (483.28). The phrase is followed by "a self a sign" (483.28), thus linking the nose and I ("self-sign = speaking of oneself" VI.B.30.73). In Chinese, the character for nose is used for "self."[14] Another Chinese expression for the first person singular is derived from the sign for "cocoon" (cf. VI.B.30.73 "cocoon sign and mouth = egoistic").[15] This is the key to "ick (ickle coon icoocoon)" 483.35 ("ickle" = "little" in children's speech; Old English *ic*, Gothic, Dutch *ik*, I; Irish *caca*, I shit; Japanese *ikko*, oneself; *-kun*, Mr.)

The "counterfeit Kevin" (483.05) is really a sham Patrick, a circumcised Jew ("circumcised my hairs" 483.33) with a tonsure on his head and arse. Patrick's tonsure brought him the nickname "Adzehead" ("you tripartite and sign it sternly, and adze to girdle" 486.28).[16] As Kevin goes through the Canonical hours of the Divine Office on pages 605-606: "matins," "prime," "third moon hour," "sextnoon," "ninthly," "vesper," "compline"), so does our hero: "Oh laud" (483.34) [the old man is deaf; Lord; Latin *laud-* praise; lauds are sung at dawn, the second, or with matins the first, of the canonical hours]; "primes" (483.21; prime = the first of the daytime canonical hours); "thrice" (483.31; terce or tierce = the third canonical hour); "sexth" (487.07; sext = the fourth canonical hour); "none" (484.15; nones = the fifth canonical

---

14 Chinese *tsi* 自 (self); Bernhard Karlgren, *Analytic Dictionary of Chinese and Sino-Japanese* (Paris: Librairie Orientaliste Paul Genthrer, 1923) 310. Similarly in Sanskrit, where *atman* means both "breath" and "self"; cf. "at man like myself" (481.23).

15 Chinese *si* 厶 private (from a picture of a silk cocoon); Karlgren, *Analytic Dictionary of Chinese and Sino-Japanese*, 241. This character + a character for "mouth" 口 = 台, meaning "I, myself," and pronounced in Chinese "i"! (Karlgren 79).

16 Stokes, *The Tripartite Life of Patrick*, clxxxiv.

hour); "vespian" (484.17; vespers = the sixth canonical hour); and "comeplay" (484.18; compline, French *complie* = the seventh canonical hour).

Of the Seven Sacraments, Holy Orders, Baptism, Confirmation, and Penance are particularly important in this passage, but Marriage, Extreme Unction, and the Eucharist are also alluded to. The penitent Patrick weeps ("offering meye eyesalt" 484.05; "my thrain tropps" 483.04; German *Träne Tropfen*, tear drops), hears the Scripture in the presence of *audientes* ("attaching Audeon's" 484.03; audiens = a catachumen in training), and prostrates himself ("prostratingwards" 484.04). He beats his breast and cries: *mea maxima culpa* ("meas minimas culpads!" 483.35). The smelly monk ("making so smell" 484.01; Japanese *so*, a bonze) makes himself small.

"[S]mell partaking myself" (484.01) again equates the nose and ego, but it is the dirty linen of ALP, the "unwachsibles," which is brought to the nose as well. From VI.B.15.151 we know that "Ⅲ ear, △ nose, ∧ taste, ⊏ touch, ⊣ sight." All the five senses appear here as "Audeon's" (484.03; Latin *audio*, I hear), "smell" (484.01), "mouthspeech" (484.02), "fingerforce" (484.02) and "meye eyesalt" (484.05; Japanese *me*, eye, female; eyesight; Iseult). After finding Iseult, it is easy to discover Tristram as well. He is the "Nephew" (484.09) of King Mark. Tristram is from Lyonnesse ("kalblionised" 483.22) and he was hated by the four Barons at Mark's court. Poor Iseult was thrown to lepers ("my leperd brethern" 483.21). The speaker is therefore Tristram-Patrick, since he defends himself against Mark Lyons.

Another Sino-Japanese pun on the first person singular is hidden in "mouthspeech allno fingerforce" (484.02). Joyce was first thinking about the sign 吾 ("five and a mouth = weak and defensive" VI.B.30.73, i.e. 五 five and 口 mouth → 吾, *ware*, I. However, he had to notice that a more complex character for speech 語, could be decomposed into the figure for four plus 口 (mouth), 言, and 五 (five) and 口 (mouth), 吾, and he used both ("fingerforce" = finger four, but also five fingers).

"I (the person whomin [womb; woman] I am now) did not do" (484.05) was entered in VI.B.12.14 as I (ten persons in whom I am man) alone did it." This entry was followed immediately by a list of various expressions in Japanese for the first person singular, now listed in 486.26, which are discussed below. This missionary of a dubious sex ("Mezosius" 483.32, Japanese *mesu*, female; *osu*, male), mock-meet

Mansuetus ("mansuetude" 484.03; British bishop from the 4ᵗʰ century, Mansuetus, "Meek") pretends to be J.C. "Ecce rex tuus venit tibi mansuetus, sedens super asinam" (*Matthew* 21:5); but he was more likely an Anthropomorphic, Audean heretic, contemporary to St. Patrick ("Audeon's" 484.03; also alluding to St. Audoen's Church in High Street (482.19) and Aed Donn, the king of Ulster).

The time is between Maundy Thursday and Good Friday. The psalm *Deus, Deus Meus* (*Psalms* 21) is heard throughout: *locuti sunt* ("locutey sunt" 484.07) *speravit in Domino* ("*Spira in me Domino*, spear me Doyne" 485.19) *circumdederunt me vituli multi ... quoniam circumdederunt me canes multi* ("circumdeditioned me" 484.24) during the Stripping of the Altars (and Patrick's). On Good Friday the Mass of the Catechumens takes place ("catachumens" 484.13; catechumens are candidates for baptism. Their head was already tonsured and washed in preparation for their Confirmation on the Easter Sunday ("circumcised my hairs" 483.33; this took place on Maundy Thursday), now the priests and ministers prostrate themselves in prayer before the altar "prostratingwards" 484.04). During the Mass, the prophecy of Osee is read ("he to say essied" 484.06, at least he tried to mumble it aside; French *essayer*, to try). After the Stripping of the Altar, the Washing of the Feet takes place ("Washywatchy" 484.26). The Mass is Black (vestments for Good Friday are black) and sexy ("my sexth best friend" 484.07; Patrick came to Ireland during the first year of Pope Sixtus III) and the celebrant is in his birthday suit ("quoniam you will celebrand my dirthdags quoniam" 484.13; quoniam = female pudend; celebrand = someone to be celebrated, modelled on "confirmand" i.e. a candidate for confirmation; "quoniam" can also be "a drinking cup" according to Partridge). Henry VI ("sexth") is lurking here too (note the contemporary War of Roses in "Rose Lancaster and Blanche Yorke" 485.12) since he was a nephew of the Good Duke Humphrey, ("Humphrey hugging Nephew" 484.09), and in the Roman context, Sextus Pompeius, surnamed Magnus ("Pumpusmagnus" 484.35). Patrick, the celebrant, babbles on ("blabber" 484.08; Old Irish *Babloir*, a nickname for Patrick—French *babiller*, babble,[17] Anglo-Irish *blather*, to blarney) between sobs (blubber = weep noisily; "snub" 484.11 = sob) the "sob story to your lamdad's [Father of the Lamb = J.C.; lamda, Λ = "man" in Japanese, i.e. Shem's story delivered by Shaun] tale" (486.01).

---

[17] Stokes, *The Tripartite Life of Patrick*, 569.

Originally Humphrey and Nephew was a firm where Shaun was looking for a post, but he was not successful as he was not Irish ("uppish & not mere Irish").[18] Patrick was a blow-in, a bloody foreigner, British and Roman, spreading strange doctrines, such as irredentism ("ersed irredent" 484.09; i.e. seeking Irish unity on an Italian model, and pretending to be more Irish than the Irish themselves (*Hibernis ipsis Hiberniores*, "none meer [German *nunmehr*, by this time; Dutch *meer*, more] hyber [hibernian; hyper; German *über*, above] irish" (484.15). He knows that the four are waiting to run their knives into him.[19] The "mockbelief insulant" (484.15) is afraid of the four Irish representatives, "erse-irredented" into one, Mamalujo (Matthew, Mark, Luke, John; "Momuluius" 484.11; Old Irish *Mumu*, Munster; *Lugh*, who blinded the Cyclopean monster Balor with a spear). This could be his deathday ("dirthdags" 484.14; Good Friday, when J.C. was pierced with a spear; Dutch and Scandanavian *dag*, day) "forasmuch as many have tooken [Japanese *token*, spear] in hand to [Japanese *to*, and]" (484.16). Compare with St. Luke's [Lugh's]: "Forasmuch as many have taken in hand to" (*Luke* 1:1) or in the Vulgate version: "*Quoniam* ..." Muirchú's "Life of Patrick" in the *Book of Armagh* also starts with *Quoniam quidem, mi domine Aido* [Aedh, cf. "Aud" (484.21)].[20] The obscene meaning of "quoniam" is attested in "her quoniam" (VI.B.17.44) and "the quoniam fleshmonger" (144.30).

"The spear in hand = emphatic" (VI.B.30.73), the pervasive Noman's motive, refers, in fact, also to the first person singular in Sino-Japanese: 我 interpreted as "two lances in opposite direction."[21] (The last entry in VI.B.30.73: "conceal = selfish and private" I cannot identify, though it should be another first person singular in Sino-Japanese characters: this appears after the second "quoniam" as

---

18 Hayman, *A First Draft Version of Finnegans Wake*, 235.29.
19 "But don't you remember," said Joyce to Italo Svevo, "how the prodigal son was received by his brother in his father's house. It is dangerous to leave one's country, but it is still more dangerous to go back to it, for then your fellow-countrymen, if they can, will drive a knife into your heart." Padraic Colum, in *The Joyce We Knew*, ed. Ulick O'Connor (Cork: Mercier, 1967) 79. Compare a similar sentiment expressed by Joyce in his note to *Exiles*: "A nation exacts a penance from those who dared to leave her payable on their return. The elder brother in the fable of the Prodigal Son is Robert Hand." *Exiles*, ed. Padraic Colum (London: Signet, 1968) 150. Cf. Hayman, *A First Draft Version of Finnegans Wake*, 235.29: "waiting your chances to run yr knife into me."
20 Stokes, *The Tripartite Life of Patrick*, 269.
21 Karlgren, *Analytic Dictionary of Chinese and Sino-Japanese*, 209.

"concealed a concealer" 484.14).

"Well, chunk your dimned chink" (484.15) refers to the Sacrament of Confirmation. Immediately after confirming the "celebrants" the bishop gives them a slight blow on the scheek ("chunk" → chuck) to give a pat, "dimned chink" → dumb cheek). "Chunk ... chink ... kinatown [Chinatown]" (484.15-16) parodies "Chin, Chin, Chinaman" (chink = Chinese, but also female slit) with its Pidgin English and the laundry theme: "Washee-washee once me takee washee-washee wrong"[22] (cf. "Washewatchy" 484.26). The Pidgin Druid is like a wasp ("that vespian," Latin *vespa*: 1. wasp; 2. one who attends the dead, one who carries out the bodies of the poor at night; French *vespasienne*, public urinal, named after the Emperor Vespasian). Patrick gets quite excited and the pockets of his suit ("comeplay" 484.18: French *complet*, suit) are full (French *complet*, full) of "come." The four are prancing around him: "ap [Sanskrit *ap*, water] rincer [rinse, prince = Matthew] ap rowler [ruler, prowler = lion = Mark], ap rancer [prancer = calf = Luke], ap rowdey! [rowdy, proud eagle = John]" (484.19).

"Improperial!" (484.20). Improperia (Reproaches) are sung during the Adoration of the Cross on Good Friday. There are nine of them altogether, and they have a common pattern: "I did something good to you and you did something wrong to me in return." Joyce makes up three new reproaches in this mode:

1. "I saved you fore of the Hekkites [Hittites, hekates (witches)] and you loosed me hind bland Harry to the burghmote [Old English *mot*, meeting of town freemen; Japanese *hari*, beam; Blind Harry;[23] Japanese *me*, eye: "Let me pull the mote out of thine eye; and, behold, a beam is in thine own eye?" *Matthew* 7:4] of Aud Dub [Oul' Dublin; Aed Dub, king of Ulster, killed Diarmait, king of Tara; another Aed Dub was a bishop of Kildare in the 7th century, cf. "Chelly Derry" 484.33]" (484.20).

2. "I teachet [taught, touched] you in fair [four] time, my elders, the W.X.Y.Z. [? waxies, wax-ears] and P.Q.R.S. [French *piquers*, pricks, piercers] of legatine powers [in both Roman and ecclesiastical

---

22 For full text of "Chin Chin Chinaman," including the music, see *The James Joyce Songbook*, ed. Ruth Bauerle (New York: Garland, 1982) 333.

23 A 15th century Scottish poet (*Census III* 119) + Henry II or Henry VI; "blond hair."

senses] and you Ailbey and Ciardeclan,[24] I learn [Bishop Laoirn],[25] episcoping me [Greek *episkopeo*, observe; Latin *episcopus*, bishop] altogether [= naked], circumdeditioned me [Latin *circumdedi*, I have surrounded]" (484.21).

3. "I brought you from the loups of Lazary [Bishop Lupus accompanied Bishop Germanus of Auxerre[26] to Britain to combat the Pelagian heresy; French *loup*, wolf; a wolf of Lozere;[27] Latin *lupa*, prostitute; Maison St. Lazare in Paris;[28] lupus is a skin disease similar to leprosy; lazars = lepers; Italian *lazaroni*, the mob] and you have remembered my lapsus langways [*lapsus linguae*, a slip of the tongue; Chinese *lang*, wolf]" (494.24).

"Washywatchywataywatashy! Oirasesheorebukujibun! Watacooshy lot!" (484.26) culminates the washing ritual, washing of the original sin by Baptism, washing of the feet and washing dirty linen ("Ir. [ish] wash on Friday" VI.B.14.112; "S.P. [St. Patrick] waterworship" VI.B.14.59). In Japanese, the first expression is composed from the first person singular pronouns, which could all be used by women, while the second expression contains only male first person singular pronouns. The third (*watakushi*) is neutral. There are many more expressions for the first person singular pronouns, some of them listed by Joyce in VI.B.12.14 and VI.B.30.72-75. *Washi* (used by senior or superior), *wachi*, *watchi* (a neutral dialect form), *watai* (used by prostitutes), *watachi* (a neutral form, abbreviation of *watakushi*). *Oira* (a variant of *orè*), *seshe* (archaic, used by samurai), *ore* (neutral or used to inferiors), *boku* (used by children), *jibun* (used by soldiers in the Meiji and Taisho eras), *watakushi* (used by both sexes, neutral form).[29] Another form, *temae*, ("temaye" VI.B.12.14)

---

24 St. Ailbe of Emly, St. Ciaran of Saigir, and St. Declan of Ardmore, three "pre-Patrician" Munster saints, here presented as 2 names, 3 persons, and 4 letters ABCD. 432 is Patrick's number. In the *transition* draft, Joyce originally used 4 names, including St. Ibar ("Ailbeybar and Ciardeclan," BM 47484a.254).

25 "Bishop Loairn, who dared to blame Patrick." Stokes, *The Tripartite Life of Patrick*, 40-41.

26 "S.Ger.L'Auxerr" VI.B.14.63, i.e. St. Germain of Auxerre.

27 Famous wolf of Gevaudon in the district of Lozere, 18C (*Larousse*).

28 A prison for women, originally "College de Saint Lazare," the headquarters of the "Congregation of the priests of the Mission," known as "lazarists," plundered by the mob during the French Revolution; also the order of "Lazarists" (*Hospitaliers de Saint Lazare*), from the time of the Crusades, whose chief duty was to care for lepers.

29 I am grateful to Professor Yukio Suzuki from Waseda University, Tokyo, the translator

appears in "time thing think [Chinese *tsien sing*, humble name]" (484.27).

"Mind of poison is." (484.27) refers to a poisonous spear, since Old Irish *mind* is a name applied to the relic of St. Patrick's crozier.[30] And it was druid Lucat ("luckat" 485.09) who tried to poison Patrick.[31] French *poisson* also comes to mind, as a symbol of J.C. ("Ichthyan!" 485.10; i.e. **I**essous **C**hristos **th**eou **h**yios **s**oter, Greek *ichthys*, fish).

"My ruridecanal caste" (484.28) identifies the speaker as Dean Swift at St. Patrick's Church, the itchy dean ("Itch dean" 485.03). *Decanus ruralis* (rural dean) was in charge of a rural deanery (*plebs*; cf. "Gags be plebsed!" 485.10). Patrick himself was "rural" ("I was once rustic, exiled" *Confession*, 12) and of an honourable rank ("I am the son of a decurion, but I sold my noble rank" *Letter to Coroticus*, 10). He likes to reminisce about his Roman origin ("Aye vouchu to rumanescu" 484.29; a pseudo-Rumanian phrase "I wish to remain"; Italian *romanesco*, Roman). He is "cut above you peregrines" (484.28; *peregrinus*, foreigner, pilgrim; Irish monks were famous by the peregrinations). "See the leabhour of my generations!" (484.29; refers to both the beginning of Matthew's Gospel: *Liber generationis Iesu Christi*, *Matthew* 1:1 and to "Now these are the generations of the sons of Noah" *Genesis* 10:1; Irish *leabhar*, book; labour).

The baptismal motif returns with the dove of the Holy Spirit ("the spirit is form the upper circle" 484.31; "And Jesus, when he was baptised, went up straightway out of the water; and lo, the heavens were opened unto Him, and He saw the Spirit of God descending like a dove" *Matthew* 3:16). "And lo, a voice from heaven" *Matthew* 3:17, is paraphrased as "Theophrastius" (483.30; Theophrastus was a pupil of Aristotle; the name could be translated as "Divine Speaker"). Similarly, "Spheropneumaticus" (484.30) has both Aristotelian (heavens as series of concentric circles; pneuma = vital spirit) and Christian connotations (the *Pneuma*, the Holy Spirit, in the New Testament).

"I am of ochlocracy [= mob rule] with Prestopher ["Presto" was the name of Swift in *Journal to Stella*; presbyter, Christopher] Palumbus [Latin *palumbus*, wood-pigeon; *columbus*, dove, pigeon, St. Columba, Christopher Columbus] and Porvis Parrio [carrion crow, Latin *corvus*, raven, crow; Latin *parvus*, low, humble; "pariah" = member of a low

of *Finnegans Wake* into Japanese, for a helpful letter, explaining the subtle nuances of these forms.

30 Stokes, *The Tripartite Life of Patrick*, cxciv, 86.
31 *Census III* 174.

caste, outcast]" (484.31). The birds are the birds of Noah—raven and dove—corresponding to the colour of the passage, which is black-and-white (e.g., "Ailbey [Latin *albus*, white] and Ciar" 484.23 [Irish *ciar*, black] with the Irish iridescent green ("ersed irredent" 484.09; Patrick's green and Noah's rainbow).

"Soa koa Kelly Terry per Chelly Derry lepossette" (484.32) contains Pidginised Paternoster ("sicut in caelo et in terra" *Matthew* 6:10) and possibly also "the heaven and the earth" ("caelum et terram" *Genesis* 1:1) "Soa koa" anticipates the so-called "Sagart" (485.01: Irish *sagart*, priest) and his invitation 'suck it!' ("Suck at!" 485.07). Several Irish locations are hidden here: Kerry, Derry, Kildare (Aed Dub was the royal bishop of Kildare [Old Irish *Cille Dara, Cell Dare*] and Tara, the place of the encounter between the Pidgin Druid and the Japanese Patrick (Japanese *so*, bonze; Chinese *sou*, old man; blind; Japanese *kua*, Chinese *ko*, spear). A Terry Kelly was a Dublin pawnbroker.[32] The Easter bunny is the "lepossette" (484.33; Latin *lepus*, hare). "Chelly Terry" is also the Japanese cherry tree (cf. "japi jap cheerycherrily ... tree" 031.30-31), in Pidgin pronunciation of Irish *coll-dair*, i.e. hazel and oak. (In Irish, "hazel" is a symbol of Christ, *an coll cumhra*, the fragrant hazel = Christ.)

The Chinese first person singular pronoun *o* ("Ho" 484.33; cf. "High" 484.34 [I]) was inserted together with the Sanskrit *aham*, "I" ("ahem" 484.36; in earlier drafts "aham") and "watacooshy" (484.26), already around 1926 (BM 47484a.128). The god of postmen, Mercury (also a god of eloquence), identified with the Celtic god Lugh ("look" 484.33), is alluded to in: *"Eggs squawfish* ["sacred" pike, i.e. Sacramento pike with Easter eggs for menu] *lean yo nun feed* [?] *marecurious"* (484.36), paraphrasing the Roman proverb: *Ex quovis ligno non fit Mercurius,* i.e. you cannot make a statue of Mercury from any piece of wood, or, in Hiberno-English "no making of a wise man." We could not see the wood for trees. Can we find the Tree-stone (Tristram) in the wood of opposites, between the heaven and the earth, between Kerry and Derry (South and North), with the help of the Easter Rabbit? It sits opposite the tree ("lepossette" 484.33; *a l'opposite de*; Latin *lapis*, stone)! The tree from which Mercury-Lugh made his spear (Greek *doru*, spear).

The Gallo-Roman pair, "Pappagallus and Pumpusmagnus" (484.35)

---

32 *Census III* 280; cf. "to heaven through Tirry and Killy's mount of impiety" (206.19; *coelum*, heaven; *Mont-de-Piété*, French pawnbroking establishment).

is the Father of the Gaels ("primate of the Gaels" VI.B.46.29, i.e. St. Patrick) and Pompeius Magnus, the cock and the hen (Latin *gallus*, cock). The hen (French *poule*, hen) from Guinea (guinea fowl) pulls the pump and fills the pint ("a Guinea, gagag, Poulepinter" 484.18; French *pinter*, to drink immoderately) of Guinness. Thus "Pumpusmagnus" is "Pump-us-a-Guinness Magonius."[33] (And the cock happened to be sacred to Mercury.) Poor Patrick was surrounded with "*pueri Patricii*, the boys who accompanied him, being trained for the clerical state which they wished to embrace."[34] The Gaelic "Pappa" embraced them instead (French *papaout*, pederast). Pump was good but the sucker (*sagart*, priest; "Sagart" 485.01) was dry, as in the old catch-phrase.

Not surprisingly, his original name was "Sucat" ("Suck at!" 485.07). The druid cannot say r's, and so the Roman Catholic Patrick becomes "Lowman Cathlick's" (485.01), i.e. Cothraige, a slave to the four (cf. lowman = servant, slave),[35] though he was a free Roman citizen (*patricius*). In his arms he holds his "thrupenny croucher" [crozier for three pennies, but also the three-pin Devil's fork]" (485.17), "tripenniferry cresta" (485.02) of three ostrich feathers from the crest of the Prince of Wales, pretending to be Christopher or Christ Himself ("ferry cresta" 485.02). But the tail itch was the beginning of his end (Latin *cauda*, tail, end, penis) as his "caudal mottams" (485.03; Japanese *moto*, beginning) showed: "Itch dean" (485.03). There was something fishy in his claim to be Christ ("Ichtyan!" 485.10), he was neither fish (Prince of Wales—"Eich dyn") nor flesh (King of Bohemia—"Ich diene"), the exile from across the sea (Ictian sea = *Muir nIcht*, i.e. the English Channel, "fr'over the short sea" 3.04; cf. "Muir n'Icht" VI.B.14.73).

Since "Russian prays to S.P." (VI.B.14.41), the language method of Gaspey, Otto and Sauer (edited by Motti, "mottams"[36]) becomes a Russian gasp: *Gospodi* (O Lord!; "Gaspey otto") and *Tzar* ("sauer"). The 21st Psalm *Deus, meus Deus* resounds in Russian *Bozhe, Bozhe* (O God, God!; "boissboissy." 485.06; cf. "evangelical buzzybozzy and the rusin"

---

[33] "He had four names upon him: 'Sucat,' his name from his parents; 'Cothraige,' when he was serving the four; 'Magonis,' from Saint Germanus; 'Patricius,' that is *pater civium*, from Pope Celestine." Stokes, *The Tripartite Life of Patrick*, 17.

[34] John Ryan, "The Two Patricks," *Irish Ecclesiastical Record* (1942): 60, 251.

[35] "[H]e got the name 'Cothraige,' because he served in four households." Stokes, *The Tripartite Life of Patrick*, 17.

[36] *Census III* 102.

40.07). His name be praised! ("the first praisonal Egoname" 485.05; the first personal pronoun; I AM THAT AM; Russian *ego*, His; Latin *ego*, I). It was a Russian Adam who was the first to bear arms ("of the first was he to bare arms" 5.05; cf. "He was the first that ever bore arms" *Hamlet* V.i.33), Vasilii Buslaev.[37] Here Patrick-Hamlet's Eucharist dilemma is "eat or not eat body Yours" (485.04) ("To be or not to be" *Hamlet* III.i.56) Shake the spear. "Hastan the vista!" (485.06; Latin *hasta*, spear, penis; Spanish *hasta la vista* = au revoir; *vista*, sight) means "hurry (hasten) and blind him with the spear!" make a blind Harry of him ("bland Harry" 484.21). Hasten his doom! Down with Cyclops!

"In Moy Bog's domesday" (485.06; Russian *moi Bog*, my God) refers to God's Doomsday, i.e. Good Friday. Pierce His side with the spear! "My God's doom!" was a favourite exclamation of Patrick's.[38] "Moy Bog's" (485.06) is Ireland (i.e. my bog), specifically *Mag Breg*, the site of Patrick's challenge to Irish druids.[39] God's death on Good Friday secures resurrection of all on Doomsday, when Patrick will judge the men of Ireland.[40] Here Patrick's nightmare confession and his dream that he reads Shem's letter delivered to him by Yawn ends. "Aye vouchu to rumanescu" (484.29; I wish to remain), "Yours am" (485.05), "echo stay so" (485.04; Italian *ecco stesso*, here it is the same; I stay = I remain), *hasta la vista!* In this dream he is both Shem and Shaun (Yawn), as well as their father HCE—the shamrock Trinity, the false unity of False Reynard (= Unitarians in *The Hind and the Panther* by Dryden).

---

37 Petr Škrabánek, "Wassaily Booslaeugh (of Riesengeborg)," *AWN* 14.6 (1977): 100.
38 Stokes, *The Tripartite Life of Patrick*, 139, 225, 235, 467, etc.
39 "Now, when the high-tide of Easter drew near, Patrick thought ... no place fitter ... for celebrating Easter than in Mag Breg ... the chief abode of the idolatry and wizardry in Ireland, to wit, in Tara." Stokes, *The Tripartite Life of Patrick*, 41.
40 One of Patrick's four wishes for Doomsday. Cf. Stokes, *The Tripartite Life of Patrick*, 477.

NOTES ON 29 DEATH WORDS (499.05ff)

The exclamations in 499.05-499.11 are grouped into 14 echoic pairs. They imitate the practice of hired keeners at Irish wakes. "The mourner at the head [of the bed or table on which the corpse was laid] opened the dirge with the first note or part of the cry; she was followed by one at the foot with a note or part of equal length" (Eugene O'Curry, *Manners and Customs of the Ancient Irish* (London: Edmund Burke, 1873)).

Incomplete and scattered notes for this passage can be found in the Buffalo Notebook VI.B.4.81-108. The first entry is *Hmvs* on page 81 of the notebook, following a short list of Hebrew words. *Hmvs* are transcribed Hebrew consonants of the word for "death." On page 84, Joyce wrote: "29 Hemovs! 28 Hamovs!" he obviously liked the pun of "he moves" contained in a word for "death" and intended to use 28 expressions for "death," followed by the 29th "leap" of the corpse. On the following page 85, however, Joyce started to list expressions for "death" in various languages, but stopped short at number 14, though he already made a column of numbers on the left margin from 1 to 16. Perhaps he already considered the structure of 14 echoic pairs as it appears in the final text. On pages 104-108 of the notebook there are a number of expressions for "death" in various languages. Some of them are crossed out, but he also used several uncrossed expressions.

The following comments are based on this notebook and notebook gaps are filled by guessing.

1. Mulo mulelo!
Romani *mulo* "dead" (past participle of the verb *merav*). *Mulo* is also the Gypsy vampire (pural *Mule*). *Melalo* is the dreaded monster of Gypsies, which tears out hearts and lacerates bodies. (Jean-Paul Clebert, *Les Tziganes* (Paris: Arthaud, 1961)). In Anglo-Irish *muley, mooly* = "hornless," perhaps alluding to the dead member, or to the missing piece of the dead Osiris, "pending a rouseruction" (499.01). In Swahili, *malale* is "sleeping sickness." Finnegan has a kind of the Sleeping-Beauty disease. *Mulelo* = ? The notebook does not help.

2. Homo humilo!
Latin *humo* "I bury," *humilis* "humble" (i.e. literally "close to earth," "low," "earthly"). Hence "homo humilo," "man of earth," i.e. "buried man." *Humus* is decomposed organic matter in earth.

3. Dauncy o deady O! 4. Dood dood dood!
Dance for your (dead) daddy! *Dauncy*, dial. var. of *donsie* "unlucky." Dutch *dood* "death," "dead." In slang, *dead oh!* Means "in the last stage of drunkenness" (Partridge). *Dodo* is an extinct bird, also "stupid." French *faire dodo* to go to sleep.

5. O Bawse! 6. O Boese!
Irish *bás* "death." Flemish *boezen* "to booze." *Bowse*, dial. var. of "booze." Anglo-Irish *bowsie* "a layabout." Also "obese" (note that Joyce entered both "O Boese" and "adipose" in his revision of a *transition* version, MS 47486a.104). German *böse* "bad," "wicked."

7. O Muerther! 8. O Mord!
Spanish *muerte* "death," Hindustani *murdár* "dead body." German *Mord* "murder," in Old High German, *Mord* also "death." Also echoes of lamentation—"O Mother!," "O Mercy!" and Anglo-Irish expletive *melia murther* (*U.* 12.1345/329.13).

9. Mahmato! 10. Moutmaro!
Armenian *mah* "death" (VI.B.4.106: "mah"), Arabic *mamat*, mout "death," Egyptian *m(w)t* "death," Welsh *marw* "dead," Breton *marv* "death," Irish *marbh* "dead." Also *mammoth*, like dodo, extinct species.

11. O Smirtsch! 12. O Smertz!
Polish *śmierć* "death," Czech *smrt* "death," Russian *smert* "death," Italian *smorzare* "to die away." Perhaps also scatologic *smirch, smear*, and *merde.* German *Schermz* "pain." (God)'s mercy.

13. Woe Hillill! 14. Woe Hallall!
Valhalla (where Odin receives the souls of the dead), woe, howling, and ululation. Hungarian *halál* "death," Welsh *hollol* "dead."

15. Thou Thuoni! 16. Thou Thaunaton!
Irish *thuit* "died," *do thóin* "your arse," Greek *thuō* "I sacrifice by killing," *thánatos* "death," Finnish *tunteeton* "dead," *tuoni* "death."

17. Umartir! 18. Udamnor!
Czech *úmrtí* "death." VI.B.4.106 has "Pol. umart" (Polish *umarł* "he died": Joyce or the printer mistook the Polish crossed *ł* for the crossed *t*). Sanskrit *mrta* (VI.B.4.107). *Damnor* is, according to VI.B.4.104, Cambodian (Khmer), but I did not find it in a Cambodian dictionary. It gave only *dam* "to hit with a hammer."

19. Tschitt! 20. Mergue!
Annamese *chêt* "to die" (cf. VI.B.4.105: "Ann. chet"). Persian *merg* "death." Also puns on "morgue" and "*merde!*" Japanese *shitai* "corpse."

21. Ealumu! 22. Huam Khuam!
Turkish *ölüm* "death"; old transcription from Turkish written in Arabic letters was *eulüm*). Slang *lumme!* contracted exclamation from "love me!" Siamese *khuam* "death" (given thus in VI.B.4.105 together with Laotian *khuamtai*). *How come* (you so)? = "drunk" (Partridge).

23. Malawinga! 24. Malawunga!
VI.B.4.108 has Samoan *maliu* (= death) and *maliuga* (= arse).
Wing'd is a slang word for "drunk."

25. Ser Oh Ser! 26. See Ah See!
Chinese *sé* "death" (VI.B.4.104), in Morse (Latin *mors* = "death"): S.O.S., Slang *so-so* "drunk." Japanese *shi* "death" (VI.B.4.104, where also Japanese *sei-shi* "life and death" appears). *Séance* (of spiritualists to communicate with the spirits of the dead).

27. Hamovs! 28. Hemoves!
Hebrew *hamoves* "death" (Ashkenazi pronunciation). He moves! The candle of life comes back to life: "Ther's leps of flam in Funnycoon's Wick" (499.13). *Funny* = drunk. "The keyn has passed." "Keyn" = keen, king, key (penis). "Rouseruction of his bogey" ends the cycle. It is both the resurrection of the dead penis and of God (Russian *bog* "god").

29. Mamor!

One of the keeners notes the movement of the corpse, "Bedad he revives, see how he rises" of the ballad. She exclaims: *Ma mort!*

29 PACIFETTES (470.36ff)

Explanations of passages in *Finnegans Wake* supplied by Joyce in his letters to Miss Weaver are characteristically superficial, tantalisingly inaccurate, or perhaps even deliberately misleading. After all, *Finnegans Wake*, whether taken as a riddle or a joke, would lose its *raison d'être* by being explained. On August 8, 1928, Joyce informed Miss Weaver (*L* I.263) that the 29 words for "peace" incorporated into the parody of the Maronite liturgy on page 470-71 "are modeled on the following tongues and variations: German, Dano-Norwegian, Provençal, French, Greek, French variations, Malay, Echo, Gipsy, Magyar children's, Armenian, Senegalese, Latin variation, Irish, Diminutive, N. Breton, S. Breton, Chinese, Pidgin, Arabic, Hebrew, Sanskrit, Hindustani and English ... This word was actually sighed around the world in that way in 1918." However, as many readers have noticed before me, this list of languages is too short for the 29 words and thus does not quite match the text in *Finnegans Wake*.

The formal structure of "peace" words resembles a similar setting of the 14-pair antiphonal threnody on page 499. In both "the choir of girls split in two = those who pronounce Oahsis and those who pronounce Oeyesis" (*L* I.264) wails over the dead body of Osiris-Jesus-Shaun-Finnegan, one group standing at the head and the other at the feet of the corpse. Issy, the leap-girl; dismisses them by the last, 29th, word. In this context, "peace" is the peace of the dead (as suggested by Mrs Glasheen in *Census III* 293) but the peace words are also pieces of dismembered Osiris, bewailed and later reassembled by Isis.

However, as part of a mock-Maronite liturgy on page 470, the leap-year chorus-girls exchange the kiss of peace, the "pax," symbolised by an embrace at Mass ("exchanged the pax in embrace or pogue puxy as practiced between brothers of the same breast" 83.32).

1. Frida! 2. Freda!
"Freda" is a plate with an embossed crucifix, kissed first by the priest and then by congregation. German *Friede* (peace), Danish and Norwegian *fred* (peace) may possibly also pun on Joyce's own name, since German *Freude* = joy. Cf. "exclaiming one another's name

joyfully" (*L* I.264). "Frida" suggests "Friday" ("On Good Friday the body of Jesus is unscrewed from the cross ... while girls dressed in white throw flowers at it and a great deal of incense is used")[1]

3. Paza! 4. Paisy!

Provençal *patz* (peace), but Spanish and Portuguese *paz* (peace) is closer. English *peace* and French *paix* derive from Old French and Middle English *pais*, etymologically related to Latin *pax* ("peace," or specifically, "the kiss of peace"). Greek *pais* = child, virgin (of both sexes). Pidgin *pis* (fish) may allude to *ichthys* = Christus.

5. Irine! 6. Areinette!

Again, the expressions may be read as girls' names. Greek *eirēnē* (peace) is used by ecclesiastical writers for the "holy kiss," "kiss of peace." Irena personified Ireland in Spencer's *Faerie Queene*. French *reinette* alludes to *reine* (queen) (cf. "areine" VI.B.22, back cover recto (2)) and appears as Issy's epithet in "Reinette" (373.22) or "reinebelle" (527.30), the little rainy cloud before it becomes Anna Livia. Peacing (pissing) rain in associated with the rainbow the peace "heptarched span of peace" 273.04) represented by 28 iridescent girls of seven colours ("several successive-coloured serebanmaids" 126.19; "*his Arcobaleine forespoken Peacepeace*" 175.16). The source of piss is the kidney (French *reine*).

7. Bridomay! 8. Bentamai!

"My bride, bend to me" is an echo from the "Song of Songs" of Solomon. Malay *berdamai* (at peace, to make peace) is recorded in VI.B.22.150, but VI.B.21.153 has "bridomai," while the margin of the second set of galleys for *transition 13* (BM 47483.211) and VI.B.22.151 have "Birdomay."[2] Joyce preferred at the end a spelling alluding to Issy as a bride Bridget Brinabride. Dead Finnegan, however, looks more like the stuffed corpse of Jeremy Bentham, preserved in University College of London, than a bridegroom.

---

[1] William E. Addis and Thomas Arnold, *A Catholic Dictionary*, 10th ed. (London: Virtue, 1928) 505.

[2] All references to the Buffalo notebooks are transcribed from *The James Joyce Archive*, ed. Michael Groden, *et al.* (New York: Garland, 1978).

9. Sososopky! 10. Bebebekka!

This is the first of two successive pairs in which not the sound but stammering is imitated. The spelling "sososopky" could be a printer's error, since Joyce's notebooks and proofs give three times "sososokky" (VI.B.21.153, VI.B.22.151; BM 47483.211). Cambodian *sok(h)* (peace); cf. "soc" listed as Cambodian in the preparatory peace vocabulary in VI.B.22.150. Irish *sos* (rest, peace). In death language (Morse or Latin *mors*): S.O.S. "Soso ..." also alluded to Issy and her mirror image (French *sosie* a person's double, twin, as in "sosie sesthers" 3.12, or "I call her Sosy because she's sosiety for me and she says sossy while I say sassy" 459.10). The English dialect expressions *soss* (to fall heavily, a thud) and *sossed* (drunk) fittingly describe the fall of Finnegan, and the staccato hammering "sososo" echoes the banging of the body against the rungs of the ladder during the descent of the tongue-tied Finnegan. Hungarian *béke* (peace) is babbled by Hungarian babies and French *bébé* combines with *bécot* (little kiss).

11. Babababadkessy! 12. Ghugugoothoyou!

The kiss is bad—a hug to you. To avoid the dangers of abuse of the kiss of peace, the *Apostolic Constitutions* (viii, 11) ordered strict separation of sexes in church and later, to be safer still, an embrace was substituted for the old kiss.[3] Romani (Gipsy) *baxt, bacht* (luck, happiness) in "bababadkessy" puns on Anglo-Irish *Bad cess to you* (bad luck to you). "Ghugugoothoyou" is Armenian *xaġaġawt'yown* (peace) (cf. "khagagouthioun" VI.B.22.150).

13. Dama! 14. Damadomina!

Dama dama is the zoological name for fallow deer. This also alludes to the "Song of Songs," in which the bridegroom is "like a roe or a young hart" (*Songs* 2:9; 2:17) and his bride urges the daughters of Jerusalem (i.e. the city of peace, according to etymologists) "I charge you, O ye daughters of Jerusalem, by the roes and by the hinds of the field, that ye stir not up, nor awake my love, till he please" (*Songs* 2:7; 3:5). In a Senegalese language, Volof (or Wolof) *dama* = peace (cf. VI.B.22.150: "volof = senegalais dama"). Latin *Dominus* (the Lord) is here feminised as *Domina* (lady, queen). As the language deteriorates, the dames become blasphemous: "Damn the Lord!"

---

[3] Addis and Arnold, *A Catholic Dictionary*, 505.

15. Takiya! 16. Tokaya!

Lithuanian *taika* (peace). VI.B.22.150 has "japonais takiya." This could be Japanese *tokeai* (to restore friendship) but none of the usual Japanese expressions for "peace" fits. It is unlikely that Finnegan got drunk on the Hungarian wine Tokay in Tokyo. In Russian *takaya* (such a ...).

17. Scioccara! 18. Siuccherillina!

Irish *síoth*-char (peace-loving), *síoth* (peace), *cara* (dear), *socair* (at peace, tranquil). "Sugar" (Irish *siúcaire*) may be a euphemism for "sh.." Possibly also Laotian *śuk* (listed among peace words in VI.B.22.150). Italian *sciòcco* (fool, foolish), *scioccheria* (foolishness, nonsense), *scioccherellone* (fool). Cf. "sciuccherellina" BM 47483.211 and "sciocca siucca" VI.B.22 back cover recto).

19. Peocchia! 20. Peucchia!

Breton *peoc'h* (peace). The variant *peuc'h* is recorded from the provinces Tregor (Northern Brittany) and Vannes (Southern Brittany). In slang, *peach* = an attractive girl. In Czech and Slovak, *píča* (pron. peecha) = cunt. Polish *pokoj* (peace), Russian *s pokoem* (in peace), cf. "Spockoya" VI.B.22 back cover recto.

21. Ho Mi Hoping! 22. Ha Me Happinice!

Chinese $ho^2\ mu^4$ (domestic peace) and $ho^2\ p'ing^2$ (national peace), ho^2 (harmony), $p'ing^2$ (peace). VI.B.22.150 has only "chinois hoping." Combined with the preceding pair, we get a glimpse of *ecce homo!* from Good Friday. Pidgin *pinis* (end), hence "happenice" is also "happy end."

23. Mirra! 24. Myrha!

"Tchequoslovaque mir, bulgare mir, serbe mir" (VI.B.22.150) makes it impossible to attribute a single language for "mirra" and it can be only glossed generally as Slavonic. Entry 24, however, could be Ruthenian (i.e. Ukrainian) *myr* (peace). Myrrh alludes again to the "Song of Songs": "a bundle of myrrh is my wellbeloved unto me; he shall lie all night ..." *Songs* 1:13) and, according to Joyce, myrrh was used by the Maronite girls for pelting and incensing the body (*L* I.263). The words 23 and 24 also suggest "mirror," the double image of Issy. Myrrha, like Issy, had an unnatural love for her own father, Phoenix.

25. *Solyma! 26. Salemita!*

Solomon and Shulamite of the "Song of Songs." "Let him kiss me with the kisses of his mouth" (*Songs* 1:2) and, later: "Return, return, O Shulamite; return, return, that we may look upon thee" (*Songs* 6:13). Shelomith from 1 *Chronicles* 3:19 had two brothers like Issy, and Shelomith from *Leviticus* 24:11 was the mother of a man who blasphemed the name of the Lord and cursed, like Joyce or his protagonists. Salome was the mother of James and John (*Matthew* 27:56; *Mark* 40:40), i.e. of Shem and Shaun. Another Salome asked for the head of John Baptist. Arabic *salaam* (peace), *salaama* (peacefulness), Hebrew *shalom* (peace), *shelomith* (peaceful, love of peace).

27. *Sainta! 28. Sianta!*

The two penultimate languages in *L* I.264 are Sanskrit and Hindustani. Sanskrit *śānti* (peace) and Hindustani *shanti* (peace). VI.B.22.150 gives Bengali "sainta" and Hindustani "sianta."

29. *O Peace!*

"English = O for goodness sake leave off" (*L* I.264), i.e. "peace off" (piss off!). In slang, *piece* = a sexual partner, coitus, male or female genitals. Isis finally found the missing piece, according to the *Book of the Dead*, the *membrum virile* of Osiris,[4] the *pièce de résistance*. The date of the Armistice Day in 1918 was set on November 11, at 11.00 p.m. The date duplicates the renewal number eleven.

---

[4] James S. Atherton, *The Books at the Wake* (London: Faber and Faber, 1959) 19.

NOTES ON ARMENIAN IN *FINNEGANS WAKE*

The transliteration of Armenian which Joyce used in Buffalo Notebooks VI.B.30.19-26 and 46-47, VI.B.45.99-101 and 128-29, and VI.B.47.89-92 is inconsistent and inaccurate. More often it is an approximate phonetic transcription, using a French phonetic system, which would suggest that some expressions were supplied by an acquaintance with a knowledge of Armenian. The transliteration used in these notes follows the French system for Western Armenian in Frederic Feydit's *Manuel de langue arménienne* (1935; Paris: Editions Klincksieck, 1969).

The main difference between Eastern Armenian (spoken in Soviet Armenia) and Western Armenian (spoken initially in Turkey, and now also by the diaspora) consists in the exchange of voiced and unvoiced consonants. The transliteration used by MacArthur, Nersessian and Rose in *AWN* 13.3 (1976): 48-51 (MNR 1), and 17.2 (1980): 26-27 (MNR 2) was based on Classical Armenian, which is close in form to Eastern Armenian. Thus, for example, Տիկին (VI.B.45.128: digin) is transliterated as *digin* in Western Armenian and *tikin* in Eastern Armenian.[1]

8.28 arminus-varminus
In the military context, the phrase suggests the war between Arminus and Varus in 9 A.D. *Armina* was the earliest form of Armenia as it appeared in the Achaemenid inscription of Darius Hystapes in 521 B.C. In 1915 the Young Turks planned the mass deportation and extermination of what they called the Armenian "vermin."

38.11 (no persicks and armelians for thee, Pomeranzia!)
Prunus persica = peach tree; *Prunus armeniaca* = apricot tree; German *Pomeranze* (bitter orange).

69.08 Ere ore or ire in Aarlund. Or ... or
VI.B.45.128: oré or (au jour de jour); MNR 1: oré or (day by day) *ore or* (daily, day by day).

---

[1] See the French transliteration table at the end of this article.

69.08 Dair's Hair
VI.B.45.128: Der (Mr) Hair (Fr); VI.B.46.91: hair (père); MNR 1: hayr (father); *der* (Sire, Lord), *hayr* (father). Feydit in his *Manuel* writes that *der* is used when addressing *clergé séculier* and *hayr* for *clergé régulier*.

69.09 Diggin Mosses
VI.B.45.128: digin (Mrs); MNR 1: tikin (Mrs); *digin* (Mrs); the phrase may echo Franz Werfel's *Die vierzig Tage des Musa Dagh* (1933), the harrowing account of the Armenian persecution by the Turks. Additional Armenian allusions may be to *Moses* of Koren, the "father of history," who was the first Armenian chronicler, and to *Massis*, the higher of the two Ararat peaks.

69.09 horde of orts and oriorts
VI.B.45.125: oriort (Mlle); VI.B.46.89: orti (fils); MNR 1: oriord (young woman), ordi (son, young man); *orti, oriort*.

69.11 doun
VI.B.45.129: doun (house); MNR 1: toun (house); *doun.*

69.11 to see for menags
VI.B.45.129: menags (moi seul); MNR 1: menak (solitary); *minag* (alone); Joyce intended to convey the sense "to see for myself."

69.12 strikes a lousaforitch
VI.B.45.128: Krikor Lousaforitch; MNR 1: Lousavorič (Illuminator, title given to St. Gregory); St. Gregory the Illuminator was the first Armenian patriarch, also known as the Apostle of Armenia (c.260-c.330). The phrase indicates striking a "lucifer" match.

69.13 baregazed shoeshines
VI.B.45.129: chouchane (Suzy) (baregazed); MNR 1: barekeac (living a good life), Šoušan (feminine name); *Chouchan* (Susanna). Gazing at bare Susanna is the subject of the apocryphal biblical book *The History of Susanna*.

69.13 shoodov a second
VI.B.45.129: shoudov (vite); MNR 1: šoutov (quickly); *choudov.*

72.11 Armenian Atrocity
A reference to Armenian massacres by the Turks.

75.02 Ariuz forget Arioun
VI.B.46.92: airuz (lion); 91: arioun (sang); MNR 1: ar̄uyc (lion), ar̄yun (blood); *ar̄iudz, ariun.*

75.02 Boghas the baregams
VI.B.46.89: Boghos; MNR 1: Połos (Paul); VI.B.46.90: baregam (ami); MNR 1: barekam (neighbour); *Boghos; paregam* (friend) [with one exception—see note on 107.22, below—Joyce transcribes the letter *Ƿ* always as b].

75.03 Marmarazelles from Marmeniere
VI.B.46.90: marmarazan (corporel); MNR 1: marmnakan (corporal); *marmnasēr* (carnal, sensual, voluptious), *marmin* (flesh, body). "Mademoiselle from Armentières" was a song of the British Soldiers. (Two gamy versions are printed in *Bawdy Barrackroom Ballads* by H. de Witt (London: Tandem, 1970)). The old whores have bare gums and bare gams (= legs).

107.19 kidooleyoon
VI.B.46.91: kidoutioun (science); MNR 1: gidut'yun (knowledge); *kidout̄iun* (science).

107.19 madernacerution
VI.B.46.89: madenakroutioun; MNR 1: matenagrut'yun (bibliography); *Madenakrout̄iun* (literature).

107.19 lour
VI.B.46.91: lour (nouvelles); MNR 1: lur (news); *lour.*

107.20 so herou from us
VI.B.46.91: herou (loin); MNR 1: her̄u (distant); *her̄ou* (far)

107.20 kitchernott
VI.B.46.91: kichère (de nuit) kicher (nuit); MNR 1: gišer (night); *kicher*

(night), *kicheri* (nightly); Italian *notte* (night), Old Norse *nött* (night)

107.21 *hasard*
VI.B.46.91: hasar (1000); MNR 1: hazar (thousand); *hazar*

107.22 *Zerogh*
VI.B.46.91: zerogh (jour); MNR 1: tserek (day); *zereg*

107.22 *pou owl giaours*
VI.B.46.89: pou (owl); MNR 1: bu (owl); *pou*; VI.B.46.89: gouir (aveugle); MNR 1: kouyr (blind); *gouyr;* giaour comes from Turkish *gâvur* (infidel), a term likely to be applied by the Turks to the Armenians; "pou owl" approximates a drawled pronunciation of "poor old ..."

107.23 *aysore today*
VI.B.46.90: "aisor (aujourd'hui)"; MNR 1: "aysor (today)"; *aysör;* Joyce's eye was sore when he wrote this.

107.23 *Amousin*
VI.B.46.89: amousin (mari); MNR 1: amusin (husband); *amousin;* also slurred English *amazin'.*

107.36 *baroun lousadoor*
VI.B.46.89: barun [illegible entry]; MNR 1: paren (reserve food stock); VI.B.46.89: lousador (lumineux); MNR 1: lousavor (bright); *baron* (Mr), *lousavor* (bright), *lousadarr* (luminous); *lousadour* (the giver of light); i.e. Mr Lucifer.

107.36 *hallhagal*
VI.B.46.89: hagal (play); MNR 1: xałal (play); *khagal* (to play); overtones of Hell and Valhalla.

108.17 *Kinihoun or Kahanan*
VI.B.46.92: kini (vin); 90: kahana (prêtre); MNR 1: gini (wine); kahana (priest); *kini* (wine); *kinedoun* (tavern); *kahana:* it seems the passage refers to Jesus's first miracle at the wedding in Cana, changing water into wine (*John* 2:3-10).

108.17 giardarner or mear measenmanonger
VI.B.46.90: giardar (habile); 91: misen (viande); 91: manoug (garçon); MNR 1: čarter (clever, albe); misen (meat); manuk (child); *djardar, mis-en* (the meat); *manoug.*

108.18 darnall
VI.B.46.90: darnal (retourner); MNR 1: darnal (return); *tarnal* (to return) [this is the only example of Joyce transcribing 𝟳 as "d"].

108.19 at the barbar of the Carrageehouse
VI.B.46.90: barbar (language); MNR 1: barbar (dialect); *parpar* (speech, language, voice, dialect); VI.B.46.90: karagiour (beer); MNR 1: garejur (beer); *karedchour* (beer).

108.27 glorisol
VI.B.46.89: glor (rond), sox (oignon); MNR 1: glor (round); Sox (onion); *glor, sokh.*

108.27 Aludin's Cave
VI.B.46.89: abadin (refuge); MNR 1: apaven (refuge); *abaodan* (asylum, refuge); *abauēn* (asylum, refuge).

108.28 cagacity
VI.B.46.89: cagac (ville); MNR 1: k'ałak' (town); *kaghak.*

113.03 Grabar
The literary language, used between the 5th and 19th centuries by the Armenian writers and poets, and retained for use in Church.

113.03 old armeanium adamologists
The old etymologists of Armenian were German (French *allemand*, German). Adam of the Garden of Eden was Armenian.

113.04 Dariaumaurius and Zovotrimaserovmeravmerouvian
VI.B.46.92: zov (mer), 91: maserov (hair), 90: merav (il est mort); MNR 1: mazerov (by the hair); merav (he is dead); *zov* (sea), *mazerov* (with hair); *metav* (he, she, it is dead). Persian *daryā* (sea), *muye* (hair). One of the "old German etymologists," Georg Curtius (*Principles of Greek*

Etymology, trans. A.S. Wilkins and E.B. England, vol. 1 (London: 1875) 413, makes a connection between "sea" and "death": Latin *mare* (sea), Irish *muir* (sea) with Latin *morior* (to die), Irish *marbh* (dead) etc. In the second edition of *Esquisse d'une grammaire compareé de l'Arménien classique* (1936), A. Meillet thanks Father Mariès ("maurius") who devoted a large part of his life to Armenian. The first time we hear of Armenia (Armina) as the name of the country is in the Persian King Darius Hystapes' inscription on the cliff at Behistun from the 6th century.

181.22 not even the Turk, ungreekable in purscent of the armenable
A reference to foxhunting: "the unspeakable in full pursuit of the uneatable" (Oscar Wilde), and to the hunting of Armenians by the Turks.

182.12 a ghinee a ghirk
VI.B.45.128: ghine (price), ghirk (book); MNR 1: gine (price), girk' (book); *kine* (the price), *kirk* (book).

190.25 as popular as an armenial with the faithful
A reference to the enmity between the Christian Armenians and the Muslim Turks.

240.27 Anaks ... centy procent Erserum spoking
Anak was the father of St. Gregory the Illuminator. Erzerum was an important Armenian centre. Greek *anax* (king, lord).

241.32 osghirs
VI.B.45.128: osghi (gold); MNR 1: oski (gold); *osgi*.

242.02 Adenoiks
VI.B.45.128: adenok (jadis); MNR 1: atenok' (formerly); *adenok*.

242.09 nerses nursely, gracies to goodness
VI.B.45.128: Nerses gracious; MNR 1: Nerses the Gracious (Arm. poet). Nerses also the name of the 69th patriarch of Armenia (1098-1173): 11th *EB*, "Armenian Church": "On the death of Nerses the right of saying grace at the royal meals, which was the essence of the catholicate, was transferred...to the priestly family of Albianus, and

thenceforth no Armenian catholicus went to Caesarea for ordination."

243.10 zoravarn
VI.B.45.128: zoravar (gen.); MNR 1: zoravar (general, commander); *zōravar*, cf. VI.B.30.19: saravor (powerful); *zaurauor*.

243.33 Hrom
VI.B.45.128: Hrom; 129: Hroma on Kagakik; MNR 1: Hrom (Rome); *Hrom*, *kaghakik* (small town); cf. 108.28.

267.F6 All abunk for Tararararat!
An allusion to Noah's landing on Ararat.

296.04 by Araxes, to mack a capital
VI.B.45.99: Araxes; MNR 1: Arax (name of river; feminine name); The river Araxes (Aras, *Eraskh*) is for Armenians what the Liffey is for Dubliners. The Araxes rises south of Erzerum and flows east through Armenia. On an island in the river stood Artaxata, the capital of Armenia from 180 B.C. to 50 A.D.

296.08 Airmienious
Greek *Armenios* (Armenian).

296.19 yaghags hogwarts
VI.B.45.99: Yaghags Hogwatz; 100: Yaghags (soul), hogwatz (illegible word) hogwats (soul); MNR 1: yałags (for, about); yok'voc (for the souls); *yaghaks* (concerning, on, upon the subject of); *hokuots* (souls, gen. dat. abl.); "On the Subject of Souls" (an Armenian theological tractate?).

296.20 arrahquinonthiance
VI.B.45.100: arhaqinonthiantz (virtue); MNR 1: ařakinout'yanc (virtue); *ařakinoutiun* (virtue).

296.23 bironthiarn and hushtokan hishtakatsch
VI.B.46.101: bnouthian hrshtakaz (nature of angels); 100: hereshtakatz; 99: hereshtakatz; MNR 1: transcribed the entry as "bironthian (nation) hreshtakatz (of angels)," identifying "hreštak" (angel) but failed to find

the equivalent for "nation." *Bnoutiun* is the key word in Armenian theology. "The chief, and almost the only cause of the occasional discussions, occurring betwixt the Greeks and Armenians is the ambiguity of the Armenian word *bnoutian* (Greek *physis*, nature)" (Archdeacon Dowling, *The Armenian Church* (London: 1910) 61.) The Armenian Church belongs to the Monophysite churches who rejected the definition of the Council of Chalcedon on the two "natures" of Christ. *Hreshtak* (Classical Armenian transcription) was a good spirit in pre-Christian Armenia. The term was later adopted to mean an angel. *Hreshtak-atz* means "of the angels."

296.F3 *Thargam*

VI.B.45.99: Jacobis thargman; VI.B.45.91: targman (interpreter); MNR 1: targman (interpreter); *tarkman* (translator, interpreter), cf. 340.32 dragoman (i.e. an interpreter and guide in the Middle East).

296.F3 *Suksumkale!*

VI.B.45.99: suk sumkale; MNR 1: Suk Sum Kale (Turkish place name); Sukhumi (Sukhum-kaleh) is a seaport on the Black Sea in what is now Georgia. It had an Armenian population, as also Batum (Batumi), another Georgian Black Sea port (*cf.* "batom" 296.06). Armenian *souk* (devil), Turkish *kale* (fortress).

321.23 *giel as gail*

VI.B.46.89: giel (hâte); 92: gail (loup); MNR 1: gayl (wolf); Armenian *djeb* (haste) was probably the word which Joyce copied and transcribed as "gieb," later on mistaking "b" for "l"; *kayl* (wolf).

321.23 *Odorozone, now ourmenian servent*

VI.B.46.92: odarazan (étranger); MNR 1: otarakan (stranger); *ōdaradzin* (stranger); the Serpent in the Armenian Garden of Eden.

337.32 *We want Bud Budderly boddily.*

VI.B.30.46: beat/batter(d) budrel badel badrel baderel; *badrel* (to tear apart), *bardel* (to beat, conquer).

338.23 *Satenik ... Siranouche*

VI.B.46.91: Satenik Siranouche; MNR 1: feminine names; Sathenik was an Armenian queen in the first century A.D. She has been celebrated by Armenian poets and historians.

339.29 Erminia's capecloaked hoodoodman!
V. Nersessian in a note to MNR 2 suggests that this phrase refers to the hood-like head-dress of *vardapets* (Armenian priests).

340.34 Zaravence
VI.B.46.92: zara (servant); MNR 1: caȓa (servant); *dẓaȓa*; i.e. "ourmenian servent" (321.23).

344.01 unglucksarsoon
VI.B.46.90: sarsoun (frisson); MNR 1: sarsoun (shiver); *sarsoun*; "sarsoun" may allude to the Armenian epic "David of Sassoun" and possibly to the well-publicised Sasun massacre of Armenians by Turks in 1894.

344.31 meac Coolp, Arram of Eirẓerum
An Armenian disguise of Finn MacCool. Kulp, in the Ararat region, was a place with famous salt mines exploited from ancient times. VI.B.46.92: Aram; MNR 1: Aram (masculine name); Aram was the sixth in succession from the mythical Haik, the first to assume the title of King and to assert his authority over the whole of Armenia (see W. St.Clair-Tisdall, *The Conversion of Armenia to the Christian Faith* (London: 1897)).

344.32 Deer Dirouchy
VI.B.46.92: Der Dirouhi; MNR 1: Der Dirouhi (expression used in addressing a priest and his wife); *Der:* see 69.08; *Dirouhi:* the feminine form of *Der*, also a feminine Christian name.

344.33 Saur of all the Haurosians
VI.B.46.92: saur (épée), haur (feu); MNR 1: saur (sword), hur (fire); *sour* (sword); *hour* (fire); Haroutian is a Christian name, e.g. Haroutioun Vehabedian, Armenian patriarch of Jerusalem, or Harootheun Argerian, the Armenian linguist who taught Lord Byron Armenian. The name means "resurrection."

344.34 arge
VI.B.46.92: arge (ours); MNR 1: arj(e) (a bear); *ardch.*

345.01 my Irmenial hairmaierians ammongled his Gospolis fomiliours
MNR 1: hayrmen (the Lord's Prayer); *hayrmer* (lit. Our Father);
VI.B.46.91: Gospolis Bolis; *Polis* (Istanbul); Church Slavonic *Gospodi
pomilui* (Kyrie eleison): Armenian *vs* Orthodox Church.

345.02 achaura moucreas
VI.B.46.89: axaur (triste); MNR 1: txour (sad, morose); *dkhour* (sad);
Hiberno-English *achara machree* (my darling).

346.20 A hov and az on and off like a gow!
VI.B.46.92: hov (vent), zov (mer), gov (cow); MNR 1: hov (breeze), cov
(sea), kov (cow); *hov, dzov, gov.*

346.23 hay
hay (Armenian); Armenians call themselves "Hay" (pl. "Hayk") after
their traditional first hero, Haig, son of Togarmah, grandson of Japhet
(*Genesis* 10:3).

347.06 hegheg
VI.B.46.89: hegheg (torrent); MNR 1: hełeł (torrent, flood); *hegheg;* cf.
"hooghoog" (69.07).

348.36 ohosililesvienne biribarbebeway
VI.B.46.89: leseu (lesvi) langue; 91: xosel (parler); MNR 1: xosel (to
speak), lezou (language); *khōsel, lezou* (pronounced: lesvi); cf. "barbar"
(109.19).

350.02 garerden
VI.B.46.91: garer (tree); MNR 1: dzar (tree); *dzar.*

353.15 Unknun!
oungn (ear); Classical Armenian transcription: *unkn.*

354.20 oudchd
VI.B.46.89: ouxd (voeu); MNR 1: uxt (vow); *oukhd.*

354.20 astoutsalliesemoutioun
VI.B.46.89: asdouzaliamoutioun; MNR 1: Asdouac (God); *Asdouadz* (God); this Armenian word remains unexplained.

354.21 cococancancacacanotioun
VI.B.22.150: khagagouthioun (paix); VI.B.46.90: xagagoutioun (paix); MNR 11: xałałat'yun (peace); *khagaghhoutiun*; cf. "Ghugugoothoyou!" (471.02), and "Hagakhroustioun!" (396.19).

387.10 yaghoodurt
VI.B.46.92: yaghoodourt; VI.B.30.46: yaghoodurt (people); MNR 2: žołovourd (people); *joghovourt* (people); English readings of "yaghoodurt" give "Yahoo-dirt" and "yoghourt." Yoghourt (yogurt) is a Turkish word for fermented cow's-milk. Another type of fermented milk popular in central Asia is koumiss, prepared from mare's-milk, which could be the yogurt of the Yahoos.

387.11 hayastdanars
VI.B.45.128: Haiasdani; *Hayasdan* (Armenia).

388.28 gloriaspanquost
VI.B.30.26: Park glory; MNR 2: p'ark' (glory); *park*.

388.28 on anarxaquy out of doxarchology
VI.B.30.24: naxaka (president); doxarca (illegible word); MNR 2: naxagah (chairman); *nakhakah* (president, chairman); "doxarca" remains unexplained.

389.22 gaze, gagagniagnian
VI.B.30.47: gagagnagnian; *gagaz* (stammer).

389.32 Mahazar ag Dod!
VI.B.30.20: mahaza (mortal), agdod (dirty); MNR 2: mah (death); ał tot (dirty); *mahatsou* (mortal); *aghdeghi* (dirty), *aghdod*.

390.13 Tarpey ... 23 terpary
VI.B.30.46: terpay (a word illegible); MNR 2: Ter bari (kind lord);

derbay (adverb); *terpay* (an Armenian grammatical category; a term for impersonal verb forms, such as the infinitive, or participles).

391.01 Erminia Reginia!
An allusion to Armenian regalia and regal ermine.

391.05 Hohannes!
VI.B.30.46: Hohannes; MNR 2: Hovhannes (John); *Hovhannēs.*

391.08 in chors, with a hing
VI.B.30.47: chors = 4, hing = 5; MNR 2: cors (four), hing (five); *tchors, hink*

392.06 hevantonoze
VI.B.30.21: hivantanoz (hospital); MNR 2: hivandanoc (hospital); *hiuantanots.*

393.29 dthclangavore
VI.B.30.47: ddangavor (terrible); MNR 2: vtangavor (dangerous, noxious); *vdankauor* (dangerous).

395.36 aragan throust
VI.B.30.22: aragan (masculine); MNR 2: arakan (male); *aragan*; hurricane (French *ouragan*) thrust of the male organ.

396.03 Alris!
VI.B.30.26: abris/bravo!; MNR 2: apris (bravo); *abris* (French *vives-tu!*); it seems that Joyce read his "b" as "l."

396.06 A mot for amot.
VI.B.30.23: amot (shame); MNR 2: amot' (shame); *amot*; Hiberno-English *mot* (girl), French *mot* (word); A girl for a word. Word for word.

396.06 meng, and douh
VI.B.30.47: Meng = We, Douh = you; MNR 2: menk̄ (we), dou (you); *menk, tou.*

396.16 hairyg
VI.B.30.20: hairig/father; MNR 2: hayrik (father); *hayrig* is a diminutive of *hayr* (father). It is an affectionate term, used in Joyce's time as an epithet of Meguerditch I, the Armenian Church leader.

396.19 Hagakhroustioun!
VI.B.30.24: haga = anti; 20: haigasian (corrected to "haikasian"); MNR 2: haka (anti, against); haga- (anti-); *krisdonēouťiun* (Christianity), *hayakidouťiun* (armenism): for Haig/Hayk see the note on 346.23.

397.21 xmell
VI.B.30.46: zmell = xmell = drink; MNR 2: xmel (to drink); *khmel.*

397.27 magnegnousioum
VI.B.30.24: mag = super; 22: megnoutioun/commentary; 26: megh sin; 26: mega malheur: 47: meg meg; MNR 2: mec (big), meknout'youn (commentary); *megnouťiun* (commentary); *medz* (big), *megh* (sin), *mega* (French *malheur!* lit. *j'ai péché!*); *meg meg* (one one).

530.36 tuckish armenities
An allusion to Turkish atrocities in Armenia.

559.25 Armenian bole
A colouring clay of bright red colour, used in make-up.

WESTERN ARMENIAN: FRENCH TRANSLITERATION TABLE

Ա	ա	a		Ձ	ձ	dj
Բ	բ	p		Մ	մ	m
Գ	գ	k		Յ	յ	y
Դ	դ	t		Ն	ն	n
Ե	ե	e		Շ	շ	ch
Զ	զ	z		Ո	ո	o
Է	է	ē		Չ	չ	tch
Ը	ը	ə		Պ	պ	b
Թ	թ	t̄		Ջ	ջ	dch
Ժ	ժ	j		Ռ	ռ	r̄
Ի	ի	i		Ս	ս	s
Լ	լ	l		Վ	վ	v
Խ	խ	kh		Տ	տ	d
Ծ	ծ	dz		Ր	ր	r
Կ	կ	g		Ց	ց	ts
Հ	հ	h		Ւ	ւ	u
Ձ	ձ	tz		Փ	փ	p̄
Ղ	ղ	gh		Ք	ք	k̄
				Օ	օ	ō

Adapted from Frederic Feydit, *Manuel de langue arménienne* (1935; Paris: Éditions Klincksieck, 1969).

NOTES ON RUTHENIAN IN II.3

A cluster of Ukrainian words in II.3, heralded by "Malorazzias" (338.22) (VI.B.46.37 "malarossia") was added to a 1937 draft (BM 47480.40v—47480.44v). The Russian *Malorossiya*, literally "Little Russia," was a term used by the Muscovites for the Ukraine from the 13th-14th centuries onwards, to put it in its place beside "Great Russia." In the Wakean literature there is some confusion as to the meaning of "Ruthenian": for example, Louis Mink stated that "The Ruthene language resembles Ukrainian."[1] The Ruthenian language is, in fact, a synonym for the Ukrainian language. *Rutheni* (or *Ruteni*) was the medieval Latin name for the inhabitants of Russia, which was later borrowed into other languages, e.g. German *Ruthene*, French *Ruthène*. While Ruthenia in the narrow sense was a part of the Eastern Ukraine, it also stood for the whole of the Ukraine. The dictionary of the Ukrainian language Joyce most likely used was a German or a French one, either of which would call the language "Ruthenian." Russian and Ukrainian have the same ancestor—old Russian, which was the language of Kiev Rus until the 13th century.

A list of Ukrainian words in VI.B.46.67 was transcribed by Rose.[2] I have identified many of the words in my Slavonic list,[3] without recourse to the Buffalo notebooks, but even with the easily available holograph edition of the Buffalo notebooks,[4] there remain still a few loose ends to be tied up.

338.35 switches
Rose gives "svitylny (light)," but the correct Ukrainian word is *svichky* (candles, lights). Cf. VI.B.46.67: "switchskes (light)." "Switches" is closer to the Ukrainian *svichy* (candles), given an English plural ending.

---

[1] Louis O. Mink, *A Finnegans Wake Gazetteer* (Bloomington: Indiana University Press, 1978).

[2] Danis Rose, *James Joyce's The Index Manuscript: Finnegans Wake Holograph Workbook VI.B.46* (Colchester: *AWN* Press, 1978).

[3] Petr Škrabánek, "355.11 Slavansky Slavar, R. Slavyanskii Slovar (Slavonic Dictionary)," *AWN* 11.4 (1972): 51-68.

[4] *The James Joyce Archive*, eds. Michael Groden, *et al.* (New York: Garland Publishing, 1977-78).

In the context of 338.35, "switches" could mean candles in Butt's Japanese lantern.

339.31 *aleal lusky Lubliner*

One of the many echoes of "Dear Dirty Dublin," which here hides a lisping allusion to the Ukraine, Little Russia, "a little Russki Lublin." In 1569 the Ukrainian territories became part of Poland by the Act of Lublin Union. This included willy-nilly also Lithuania with her capital Wilnius ("wilnaynilnay" 339.33), White Russia with the capital Minsk ("minsk" 339.34 and "monkst" 339.35), and Volynhia with the capital Lutsk ("lusky" 339.31). In 1831 Lublin was taken by the Russians, but is now Polish.

340.01 *oukraydoubray*

Another allusion to the Ukraine (cf. VI.B.46.63 "rutene, ukrene"). Ukrainian *dobre* (good).

340.02 *lyudsky ... fitchid*

Rose supplies "lyudsky (human)." Joyce has in VI.B.46.67 "lyudsky wischod" (or possibly "wischid"), i.e. Ukrainian *lyudskyi vischod* (Origin of Man). *Vischod* also means "germination of seed," which may be relevant in the phrase "so sewn a fitchid" (340.02).

340.03 *bogey bragge*

Probably not Ukrainian, although added together with Ukrainian words in a 1937 draft. Russian *bog* (God), Ukrainian *Boh* (God); Russian *braga* (home-brewed beer), Ukrainian *braga* (brandy).

340.05 *in rutene*

Cf. VI.B.46.63: "rutene, ukrene": i.e. in Ukrainian.

340.05 *mistomist*

Ukrainian *misto* (town, city), *mist* (bridge) suggest "the town of towns" or "the town of bridges," i.e. Dublin. The German *Mist* (dung) brings us back to "Dear Dirty Dublin," and also explains why the famous Irish liqueur "Irish Mist" does not sell well in Germany.

340.06 Lissnaluhy
Lyisna and *Luh* are tributaries of the Ukrainian river Bug. Joyce used "lissnaluhy" (VI.B.46.67: "lyiss (wood) luhy (meadow)") to represent the country (Ukrainian *lyis* (forest), *luhy* (meadows)) as a contrast to the town Mistomist. *Lisna-* is a common beginning of Irish place names. P. W. Joyce in his *Irish Local Names Explained* gives *Lios-na-Laegh* (the Fort of the Calves) as an example of the Irish form for the village Lisnalee.

340.10 Nye? ... Tak!
VI.B.46.67: "tak nyi." Ukrainian *tak* (affirmative "so"), *ne* (not), *nyi* (no).

340.14 widnows
Not in Joyce's list. Ukrainian *vidnova* (renewal).

340.16 selo moy!
VI.B.46.67: "selo." Ukrainian *selo moe* (my village).

340.33 ant's
The Slavs on the shores of the Black Sea in the area which is now a part of the Ukraine were known as *Antes* or Ants-As.[5] In the Wakean warfare, their enemies were the ancient "antiants" (343.23).

340.34 on his Mujiksy's Zaravence
Ukrainian *muzhyk*, Russian *muzhik* (peasant), Ukrainian *muzhytskaya charivnytsa* (peasant witch). VI.B.46.92 has "zara (servant)" in the list of Armenian words, which here merges with its opposite, the Tzar (Ukrainian *tzar*). Similarly, "Mujiksy" contains the muzhik servant in His Majesty's Service.

341.05 blodestained boyne
Ukrainian *boinya* (slaughterhouse).

341.07 Why the gigls he lubbed beeyed him
Ukrainian *lyuba* (love), *biy* (fear). This and the preceding entry are not in Joyce's Ukrainian list.

---

5 Francis Dvornik, *The Making of Central and Eastern Europe* (London: Polish Research Centre, 1949).

341.11 howorodies
VI.B.46.67: "howorodies." The nearest Ukrainian word is *hovoryty* (to speak), but the joke escapes me.

343.25 after his obras
VI.B.46.67: "obras." Ukrainian *obraz* (image, icon).

343.27 pulversporochs
VI.B.46.67: "poroch." Ukrainian *porokh* (dust, powder).

343.27 stooleazy
VI.B.46.67: "stooleazy." Ukrainian *stolets* (stool), *stolitsya* (capital city, metropolis).

343.30 chorams the perished popes
Ukrainian *khram* (church), *pop* (Orthodox priest).

344.14 with his nitshnykopfgoknob
VI.B.46.67: "nitshnyk." Rose gives "nyzhnyk (young man)." The Ukrainian *nichnyk* (night watchman) is more appropriate. (*Nyzhnyk* means a jack in cards). An additional Ukrainian allusion is *nichnyi* (night, adj.) which here becomes a nightcap. Cf. also German *Kopf* (head) and English slang *knob* (head). Nizhny Novgorod was founded in the 13th century. It appears elsewhere as "nudgemeroughgorude" (240.18) and "neatschknee Novgolosh" (346.02).

347.03 plain of Khorason ... 347.09 Krzerszonese
While Khorasan is a territory in Iran, the main reference is to the Crimean war ("Crimealian wall" 347.10). There was an early Greek Christian colony known as Khorsun, close to modern Sevastopol in the Crimea. The Crimea was known as the Big Chersonese (Chersonesus Taurica or Scythica) to distinguish it from the small peninsula near Sevastopol, known as the Little Chersonese (Chersonesus Heracleotica). Kherson is a Ukrainian port near Odessa. The earliest inhabitants of the Crimea were Tauri, according to Herodotus. "Ivan the Taurrible" (138.17) was the first to bear the title "the Tzar of all Russia": "the sur of all Russers" (340.35). The Irish "bull in the meadows" (353.13), i.e. Clontarf = Irish *Cluain Tarbh* = Bull's Meadow, meets the Russian Bear

("Ursussen" 353.12; Latin *ursus* = bear) the Russian Brian Born, in a "victaurious onrush" (353.12). The Irish bull "onrush" on the Russian is victorious (Latin *taurus* = bull). When the Russian Tzar uses the Irish sod to wipe himself ("wollpimsolff" 353.17), the Irish Paddy ("puddywhuck" 353.17) becomes his assassin ("ussur Ursussen" 353.12, i.e. tzar's assassin). The insult to Russian Ireland ("instullt to Igorladns" 353.18) is not only the sacrilegious use of "that sob of tunf" (353.16) but also the blasphemous fart from the royal arse intoning *in exitu Israel de Egypto* (*Psalms* 113) like a thundering Jupiter ("untuoning his culothone in an exitous erseroyal *Deo Jupto*" 353.17).

347.05 *how the krow flees*
VI.B.46.67: "krow (blood)." VI.B.46.70: "as the krow flies (cow)." The latter entry appears in the Polish list; Polish *krowa* (cow); *krew* (blood).

348.12 *wody*
VI.B.46.67: "wody." Ukrainian *vody* (waters), Polish *wody* (waters).

348.27 *Raise ras tryracy!*
i.e. up Rus, three times! VI.B.46.67: "ras, tryrasy." Ukrainian *raz* (one, once), *try* (three), *razy* (-times).

350.06 *ruttengenerously*
The Russian General posing as a Ukrainian. In "the bookley with the Rusin's hat" (290.F7), echoing the encounter of private Buckley with the shitting general (...s 'hat), the general dons a Rusin's hat. Ukrainian, Russian, Polish *rusin* (a Ruthenian, a Ukrainian).

351.09 *jisty and pithy af durck rosolun*
VI.B.46.67: "jisty, pithy rosolun." The context of "wenches ... wined ... song" suggests "eat, drink and be merry" (*Luke* 12:19; *Ecclesiastes* 3:15). Ukrainian *jisty* (to eat), *pyty* (to drink). There is no Ukrainian word "resolun," but *rosolyanka* is a Ukrainian popular soup with potatoes and sauerkraut. Italian *rosolio* is a well-known cordial. The English reading of the phrase suggests "just a bit of dark Rosaleen," with a bit of the song translated by Mangan (cf. French *manger*, to eat) a few lines below: "blued the air" (351.13), i.e. "I could scale the blue air."

CUSHITIC CANT: KANT IN AFAR

Afar is an Eastern Cushitic language, spoken by the nomadic, camel-rearing tribe of the Danakils, who live along the coast and on small islands between Adulis Bay and the Gulf of Tajura, opposite to Bab-el-Mandeb, "The Gate of Tears" (cf. "A babbel men dub gulch of tears" 254.16).

Shem ran away, when the "Irish eyes of welcome were smiling daggers down their backs" (176.23), as far as he could, "to stay in afar for the life" (176.31). "And aye far he fared from Afferik" (320.27). Shem, the bad boy, is black. The Afar/African theme is introduced by "Darkies never done tug that coon" (175.30) and embellished with "piccaninnies" (175.33), "Zip Cooney Candy" (176.14), "noyr black" [French *noir*, black, *blanc*, white] (176.24), "black fighting tans" (176.24), "bach bamp him and bump him blues" [i.e. his back black and blue][1] (176.34), "nigger bloke" (177.04). "His back life will not stand being written about in black and white" (169.07).

In VI.B.45.84 a list of exotic languages starts with "Kush afar." The term "Cushitic" is derived from Cush, the first son of Ham (*Genesis* 10:6). "Shem was a sham" (170.25) and in French Ham is *Cham*; "in chems" (177.10) combines Shem and Ham, two of the three sons of Noah, here impersonated by Tom ("weltingtoms" 176.21), Dick ("pettythicks" 176.21) and Harry ("harrily" 176.20).

"Kush afar" is followed by a sentence in Afar, all crossed out in green pencil and added to the *Finnegans Wake* galleys in 1938 (BM

---

[1] "Bach and blues" stands for the white and black music, just as white and black music is an allusion to the piano keyboard; Joyce "boxed around with his fortepiano till he waswhole bach bamp him and bump him blues" (176.34). As Albert Schweitzer, an African missionary, was a well-known interpreter of Bach, he is mentioned as "Schwitzer's" (176.35). In the 1938 galleys the original "Switzer's" was changed to "Schwitzer's." In the Dublin department store Switzer's one could buy a "bedtick"—i.e. a case in which stuffing is put for a bed—or perhaps, batik bed covers. Other musical allusions, besides various Irish songs, include the *Marseillaise* ("the marshalaisy" 176.22) and Beethoven's *Sonata* Op. 13 No. 8 in C minor, the *Pathétique* ("pettythicks" 176.21), to match the French and the German colours (see note 2). "Pettythicks" echoes "bedtick" and Paddywhack, which is one of Tom Moor's melodies and also a synonym for a shillelagh-wielding Irishman, the sort of Paddy Joyce was escaping from.

47476b-399) as "kushykorked" (misprinted as "kuskykorked" 176.30) and "in afar" (176.32), together with the Afar sentence in parentheses: "(pig stole on him was lust he lagging it was becaused dust he shook)" (176.29).

The VI.B.45.84 entry runs as follows:

ala y ok bata
camel I had was lost
wah ani-k ramili yo
I lack I am because sand I
utuk
jette? [illegible]

At the same time as the Afar entry, Joyce added "categorically unimperatived by the maxims" (176.25), alluding to Kant, the Black and Tan massacre at the Croke Park on the Bloody Sunday ("bludgeony Unity Sunday" 176.19) on November 21, 1920, and cant. The Afar sentence lost "camel" which was substituted with "pig," which in cant means "sixpence." Other cant expressions (all listed in Partridge's *Dictionary of Slang and Unconventional English*) are *lag* (to deport a convict), *dust* (money) and *shook* (stole). In cant, "have you shook?" means "have you stolen anything?" *Lagging* means a term of penal servitude, and *to lag* means also "to urinate," which fits the scatological content of the passage, when "a rank funk" was "getting the better of him" (176.25) and when "his cheeks and trousers" were "changing colour every time a gat croaked" (177.06), i.e. each time Shem heard the retort of a gun (cant *gat*, gun) his gut opened and he beshit himself in fright diarrhoea. The simple Kant/cant reading of the Afar sentence is "the lust of money made him steal a sixpence, and because of his theft he was put in prison." The scatological overreading changes "pig stole on him was lust" to "big stool he lost" from the "large ampullar" (177.04), i.e. *ampulla recti*.

The colour-changing Shem took refuge in Switzerland ("Schwitzer's" 176.35), trying his luck first in the Zürich Berlitz school ("for his bare lives, to Talviland" 176.27; cf. "ensign the colours by the beerlitz" 182.07), as Thalwil is a little town on the shores of the Lake of

143

Zürich.[2] "Changing colours" is a reference to the hesitancy of the deserting Shem as to which colours he should choose from between the warring nations—he opts for the neutral Switzerland. The colours mentioned are the German (1867-1918) (in French): "noir blank and rouges" (176.24); the French (in German): "roth, vice and blause" (176.23), and the Irish (in English): "grim white and cold" (176.24; i.e. green white and gold). The American colours, the Stars and the Stripes, are desecrated by Shem who uses them as a blanket, since "bedtick" is a U.S. sailors' slang expression for the American flag; according to Partridge, because of the resemblance to striped mattress covering. This harsh treatment could be Joyce's revenge for Samuel Roth's ("roth vice" 176.23) pirating *Ulysses*. "The bedtick from Schwitzer's" serves Shem as a macintosh under which he hides himself as an unknown dead soldier ("his face enveloped into a dead warrior's telemac" 176.35).

The puzzle of Afar was solved for me by my wife, a professional linguist. When I asked her whether there was any language "Kush Afar, she thought of Cushitic and produced a little book of the grammar of Afar by G. Colizza: *Lingua 'Afar nel Nord-Est dell'Africa* (Vienna: A. Hoelder, 1887). On page 108, Colizza has the following sentence: "*alā yōk bāta wāh aník rámili yō utúq*," which he translates as "*poichè non posso trovare la cammella che ho perduta, gettami arena!*," i.e. because I cannot find the camel I have lost, throw me some sand! A word-by-word translation of the peculiar Afar syntax, closely followed by Joyce in his interlinear translation in VI.B.45.84, is as follows: *alá* (camel) *yōk* (to me,

---

[2] "Talviland, ahone ahaza" (176.27) was inserted into the 1938 galleys with the Afar material. Milesi, in his superb analysis of Ugro-Finnic elements in *Finnegans Wake* (Laurent Milesi, "L'idiome babélien de *Finnegans Wake*: Recherches thématiques dans une perspective génétique," *Genèse de Babel: Joyce et la Création*, ed. Claude Jacquet (Paris: Editions du CNRS, 1985. 155-215) traced *talvi* as Finnish for "winter," and *hon* and *haza* as Hungarian for "at home" and "homewards," respectively, explicating the VI.B.45.84 entries, crossed out in green pencil. It may be added that "Talviland, ahone ahaza" has also an Irish reading: *talamh*, land, *ochón ochón* (*Talamh na h-Éireann*, the Irish Soil, the Irish Sod, and *ochón*, the Irish wailing at the Wake), i.e. the wailing of the Irish exile for the lost country. Furthermore, in Hungarian, the Hiberno-English *ochone ochone* (alas, alas) becomes the first part of a Hungarian proverb: *ahány ház annyi szokás*, as many countries, as many customs. While *ház* and *hon* in Hungarian both mean "house," "home," *haza* and *hon* are also used as equivalents for "native land, fatherland," *hon* being more archaic and poetic.

belonging to me) *bắta* (was lost) *wãh* (I lack, I miss, I cannot find) *aní-k* (I-because) *rámili* (sand) *yō* (to me) *utúq* (throw). Colizza explains that "sand-throwing" was a kind of divination by sand used for recovering lost objects and animals.

In the Letter chapter (I.5), littered with most unlikely languages, the Hen scratches hastily an "anomorous letter, signed," teasily, "Toga Girilis" (112.30). The recipient is the cocky HCE ("hardily curiosing entomophilust" 107.12), interested in the sex life of insects and in kinky etymologies. All she wants is his cock, she writes, a nice turgid, swollen, strutted one, and that's God's truth. ("All schwants (schwrites) ischt tel the cock's trootabout him" 113.11). He should stop strutting about like a cock of the walk, telling his cock-and-bull stories; why not have a cock-and-hen party, "to see life foully, the plak and the smut, (schwrites)" (113.13); she does not mince words ("no minzies matter" 113.13). Let's play Adam and Eve: he, the old adamologist (113.04), and she, the would-be mother of "little mollvogels" (113.16), "haloed be her eve" (104.02), would play an apple harlot (113.16), just like Isold with Tristan, or any Venus with any gentleman (or two) from Verona, Venice, or Genoa ("a Treestone with one Ysold ... any Genoaman against any Venis" 113.16-21). She would have sold herself, like Isold, cheaply; it would be a bargain, as her young watermark in her letter suggests: "*Notre Dame du Bon Marché*" (112.32).

The Hen wants to "talk straight turkey meet to mate" (113.26) and no "gobblydumped turkey" (118.22); "she is not out to dizzledazzle with a graith uncouthrement of postmantuan glasseries from the lapins and the grigs" (113.01). He would not "have the poultriest notions" (112.05) what it means. With Virgil, the Mantuan Swan, dead, what use of post-Virgilian glossaries of Latin, or even of the Greek of grigs, those short-legged hens and grasshoppers. Latin and Greek were Laughing and Grief to the Gryphon and the Mock Turtle. Let's leave these childish stories, and uncouth accoutrements of Carrollian portmanteaux for another time. Let's be plain. "She feel plain plate one flat fact thing and if, lastways firdstwise, a man alones sine anyon anyons utharas has no rates to done a kik at with anyon anakars about tutus milking fores and the rereres on the outerrand asikin the tutus to be forrarder" (113.05).[1] "And the Lord said, it is not good that the man

---

[1] Holograph added to the 2nd set of Faber Galleys, MS 47476a-210, I.5: 1.11/4.11, *JJA* 49.443, copied by the typist onto MS 47476b-358v, I.5:1.12/4.12, *JJA* 50.152. The

should be alone, I will make him an help meet for him" (*Genesis* 2:18). This is what it means to "talk straight turkey meet to mate."

The Turkey is, in fact, Ainu, a curious language of the original inhabitants of Japan, now surviving in Hokkaido, Sakhalin and the Kurile Islands. A list of Ainu words appears in VI.B.45 as follows:[2]

VI.B.45.88	INTERPRETATION
ᵍsine ainou (1 man)	shine ainu (a man, one man)
ᵍainou utara / pl	ainu utara (men)
ᵍainou anakne (l'h-	ainu anakne [nominative case] l'homme
ᵍemphatic	
ᵍleastways	? not Ainu
ᵍku kik sarine	ku kik (I strike), ku kik shiri ne (I
ᵍ(I am beating)	am striking)
ᵍa kik an (tu es battu)	e kik an (you are struck)
	a kik an (he, they are struck)
sine, tu, re, ine, ᵍasikne	shine (one), tu (two), re (three),
wan = 10 ᵍ(hand)	ine (four), ashikne (five, hand),
6 = iwan	iwan (six), tupesan (eight),
8 = sinepesan	shinepesan (nine), wan (ten)

The Hen points out that a man without anyone else is tempted into a solitary sin ("a man alones sine any<u>on</u> <u>an</u>yons utharas" 113.06) after visiting bars with cancan girls as mentioned in the ejaculatory 100-letter word. "Dancings (schwrites) was his only ttoo feebles" (113.15). His weakness makes him stutter. He is much too preoccupied with the colour of their pants: "Honeys wore camelia paints" (113.17); *honi soit qui mal y pense* is the ironic comment of the Hen, whose heart is of "Arin" (112.33). A single man should not have the right to watch girls

holograph reads "asikim," the final letter is ambiguous in the *JJA* reproduction of the typescript and could be either an "m" or an "n."

2 Joyce's spelling of Ainu is Ainou, the retention of some French equivalents, and some minor mistakes in Ainu forms suggest that he was using a second-hand, as yet undiscovered French source. This interpretation draws on *An Ainu-English-Japanese Dictionary* by John Batchelor (Tokyo: Kyobukan; London: Kegan Paul, Trench, Trubner and Co., 1926). It is tempting, following Atherton's Law, to regard Batchelor as the primary source, as "a man alones" seems to pun on his name.

kicking up high. "Has no rates to done a kik[3] at with anyon anakers about tutus" (113.07) suggests "knickers around the bottom," i.e. the "camelia" (chameleon) pants of the French cancan-dancing girls (French *tutu* means "bottom" in children's language). This reading is reinforced by "rereres" (113.08) the stuttering form of "rere" (rear); cf. "in the rere of pilch knickers" (492.25), or "dodging a rere from the middenprivet" (363.30).

The second half of the Ainu sentence, "tutus milking fores and the rereres on the outerrand asikin the tutus to be forrarder," reads in Ainu "twos making fours and the threes on the other hand (ashikne = 5 = hand), asking for the rear to be put forward," alluding both to a four-legged frolic from the fore, and the homosexual proclivities of the three Tommy Atkinses at the rear.

The first entry in VI.B.45.89, i.e. immediately after the Ainu page is "5 x 20." This refers to the Ainu vigesimal number system in which, for example, 100 is expressed by 5 x 20 (*ashikne hot ne*). This entry is not crossed, but it is tempting to read "asikin the tutus to be forrarder," immediately preceding the fifth 100-letter word, as "five by twenty to be carried forward."

---

[3] Norwegian *kikke*, to peep.

CUNNIFORM LETTERS (198.25)

The decipherment of cuneiform script is a fascinating story,[1] bearing some similarities to the work of cryptographers and of Wakean scholars. The first clues were the word for "king" and the name Darius, in trilingual inscriptions (Persian, Elamite, Babylonian) found in Persia: they were written in alphabetical, syllabic and ideographic cuneiforms, respectively. The longest trilingual inscription is the one on the Rock of Behistūn. The text describes the consolidation of the Achemenian realm under Darius I (525-486 B.C.) who conquered the Medes, the Babylonians, the Armenians, and over 20 other peoples. The expression *da-ri-ia-ma-u-iš sunkuk* (the king Darius) ("Dariaumaurius" 113.04) appears about eighty times in the Elmite version of this inscription.

The second entry is Elamite *ir-tak-ik-ša-aš-ša* ("Artaxerxes" 337.35). On a column from Susa (Susa was the capital of Elam), kept in the Louvre, there is a trilingual cuneiform inscription, which combines all the first three entries from VI.B.45.89: *ú ir-tak-ik-ša-aš-ša sunkuk ir-ša-ir-ra sunkuk sunkuk-ip-in-na da-ri-ia-ma-u-iš sunkuk-na ša-a* (I am Artaxerxes, the great king, king of kings, the son of the king Darius). This inscription refers to Artaxerxes II Mnemon (404-359 B.C.), son of Darius II (424-404 B.C.).[2]

The last two entries, presumably also in Elamite, are not crossed out. Elamite *na-ap* (Nāp) means "God." The last entry, *bumii (or *burin, or *burni) is problematic. On one Susa column (also in the Louvre), the word *bu-mi-ia* in the Elamite version stands for "earth" (i.e. *terre in VI.B.45.89), which is a derivative of the Old Persian *bumi* (earth). However, in all other trilinguals, the Elamite word for "earth" is *mu-ru-un* (murūn). As the word does not seem to be used in *Finnegans Wake*, the problem is not a burning one.

The first allusion in *Finnegans Wake* to cuneiform clay tablets appears in the context of early alphabets and writings: "the claybook ... the Meades and Porsons" (18.17-22). In the 19th century the Elamite language was called Median, or Susian.

The dynasty of the Achaemenians in Persia (cf. "achamed ...

---

[1] E.A. Wallis Budge, *The Rise and Progress of Assyriology* (London: Martin Hopkinson, 1925).

[2] F.H. Weissbach, *Die Keilinschriften der Achämeniden* (Leipzig: J.C. Hinrichs, 1911).

Perisian" 143.34-36) was represented by two Dariuses, two Xerxeses and three Artaxerxeses. In the *Third Census* they are not clearly identified. Darius II (424-404 B.C.) hides in the phrase "by nettus, not anymeade or persan" (286.07), since Nothus was his cognomen, indicating his illegitimacy (Greek *νόθος, nóthos*, bastard).[3] The two Xerxeses are mentioned in "series exerxeses" (286.08), alluding to less than serious exercises by Joyce in Persian history.

Joyce's interest in Persian history is understandable, considering that the chief protagonist of *Finnegans Wake* has a name betraying his Persian royal affiliation: Persse O'Reilly, "Perseoroyal" (358.20), (cf. French *Perse*, Persia). And it just happens that the Elamite word *sunkuk* is an ideogram 𒂍𒀫,[4] i.e. "the baffling ... sign ⫟ ... moved contrawatchwise" (119.17), i.e. ⧄.

The Elamite version of the Behistūn inscription contains 111 signs:[5] "her all cunniform letters" (198.25). "Cuneiform" is derived from the Latin *cuneus* (wedge). "Cunniform" has clear overtones to the wedged lap of ALP, which hides her *cunt*, through the courtesy of Shem's cunning. The first son of Shem was—Elam (*Genesis* 10:22).

---

[3] Cf. Škrabánek's discussion of the theme of the "noman" in "Night Joyce of a Thousand Tiers." Implied here is a linkage between the idea of il-legitimacy [*νόθος*] in the (false) name of Ulysses (itself a bastardised Latinate "translation" of the Greek Odysseus) and the tropism of the "homecoming" or [*νόστος, nóstos*] in the final book of the *Odyssey*. (Ed.)

[4] F.H. Weissbach, *Die Keilinschriften der Achämeniden.*

[5] Cyrus H. Gordon, *Forgotten Scripts* (London: Basic Books, 1968).

JOYCE IN EXILE

Patrick Kavanagh wrote the rhyme "Who killed James Joyce?" He accused foreigners of the murder. This was unfair. It was foreigners who assisted at Joyce's birth and who made him immortal. In Ireland, Joyce was dead before he was born. Patrick Kavanagh saw in Joyce's writings hate and pride, and later the delirium of a man with no more to say. But he also admitted to John Jordan that he read *Ulysses* twenty times—a curious mixture of admiration, envy and hatred.

Why did Joyce choose exile? What was he escaping from?

The first-born in a family of ten children, James was the favourite child. Since he was a gifted boy, they provided him with the best education they could afford—the Jesuit Colleges of Clongowes and Belvedere, and then University College, Dublin (UCD). Joyce was a voracious reader with a phenomenal memory and a gift for languages. His interests were literature, drama, and aesthetics, but his friends were talking about politics, religion, and whores. Oliver St. John Gogarty, a poet and a medical student, was a worthy intellectual opponent, but Joyce resented his mockery and his wealth. Joyce felt isolated, alone.

In his first published piece, privately printed because the college authorities rejected it as unsuitable for the UCD student journal, Joyce attacked the Irish nationalistic parochialism of the Irish Literary Theatre. "No man can be a lover of the true or the good," wrote nineteen-year-old Joyce, "unless he abhors the multitude. If an artist courts the favour of the multitude, he cannot escape the contagion of its fetishism and its deliberate self-deception. Until he has freed himself from the mean influences about him—sodden enthusiasm and clever insinuation and every flattering influence of vanity and low ambition— no man is an artist at all."

His stakes were high. A few years later, he expressed the same uncompromising ideas even more forcefully: "A poet must keep his soul spotless, he should not prostitute himself to the rabble. Artistic life should be nothing more than a true and continual revelation of spiritual life ... he should abstain from proffering confessions of faith ... in sum, the poet is sufficient in himself."

In *The Day of the Rabblement*, he wrote that "a nation which never advances so far as a miracle play ... affords no literary model to the artist ... The artist must look abroad." In *Dubliners*, the mitching schoolboy reflects that real adventures do not happen to people who remain at home: they must be sought abroad." In *The Portrait*, the proud and embittered budding artist makes exile one of the weapons which he allows himself to use. Nothing was happening in hibernating Hibernia, while in Europe, Sigmund Freud and Alfred Jarry had published their main works; France had broken off diplomatic relations with the Vatican; and Einstein had announced the Theory of Relativity. In 1904, 22-year-old Joyce and his companion Nora left Ireland for good, amidst sneers from his acquaintances. This was inevitable. Refusing to serve the Church and Nationalism, he had to break his social ties as well. After arriving in Trieste, Joyce said in a public lecture: "I confess that I do not see what good it does to fulminate against the English tyranny while the Roman tyranny occupies the palace of the soul."

Sixty years later, an Irish writer seriously suggested that after *Ulysses* was published there was no reason why Joyce should not have returned and relaxed in the Free State. How could Joyce have returned, when *The Dublin Review* wrote about *Ulysses*: "No Catholic publicist can ever afford to be possessed of a copy of this book, for in its reading lies not only the description but the commission of sin against the Holy Ghost," the book being "the screed of one possessed," "the devilish drench ... without grammar and sense," "a Sahara that is as dry as it is stinking," a book in which the author "splutters hopelessly under the flood of his own vomit." The reviewer—who preferred to remain anonymous—most earnestly hoped that *Ulysses* would be placed on the Vatican Index of Prohibited Books, where, till then, of all the Irish authors and heretics, only Eriugena, the Cork scientist Robert Boyle, Oliver Goldsmith and Laurence Sterne had the honour to be listed.

This was four years before the Committee on Evil Literature was set up by the Irish Government. The Irish Vigilance Association objected to the sale in Dublin shops of books by James Joyce. There was no need to ban *Ulysses* because the Irish Customs would never let it in. Although the "mediaeval legislation" (Yeats's words) of the Censorship of Publications Act has not yet seen the light of the day, *Ulysses* was on the Customs' black-list. Other English speaking countries were no better. It was the English Customs who burned *Ulysses* in Folkestone, following the example of their American colleagues who were so vigilant that they confiscated excerpts of *Ulysses* even before it appeared in book form. Book burning, under the biggest statue of Liberty in the world? And that after proofs of *Dubliners* had been burned in Dublin and *The Portrait* had been rejected by seven English printers.

When Arthur Power met Nora in Paris after Joyce's death, she complained of loneliness, and he suggested that she should go over to Ireland. "What?" she cried, her voice hysterical, "They burned my husband's books." We should not forget that *Ulysses* was a symbolic engagement present to Nora from Joyce, to commemorate their first date; later to become known all over the world as "Bloomsday."

When Sylvia Beach, who published *Ulysses* in Paris (another American who killed James Joyce?), asked Bernard Shaw for a subscription, he replied: "I have read several fragments of *Ulysses* in its serial form. It is a revolting record of a disgusting phase of civilisation, but it is a truthful one. I escaped from it to England at the age of twenty, and forty years later I have learned from the books of Mr. Joyce that slackjawed blackguardism is as rife in young Dublin as it was in 1870. It is, however, some consolation to find that at least one man has felt deeply enough about it to face the horror of writing it all down, and using his literary genius to force people to face it. In Ireland they try to make a cat cleanly by rubbing its nose in its own filth—Mr. Joyce has tried the same treatment on the human subject. I hope that it may prove successful."

It was a strange feeling for me to see in *The Irish Times* a couple of years ago a photograph of a few secondary school girls receiving copies of *Ulysses* as a prize. Did somebody get mixed up between Homer and Joyce? Or had time change so much since that article in *The Sunday Express* which described *Ulysses* as: "leprous scabrous horrors ... all secret sewers of vice canalised in its flood of unimaginable thoughts, images and pornographic words; unclean lunacies larded with appalling and revolting blasphemies." Joyce knew what he could be returning to. When Desmond Fitzgerald, the then Minister for Publicity, wooed Joyce to return to Ireland, promising that he would propose Joyce's name to be nominated for the Nobel Prize, Joyce warned Fitzgerald that he would be sacked. In fact, when Yeats got the Nobel Prize instead, it was dismissed in an Irish journal, edited by the President of the Gaelic League, as a reward for paganism, from money provided by a deceased anti-Christian manufacturer of dynamite.

It is often said that Joyce was anti-Irish. This is an Irish bull. When Nora complained that Ireland was a wretched country, dirty and dreary, where they eat cabbages, potatoes and bacon all year round, where the women spent their days in church and the men in pubs, Joyce quipped: "Dublin is the seventh city of Christendom and the second city of the Empire. It is also the third in Europe for the number and quality of its brothels. But for me it will always be the first city in the world." He aspired to become the Dante of Dublin and he wrote a human comedy of his beloved city.

As an artist, Joyce was against every state. He believed that poets were repositories of the genuine spiritual life of their race and that priests were usurpers.

Joyce left Ireland not because he hated Ireland but because he detested the Irish State which threatened the freedom of the soul. Joyce's friend, the painter Frank Budgen, perceptively noticed that *la patrie* (the fatherland) asks for our bodies in war time and for our money all the time, but Ireland demands of her sons a continual service of the soul as well. This service Joyce would not give. He would not serve. Joyce left Ireland because he felt that the economic and intellectual conditions prevailing in Ireland did not permit the development of the free artistic spirit. He saw the soul of the country weakened by centuries of useless struggles and broken treaties, and individual initiative paralysed by the influence and admonition of the church. Ireland was a house of decay, a shut door of a silent tower entombing blind bodies, a cultural desert, the dead centre of paralysis.

Joyce was also afraid to return. He once said to his friend Padraic Colum: "Don't you remember how the prodigal son was received by his brother in his father's house? It is dangerous to leave one's country, but still more dangerous to go back to it, for then your fellow-countrymen, if they can, will drive a knife into your heart."

Joyce compared his plight to that of Parnell. Irish political history was plagued by betrayals. Joyce believed that in Ireland, just at the right moment, an informer always appears. The political idol of his childhood, Parnell, was the epitome of the betrayal—by O'Shea, by the bishops, by Healy and by Piggott. Parnell going from county to county, from city to city, like a hunted deer, a spectral figure with the sign of death on his forehead. The citizens of Castlecomer threw quicklime in his eyes. "'Twas Irish humour, wet and dry, flung quicklime into

Parnell's eye." The half-blind Joyce loathed to think that something like this would happen to him. He was told that a man called into a book shop in Nassau Street and asked whether they had a copy of *Ulysses*, which they fortunately did not. "Well," the man said, "the author of that book had better not set his foot in the country again." Obviously a remark of some religious or nationalistic fanatic; but Joyce was quite right when he feared that: "It is just such an eccentric who does these things."

Joyce was afraid of the ignorant obedience of self-righteous crawthumpers and of the studied hypocrisy of the establishment. My friend, Dr Dick Walsh, still remembers Eoin McNeill citing a scornful remark about Joyce's university, a remark attributed to Mahaffy, who opposed the foundation of the new Catholic University: "Is it a university for the kind of fellas that would be standing on Butt Bridge spittin' into the Liffey?"

Joyce is often presented as an anti-religious writer. As an artist he was his own God. "I am trying in my poems," he said, "to give people some kind of intellectual pleasure or spiritual enjoyment by converting the bread of everyday life into something that has a permanent artistic life of its own." Joyce used religion, particularly the Catholic ritual, as a rich source from which to build his own myth. In his early works he was embittered and rebellious, but he mellowed with age. There is no hatred in *Ulysses* or *Finnegans Wake*. Bloom, the wandering Jew of *Ulysses*, preaches a doctrine close to the Christian teaching of love: "Force, hatred, history, all that, that's not life for men and women, insult and hatred. And everybody knows that it's the very opposite of that that is really life.—What?—Love, said Bloom, I mean the opposite of hatred." And the citizen, who represents xenophobic nationalism, gets the message, and mocks Bloom: "A new apostle to the Gentiles."

Joyce was grateful to the Jesuits for disciplining him in gathering and presenting a given corpus of material. He never missed the Easter week services. He loved singing Church songs. He memorised long passages from the gospels. However, he admitted that he professed no religion at all. "Of the two religions, Protestantism and Catholicism," he said, "I prefer the latter. Both are false. The former is cold and colourless. Catholicism is constantly associated with art; it is a beautiful lie— something at least."

He lived with Nora "in sin" (as they call it) for 25 years before marrying her. He saw matrimony as a completely personal affair; as he said: "without a clerk with a pen behind his ear or a priest in his night shirt." When he was reproached for not having his children brought up in the practice of religion, he replied: "but what do they expect me to do? There are a hundred and twenty religions in the world. Let them pick for themselves." When Joyce died in Zürich in 1941, a Catholic priest approached Nora to offer a religious service but Nora refused: "I could not do that to him." That was love beyond the grave.

In Europe, Joyce felt free. Paris had an atmosphere of spiritual effort, a race-course tension. Dadaists had just arrived from Zürich; Aragon, Breton and Soupault had founded the Surrealist movement, rising from Lautréamont's ashes like the Phoenix, and the avant-garde review, *transition*, edited by a Franco-German American, Eugene Jolas, started publishing the first extracts from *Finnegans Wake*, "this most solitary, the least affined work, meteor-like in its introduction to the world," in the words of Stephen Zweig.

"There is no work more intellectual, more disengaged from worry about contemporary matters, more estranged from Time and Space, more foreign to politics, war, the torments of a wretched Europe; none more preoccupied with the great interests of life, love, desire, death, childhood, fatherhood, the mystery of Eternal Return," wrote a member of the French Academy, Louis Gillet. *Finnegans Wake*—the boldest literary experiment ever attempted. "It is not difficult to be bold when one is young," complimented André Gide, "the finest audacity is that of the end of life." This, Joyce's testament, the work of love of seventeen years, contains nearly fifty thousand different words, three times as much as the whole of Shakespeare.

Talking to the Polish writer, Jan Parandowski, Joyce explained: "The few fragments which I have published, have been enough to convince many critics that I have finally lost my mind, which, by the way, they have been predicting faithfully for many years. And perhaps, it is madness to grind up words in order to extract their substance, to open unsuspected possibilities for these words, to marry sounds which were not usually joined before although they were meant for one another, to allow water to speak like water, birds to chirp like birds, to liberate all sounds from their servile contemptible role and to attach them to the feelers of expressions which grope for definitions of the undefined. With this hash of sounds I am building the great myth of everyday life."

Samuel Beckett was one of the first to grasp fully the mastery of the achievement. I quote: "Here form *is* content, content *is* the form. You complain that this stuff is not written in English. It is not written at all. It is not to be read—or rather, it is not only to be read. It is to be looked at and listened to. His writing is not *about* something: *it is that something itself*."

Even the Vatican *Osservatore Romano* sensed its importance and praised *Finnegans Wake* as a linguistic experiment seeking to open up new paths for the expression of human sentiments. *The Irish Times*, to their credit, recognised the power, and the moments of beauty, in *Finnegans Wake*. But the arch mocker, Buck Mulligan, could not forget and forgive. After Joyce's death, Dr Gogarty wrote that *Finnegans Wake* was a gigantic hoax written by an idiot on the backside of beauty. He went even so far as to insinuate that Joyce suffered from schizophrenia, while knowing perfectly well that there was no truth in it. Joyce, on the other hand, did forgive and forget. He died reading Gogarty's last book, *I Follow St. Patrick*.

Joyce was deeply moved by a Radio Éireann broadcast to commemorate his birthday in 1938. The Irish homage was more precious to him than any he might receive from anywhere in the world. Joyce would be amused to listen to this series of Thomas Davis Lectures. He tried to lift up Irish prose to the level of an international masterpiece and to give a full representation of the Irish genius. He went into exile to create the unborn conscience of his race. Now Ireland claims his bones. He is the Uncrowned King of the Words, who conquered Ireland by setting most uncompromising artistic criteria, by which she now must judge and be judged.

Let his restless spirit keep awake.

APPENDICES

BOOK REVIEW
James Joyce 1. "Scribble" 1. Genèse des textes, ed. Claude Jacquet (Paris: Lettres Modernes, Minard, 1988).

This collection of eleven essays, and the first volume of a planned series, is described by the editor, Claude Jacquet, as examples of the work carried out by *Le Centre de Recherches sur James Joyce de l'Université de la Sorbonne Nouvelle* and *Le Programme Joyce de l'Institut des Textes et Manuscrits Modernes du Centre National de la Recherche Scientifique*, both founded in 1980. The activities of these two impressively titled bodies include *Finnegans Wake* notebook sessions, monthly seminars, international symposia, and workshops; it is not made clear, however, whether the essays were first presented at any of these venues or whether they were commissioned by the editor.

Derrida's introductory piece "Scribble (pouvoir/écrire)" is reprinted from his introduction to an edition of W. Warburton's essay on hieroglyphs, and though it has no apparent bearing on hieroglyphs, it is even less enlightening for students of Joyce. The rest of the French contributions, however, are of a high standard, and better overall than their English counterparts.

Fritz Senn in "Distancing in 'A Painful Case'" gently probes with his sharp scalpel underneath the façade of words. Michael Beausang ("Marital Freedom and Justice in *Exiles*") disentangles a few subtle points in *Exiles* with exemplary lucidity. Hans Walter Gabler's "Narrative rereadings of *Ulysses*" is like an archeological dig after heavy rain: it gets all muddy. At the very beginning Gabler states: "On earlier occasions I have approached it from a specifically textual angle to elicit from the peculiarly—albeit not exclusively—Joycean conditioning of the literary text perspectives on the text's, as well as the work's, condition of existence." The message is garbled.

André Topia approaches the "Sirens" episode ("*Sirènes: L'expressivité nomade*") with great sensivity and an acute ear. Daniel Ferrer's "Archéologie du regard dans les avant-textes de *Circé*" is a less successful attempt, mainly because only seven pages are devoted to this greatest hallucinatory piece of theatre in world literature. Claude

Jacquet's "Les mensonges d'*Eumée*" is a masterly exposition, followed by some beautiful writing by Jean-Michel Rabaté on "Le nœud gordien de *Pénélope*."

Finnegans Wake gets only a nodding acknowledgment, but Laurent Milesi's "Vico..Jousse. Joyce..langue" displays the art of linguistic pyrotechnics. Klaus Reichart's "The Structure of Hebrew and the Language of *Finnegans Wake*," on the other hand, is more about Hebrew than *Finnegans Wake*, and Reichart's hypothesis that Hebrew—particularly the Hebrew verb system—was a model language for the *Wake* is far-fetched. The closing piece, "Joyce, Jameson, and the Text of History," by Derek Attridge, is thinly spun and comprehensible only to Fredric Jameson's friends or enemies.

Overall, *Scribble 1* deserves an unqualified welcome, and the editor our congratulations.

BOOK REVIEW

James Joyce and Heraldry by Michael O'Shea (Albany, NY: State University of New York Press, 1986)

This monograph is based on a doctoral dissertation (directed by Zack Bowen) at the University of Delaware, and is dedicated to the Rev. Robert Boyle, SJ, who first introduced O'Shea, in 1981, to *Finnegans Wake*. The back cover informs the reader that the book "demonstrates that heraldry is an essential key to the symbols of Joyce's major works," and that it is an "indispensable reference work that sheds new light on Joyce's major texts."

Less than half of the book is devoted to comments on heraldic allusions in the *Portrait*, *Ulysses*, and *Finnegans Wake*. The other material includes a general introduction to heraldry and its jargon ("blazon"), an interesting, but somewhat irrelevant chapter on the use of heraldry in English literature (Chaucer, Malory, Spenser, Shakespeare, Defoe, Dickens, Sterne, Thackeray), and a 30-page glossary of heraldic terms, not all of them pertinent to Joyce's use, with others missing, e.g. "wolf" in Joyce's crest.

As a reference book it has a serious drawback in that it does not have an index of discussed passages: this precludes a quick consultation, which is further hindered by information being scattered throughout the main text, glossary, and notes, requiring a piecemeal retrieval. While it is handy to have most heraldic references in Joyce "marshalled" into one volume, little new information is provided which could not be found in other commentaries and exegeses. It is a pity that the primary material in the Buffalo Notebooks is rarely used and not systematically treated. On page 1, the first motto is marred by an apostrophe in *Finnegans Wake*, and in subsequent chapters the opening mottoes carry on the same error (pages 41, 87) besides wrong pagination and misspellings: a minor problem, but a somewhat disturbing sign.

The version of Joyce's coat of arms that Joyce hung in his Paris flats, illustrated in the book, had a wolf in the crest ("demiwolf ducally gorged," in proper blazon), a red eagle in the shield, and the following motto: *Mors aut honorabilis vita*, i.e. honourable life or death. While O'Shea failed to locate the motto in *Finnegans Wake*, a fairly good periphrasis appears in Shem's chapter: "in honour bound to the cross of your own cruelfiction" (192.18)—Joyce's determination to stick to his guns and keep to the "Work in Progress," to maintain his artistic integrity to death, in the teeth of rumours that he had become mad. Another version appears in "his part should say in honour bound ... no matter what" (253.11).

The red eagle of Joyce's arms is lent to Stephen Dedalus in *Ulysses*: "an eagle gules volant in a field argent displayed" (*U* 15.3948). The emblem of the lion, which is in the coat of arms of Finnegan and Persse O'Reilly, can be traced to Bloom, who, through his first name, Leopold, is also a lion ("You were the lion of the night ... *Leo ferox* ... Henry! Leopold! Leopold! Lionel ..." (*U* 15.447, 712, 753))

The first full coat of arms in *Finnegans Wake* is that of Wassaily Booslaeugh of Riesengeborg: "Of the first was he to bare arms and a name: Wassaily Booslaeugh of Riesengeborg. His crest of huroldry, in vert with ancillars, troublant, argent, a hegoak, puirsuivant, horrid, horned. His scutschum fessed, with archers strung, helio, of the second." (5.05-08).

O'Shea notes "oak" in "hegoak" and links it with the oak in the second and third quarters of the coat of arms of O'Reilly of East Breffny: "an oak tree with a snake descendant proper," first identified by Manganiello.[1] The motive of Paradise and the Fall contained in this allusion is paraphrased in *Finnegans Wake* as "aslike as asnake comes sliduant down that oaktree" (100.11)—the tree in which the Serpent appeared to Eve, the Tree of Life and Death, the Tree of Knowledge, leading to Adam's fall. Adam is introduced through the joke shared by the two clowns in the churchyard scene of the fifth Act of *Hamlet*: "He was the first that ever bore arms."

However, Booslauegh's coat of arms is a superimposition of many other arms: Finnegan's, Stephen's, Dublin's and Ireland's. Moreover, it blazons the "crime" of HCE.

Vasilii Buslaev, the Russian hero-warrior, is the prototype of the Crimean Russian General in II.3. Like the other themes on page 3, he has "not yet" risen (cf. German *Riese*, ogre, giant; *Riesengebirge*, the Giant Mountains; "rising gianerant" 368.08). Wassaily Booslaeugh, the Irish hero-warrior (Irish *laoch*, hero, warrior) is the future ruler (Basileus), the young Irish private Buckley who will kill the drunken ogre (note

---

[1] Dominic Manganiello, "Irish Family Names in *Finnegans Wake*," *AWN* 16.2 (1979): 30-31.

"booze" in the name) as Odysseus killed the Cyclops. The name contains the conflict between the old and the new, between the father and the son, between the master (i.e. boss) and the servant (i.e. vassal), between life (-laeugh) and death (Irish *bás*).[2]

The first superimposed piece of heraldry is the Irish crest, with a stag springing from a castle. In blazon, "a tower triple-towered or, and from the gateway, a stag springing argent, attired and unguled of the first."[3] The bits and pieces of this scene can be salvaged in "horned," "with ancillars" (i.e. a stag with antlers), "pursuivant" (chasing, on the move), "argent" (i.e. on a silver background), the triple tower is perhaps echoed in "troublant" via "treble," "triple."

The second superimposition is that of Dublin's coat of arms, with three castles on the shield, and two female supporters, who are the "pair of dainty maidservants" (34.19), otherwise *ancillae* (Latin for "handmaidens, maidservants"). "Ancillars," in Booslaeugh-HCE's arms, however, suggests the masculine gender, more like "helping" made hands. (As O'Shea correctly notes, *ancile* was one of the 12 sacred shields of the ancient Romans.) The girls are "troublant, argent," i.e. alluring, disturbing (French *troublant*), and selling love, asking for money (French *argent*) urgently. The stag HCE chases them (French *poursuivant*, suitor, pursuer) as a satyr chases nymphs, as a he-goat ("hegoak"), half-man, half-goat, the horny Devil, with a horrid erection ("horrid, horned"). He is anxious to tumble with them in the grass (French *le vert*, grass; *vert*, green). A similar use of grass was mentioned in "laid to rust upon the green" (3.23), where "rust" means, besides the rusty colour of the Irish tricolour, to roust, i.e. to coït (Partridge).

HCE is a "hegoak," i.e. he-goak, a male cuckold. In Hiberno-English, *goak* (also spelt *gawk*, or *gowk*) means 1) a cuckoo; 2) a fool, a butt, a buffoon; and in verbal uses, "to gaze" or "to peep." This alludes to one of HCE's misdemeanours: the dirty old man, the Peeping Tom. A graffito in South Main Street, in Cork, runs: "Something in her walk makes me want to gawk." (This is, however, ambiguous, as *gawk* also means "to vomit.") HCE's cuckoldry (half-spelled out in "huroldry," which also contains wenching) is further suggested by the stag-horn image.

More serious, though, is the encounter of HCE with the boys, "the

[2] Petr Škrabánek, "Wassaily Booslaeugh (of Riesengeborg)," *AWN* 10.3 (1973): 42.
[3] Arthur C. Fox-Davies, *The Art of Heraldry* (Edinburgh: T. C. & E. C. Jack, 1904).

archers." "In vert" in blazon means the colour green, the whores in the green, but it is related to the Crime in the Park through the euphemism "inversion," used by sympathetic sexologists when referring to homosexuality, at the beginning of the century. Joyce uses it in the same sense, for example, when speaking about Wilde: "first offence in vert ... at its wildest" (34.25). (The first offence is also that of Adam, in the green, wild Eden.)

We are told that the Crime is linked to the three archers (note that German *Arsch* means arse, and French *les fesses*, the buttocks; *fesser*, to spank, *fessu*, broad-bottomed). With this knowledge we can have another look at "his scutschum fessed": in ordinary blazon, it would mean that his shield (escutcheon) had a wide bar across the middle portion (*fesse*); in the Wakean blazon, it means that a bum is displayed, that his Scots-chum (they are Welsh, or English elsewhere) exposes his "scut" (a tail of a deer, a behind), or that HCE's arse is flashed. ("Fessed," as it precedes "of the second," could be also read as "first"). The three archers peep or watch ("watch warriors of the vigilance committee" 34.04). In *Finnegans Wake* we are never quite told what exactly the crime was, taking place in the Park or in Crimea.

The interesting ending to the description of HCE's arms, "helio, of the second," has never been explained, yet, it is clear, that beside Greek *helios* (God-Sun, and Son-God) it is a clue to the colour of the drawers of the two supporting maidens, i.e. of Issy and her mirror image. The colour is—helio, i.e. heliotrope, as transpires later in II.1. But "not yet," they are "of the second," which in blazon means of the colour mentioned as the second, since tradition forbids repeating any colour twice. Thus "of the second" must be "argent" (white), since the first colour mentioned was "vert." (Cf. "withdrewers argent" in another rendering of HCE's arms, 546.06.)

Another important component of the HCE arms, missed by O'Shea, who does not venture beyond Campbell and Robinson or McHugh's *Annotations*, is "he-lio," i.e. he, the Lion, emblematic animal in Finnegan's coat of arms ("the liofant" 599.06) and doubled as a pair of lions in Persse O'Reilly's coat of arms.

"The archers" refer to the archers in Stephen's coat of arms, the Stephen who lived in and around 1132, the son of Henry. He was said to have borne on a red shield three golden centaurs, but this idea may have arisen from the "Sagittary" which was his badge.[4] In heraldry, sagittarius is a centaur carrying a bow and arrow, hence "archer."[5] Stephen and Henry; Stephen Dedalus and Henry Flower/Bloom, the son and the father.

Stephen's motto was *Vi nulla invertitur ordo* (By no force is their order altered), another "inversion" allusion. Moreover, Stephen was the first to use a badge of three ostrich feathers, according to one source which would be available to Joyce,[6] though this must not be connected with the "Prince of Wales's feathers," which have a different origin, according to the same author. The importance of the "tripenniferry cresta and caudal mottams: Itch dean" (485.02)[7] lies not in that it belongs to the Prince of Wales, but that it is the badge of the Heir Apparent. The Heir Apparent, Stephen, whose motto is "inverted" from the Black Prince's "Ich deane" to Stephen's (Shem's) "non serviam." An additional snippet of information, gleaned from the *British Encyclopaedia*, is of particular interest: Stephen renounced his hereditary claims in favour of his elder brother Theobald. Back to the familiar pattern of the *Wake*: Jacob and Esau, Shem and Shaun.

O'Shea explains how the coat of arms belonging to the Molloys became by mistake Finnegan's. As shown by Manganiello,[8] Joyce took Finnegan's coat of arms from the series of Irish family names, in *The Weekly Irish Times* (July 18, 1936). The editor, who copied his material from O'Hart's *Irish Pedigrees* (which has no coat of arms for Finnegan) found in the index a cross-reference to "The Molloys," because a Molloy was named Fiongan. However, I doubt that Joyce was unaware of this, since he links Molloy and O'Reilly (both having "lion rampant" in their arms) in "Molloyd O'Reilly, that hugglebeddy fann" (616.01), with Huckleberry Finn/Finnegan thrown in for good measure.

O'Shea glosses the Persse O'Reilly allusion "Prszss Orel" (105.10) as referring to the arms of Joyce of Galway (page 101), (i.e. a two-headed eagle, while Joyce used a single-headed version) and to the double eagle of the Tzars of Russia and the ruling houses of Prussia (page 118). The connection with Prussia is good, because of "Prszss," but O'Shea

---

[4] S.T. Aveling, *Heraldry Ancient and Modern, Including Boutell's Heraldry* (London: F. Warne, 1881).

[5] A.C. Fox-Davies, *The Art of Heraldry*.

[6] C.Wilfred Scott-Giles, *The Romance of Heraldry* (London: J. M. Dent, 1929).

[7] Petr Škrabánek, "St. Patrick's Nightmare Confession," *FWC* 1.1 (1985), 5-20.

[8] Manganiello, "Irish Family Names in *Finnegans Wake*."

misses the point that the phrase is a Polish allusion and thus refers to a Polish eagle, i.e. the single-headed Piast eagle of the Polish kings.

In the second major heraldic statement in *Finnegans Wake* (546.05-11), O'Shea is puzzled by the phrase "a tierce of lanciers, shaking unsheathed shafts, their arms crossed in saltire" and he writes "it is difficult to imagine how a terce of lancers could cross in saltire" (page 130). The problem is not insurmountable if it is accepted that "their arms" does not necessarily refer to three lanciers, or to their three lances. An inspection of the arms of Dublin, on which this coat of arms is based, provides a solution: *behind* the arms there are two "arms" (a mace and a sword) *crossed in saltire.*

One of the omissions is a gloss on "he would mac siccar" (586.29). Scott-Giles gives the following explanation: Robert Bruce, the king of Scotland, quarrelled with Red Comyn and "stabbed him in a moment of passion." Bruce's follower, Kirkpatrick, committed the actual murder, saying, "I mak sikker" (I make sure). The motto, "I mak sikker" adorns Kirkpatricks's crest around a gauntlet fist holding a dagger dripping with blood.[9] Another variant appears as "the Macsiccaries" (228.02). See also Mink's note on the same subject.[10]

When discussing the "White Horse" emblem, O'Shea deals only with the "White Horse of Hanover," without mentioning that the first Saxon "White Horse" was that of Hengist (and of Horsa—another name for Hengist), still preserved in the arms of Kent.[11]

"Or a peso besant to join the armada?" (234.04), sandwiched between Don Quixote ("tristiest cabaleer ... donkey schot") and his mate ("Sin Showpanza") seems to relate to the Spanish "invincible" Armada, sunk near the Irish coast in 1588, at the time when Cervantes, who acted as a provisioner for the Armada, was excommunicated for the misappropriation of some corn. O'Shea does not comment. It would appear that the coat of arms "or a peso besant" belongs to a penniless knight, since "besant" (or "bazant") in heraldry means a coin-like symbol known as a golden roundle. Since the field is "or," i.e. gold, the Spanish coin peso, equivalent to the English penny, made golden and placed on the shield, becomes invisible.

On page 93, O'Shea doubts that Gough in "the garden Gough

---

9   Scott-Giles, *The Romance of Heraldry.*
10 Louis O. Mink "Schwalby Words," *AWN* 9.6 (1972): 110.
11 Scott-Giles, *The Romance of Heraldry.*

gave" (271.29) is a reference to the Gough statue in the Phoenix Park, and he proposes another Gough, an author of a heraldic glossary. O'Shea places too much emphasis on Glasheen's aside in her *Census* ("I do not understand the references to him")[12] and writes that why Gough should "give" a garden "is a mystery." Gough's statue was erected near the People's Gardens in the Phoenix Park, facing Wellington's Monument. Thus Gough provides a suitable allusion to the site of the *Finnegans Wake* Garden of Eden.

---

[12] Adaline Glasheen does not make it clear that the Gough statue is an equestrian one. At Talavera (under Wellington) Gough had his horse shot under him. As the actual statue was cast in bronze, I do not know if the real horse was white, as suggested in "goff stature" (334.13) when "quite hoarse" (i.e. white horse) is mentioned. He died at the age of ninety, which may account for Joyce's description as "decayed and gouty Gough" (211.24). As mentioned recently in *The Irish Times*, in a letter by G.J.I. Costello (August 22, 1986), the Gough statue was one of four equestrian statues in Dublin, the others being William III at College Green, George II at Stephen's Green, and George I at Essex Bridge. The first three were destroyed by "the lunatic element," as the saying goes. (George I escaped via the Mansion House to Birmingham, and now stands at the entrance to the Barber Institute of Fine Art there.) The Gough Statue was unveiled in 1880, beheaded at Christmas 1944, restored, and finally assaulted on July 23, 1957 by an explosion which was heard all over Dublin, according to a news item in *The Irish Times* on August 15, 1986 in connection with the current sale of the remains to a private buyer in Britain. The inscription on the plinth said: "In honour of Field-Marshall Hugh Viscount Gough, KP, GCB, GCSI, and illustrious Irishman, whose achievement in the Peninsula War, in China, and in India, have added lustre to the military glory of this country, which he faithfully served for 75 years. This statue (cast from a cannon taken by the troops under his command and granted by the Parliament for the purpose) is erected by his friends and comrades."

BOOK REVIEW
An Anglo-Irish Dialect Glossary for Joyce's Works by Richard Wall (Galway: Colin Smythe, 1986)

The author is an associate professor of English at the University of Calgary, and the present slim volume is an extension of a paper which he presented at a conference on Anglo-Irish Literature in Galway in 1976. This paper (published in the volume of proceedings: *Place, Personality and the Irish Writer*, ed. A. Carpenter (Galway: Colin Smythe, 1977)) now forms the bulk of the preface and the introduction. What follows in the remaining 100 pages is an elementary list of "Anglo-Irish" words, as they appear consecutively in the individual works of Joyce. Most of these words can be found in O Hehir's *Gaelic Lexicon*, in standard commentaries, and in English dictionaries. Professor Wall does not explain what he means by "Anglo-Irish dialect," as some entries are Standard English and the majority of entries are simply pointers to Anglo-Irish pronunciations of common English words. Thus we are told again and again that "ould" stands for "old," and similarly that "mould" = "mold," "bould" = "bold," "sould" = "sold," "hould" = "hold," "could" = "cold," with some elegant variations, e.g., "cowld" = "cold," "owld" = "old," "sowls" = "souls." I doubt whether Joyce intended "bitter" = "better," "bitterment" = "betterment," or "yillow" = "yellow" as Anglo-Irish flavouring. I also doubt whether every initial *s* has Anglo-Irish pronunciation *sh*, as Professor Wall maintains, e.g. "shingellar" = "singular," "shunny" = "sunny," "shuit" = "suit," "shester" = "sister," "shome" = "some." But then I have not consulted Anglo-Irish word lists in the Royal Irish Academy and did not use resources of the British Library and the National Library of Ireland, as Professor Wall did.

The glossary becomes increasingly tiresome, for most entries are repetitive, and Professor Wall always refers to the first appearance. Thus, for example, the diminutive ending *-een* is glossed about sixty-five times by "see *D* 121.21," which is a reference to an occurrence in *Dubliners*, with the following piece of information: "The Anglo-Irish dim. Suf. 'een' (-Ir. *ín*) is frequently pej." It would be equally useful to say that it is frequently hypocoristic. The first -een in *Finnegans Wake*, as identified by Professor Wall is "5.23 ... een see *D* 121.21." It is not a particularly helpful note for "bedoueen the jebel and the jpysian sea." It is not clear what exactly is diminished here, as the context suggests "between the devil and the deep blue sea, Mohammed and Mountain, the mountain and the sea, the Nile (Bahr-el-Jebel) and the Egyptian sea." The last "-een" in *Finnegans Wake*, explained by "*D* 121.21," is in "pooraroon Eireen" (620.05). Does this mean that Eileen aroon was baptised Eil, and then pejoratively diminished? I would think that for transatlantic readers a more useful comment would be to point out the poignant, apposite final lines from the song as remembered by the dying ALP:

> *Never to love again, Eileen aroon!*
> *Youth must with time decay, Eileen aroon!*
> *Beauty must fade away, Eileen aroon!*

Some lemmata are spurious, e.g. "*FW* 71.11 Geit (get) see *U* 312.09 'gets.'" There is nothing under *U* 321.09, but under *U* 325.09 we get "gets ... bastards." While the overtones of the Golden Gate, guilty God, and barren goat (Dano-Norw. *gold geit*) may be discerned in *Goldy Geit* (071.11), the bastard seems to be illegitimate here.

The single phrase "hooley pooley" (581.12) is treated as two separate items: "hooley ... see *FW* 131.11" and "pooley ... see *U* 541.07." Following these instructions we end with "celebrations, uninhibited parties" and "urine (Dub. sl.)." Professor Wall seems to be unaware that Irish *húille búille* (hubbub, din) reads as a unit. I can imagine uninhibited urination but not a urinary celebration. Holypolygon!

Professor Wall glosses "rosy" in "the prankquean pulled a rosy one and made her wit foreninst the dour" (21.15) with "*U* 365.24 rossies," which leads us to "brazen women." While the Prankquean's behaviour could be described as brazen (pissing on the door), not every rose is a rossie. To pull (or pluck) a rose simply means to ease oneself in the open air.

What are we to make of the lemma "531.35 Yoke ... see *P* 182.18"? The terse note "yoke" = "vehicle" at *P* 182.18 is unlikely to throw any light on "Yokeoff" and "Yokan" (yoke off *vs* yoke on; Yacob and Johan). The pairing of these two opposite twins gets as close to the vehicle as the yoke allows. As the egg said when its companion was run over by a car: "This is no yoke!" If I may quote Professor Wall's own words from his introduction: "these errors suggest that the problems caused by Joyce's use of the dialect are serious and widespread. They range from incomplete understanding to complete misunderstanding of parts of his works."

While Professor Wall may see "dialect" where there isn't any, there must be hundreds of Hibernicisms which he did not recognise. During one idle evening, picking one random letter, I have found the following items missing in the glossary:

Taddy
(from *Tadgh*; the typical Irishman, Teague), *passim*.

táilgeann
(adzehead, a name applied to St. Patrick) may be alluded to in *talkin* ("talkin about the messiah socloover ... Trinathan Partnick" 478.24)

tanner
(sixpence), e.g. in *"Tanner and a Make"* (71.28) (Wall identified only "make" as a halfpenny)

a taste
(little), e.g. "a taste tooth psalty" (456.04), or "with a taste of roly polony" (621.12), i.e. a small portion

táthaire
(sycophant) for "tathair" (273.F8); O Hehir gives a plausible *an t-athair* (the father); another Anglo-Irish reading is *tat, tatt* (matted hair, Ir. *táth*); cf. "a slut combs the tatts from the hair" (*U* 15:40);

teeming rain
(torrential rain); e.g. "there was reen in plenty all the teem" (519.25)

teetotal
(complete; e.g. teetotal strangers); e.g. in "a tee totum abstainer" (489.17)

thick
(a blockhead); e.g. in "a thick of gobstick" (242.08)

thin wind
(cold, cutting wind); "wind thin" (587.02)

thirteen
(a shilling); from the times when a shilling was worth thirteen Irish copper pennies); "six thirteens" (248.32)

thole
(to suffer; endurance); "did I thole" (541.23); "ultimate thole" (134.02) blending with Ultima Thule

tholsel
(Lord Mayor's House in Dublin until the beginning of the 19th century); e.g. in "thollstall" (539.22)

thon
(that, those), which Wall erroneously equates with "yonder"; e.g. "cotching up on thon bluggy earwuggers" (31.10); "we've conned thon print in its gloss so gay" (334.32) etc.

thonder
(yonder); e.g. in "hinther and thonther" (365.22)

Tibb's eve
(never); "tell Tibbs has eve" (117.19); "Saint Tibb's Day" (236.08); "till tibbes grey eves" (424.29)

tinkler
(Ir. *tincléir*, tinker); "tinkler's dunkey" (405.06)

tony
(anglicised in speech and manners); e.g. "tiny manner ... tony way" (435.04)

tother
(the other); "the other way" (143.19); "in toth's tother's place" (570.13;
O Hehir points out that Ir. *toth* = female genitals); "th'other" (452.13);
"thother" (224.33)

trig
(neat); "neat and trig" (311.19)

Trojan
(a sturdy, big fellow); 381.31

twig
(to understand); *passim.*

TRANSITION (Letter to the *Times Literary Supplement*, March 5, 1982)

Sir,—Bernard Bergonzi (February 19) is incorrect in suggesting that *transition* "was not very sympathetic to Surrealism and instead boosted Joyce's *Wake*." In fact, for English and American readers, *transition* was the best source of information on French surrealism and in its twenty seven issues there were over sixty contributions by the surrealists, as compared with seventeen excerpts from "Work in Progress." The editor of *transition*, Eugene Jolas, once even signed a surrealist manifesto defending Charlie Chaplin's sex-life ("Hands Off Love," *transition* 6).

PETR ŠKRABÁNEK
Mater Misericordiae Hospital,
The Sisters of Mercy, Dublin 7, Ireland

TRANSITION (Reply)

Sir,—May I thank Petr Škrabánek (Letters, March 5) for having written the letter I intended to write to correct an earlier correspondent's misstatement concerning *transition* and the surrealists?

Eugene Jolas recognised very early that this movement, its dramas and expulsions notwithstanding, had attracted the most talented young French writers of the time. It would have been remiss indeed on his part, if as editor of a magazine devoted to contemporary experimental writing and the accompanying plastic arts, he had neglected to give this group, as well as "Work in Progress," full exposure. He regretted that their iconoclastic action left the individual word untouched, unlike the slightly older Léon-Paul Fargue, whose neologistic inventions he appreciated. But Fargue was an absolutely free spirit. He was also one of Joyce's favourite companions.

Except for Philippe Soupault, who was an early friend of Joyce, but also one of the first surrealists to be solemnly excluded from the group (there were others), there was no contact between Joyce and André Breton's movement other than the pages of *transition*.

It would be my guess today that most of the writers who accepted Breton's strict intellectual discipline, however briefly, did not live to regret it but, on the contrary, counted their gains. I myself take pride in the fact that as early as 1927, *transition* introduced these gifted French writers to the English-speaking public.

MARIA JOLAS
106 *bis* Rue de Rennes, 75006 Paris